Chocolate Creations

Chocolate Creations

Previously published as *Chocolate Sensations* by Reader's Digest Association, Inc. by arrangement with Amber Books Ltd. *Chocolate Sensations* ISBN 0-7621-0567-4

Copyright © 2005, 2015 International Masters Publishers AB

IMP are the copyright holders of the recipe material used in the book. All photos by IMP and Shutterstock.

An i-5 Press™ Book

i-5 PUBLISHING, LLC™
Chairman: David Fry
Chief Financial Officer: David Katzoff
Chief Digital Officer: Jennifer Black-Glover
Chief Marketing Officer: Beth Freeman Reynolds
Marketing Director: Will Holburn
General Manager, i-5 Press: Christopher Reggio
Art Director, i-5 Press: Mary Ann Kahn
Senior Editor, i-5 Press: Amy Deputato
Production Director: Laurie Panaggio
Production Manager: Jessica Jaensch

Library of Congress Cataloging-in-Publication Data
Chocolate sensations.
 Chocolate creations : more than 160 decadent and delicious chocolate desserts.
    pages cm
Includes index.
"Previously published as Chocolate Sensations by Reader's Digest Association, Inc. by arrangement with Amber Books Ltd."
ISBN 978-1-62008-195-2 (paperback)
1. Cooking (Chocolate) I. Title.
TX767.C5C533 2015
641.6'374--dc23
                    2015030608

This book has been published with the intent to provide accurate and authoritative information in regard to the subject matter within. While every precaution has been taken in the preparation of this book, the author and publisher expressly disclaim any responsibility for any errors, omissions, or adverse effects arising from the use or application of the information contained herein.

Eating eggs or egg whites that are not completely cooked poses the possibility of salmonella food poisoning. The risk is greater for pregnant women, the elderly, the very young, and persons with impaired immune systems. If you are concerned about salmonella, you can use reconstituted powdered egg whites or pasteurized eggs.

i-5 Publishing, LLC™
www.facebook.com/i5press
www.i5publishing.com

Printed and bound in China
18 17 16 15   2 4 6 8 10 9 7 5 3 1

Contents

Introduction

"Chcoclate is the divine drink that builds up resistance and fights fatigue. a cup of this precious drink permits a man to walk for a whole day without food."

—Montezuma (c. 1480-1520)

Deep within tropical rain forests in the warm climates of Central and South America, cacao trees flourish, quietly producing their prized seeds, cacao beans. These small beans, which grow inside football-sized pods, each containing up to fifty 7- to 8-inch-long beans, are the source of the fascinating delicacy millions in the world enjoy—chocolate. The beans are dried and then roasted, graded, and chopped into small pieces called nibs, which are rich in cocoa butter.

The cocoa butter melts in the grinding process and the thick, creamy liquid that results is chocolate liquor. The liquor is processed to form cocoa powder for baking or for making hot chocolate or, alternately, it is processed with additives such as milk, vanilla, cinnamon, and other flavors and then molded into chocolate bars. Some creative chefs even use cocoa powder and chocolate in main-course recipes.

New World Origins of Chocolate

For centuries the Aztec and Mayan Indians enjoyed chocolate. European explorers noticed this fascination the Indians had with chocolate and investigated its commercial possibilities. Christopher Columbus collected a store of cacao beans and added them to the treasure he collected on his explorations in the Americas.

The King and Queen of Spain, Ferdinand and Isabella, his royal sponsors, were suitably impressed by the stupendous treasures he brought back to them. They marveled at the gold, silver, jewels, feathers, rare spices, and other proofs of the magnificent riches he found in the Americas. They were not impressed, however, by the handful of dark brown almond-shaped beans he returned with on his fourth and last voyage to America in 1502.

It was easy to discount these small beans, lost among the magnificence of all the other recognizable riches. How could Ferdinand and Isabella have known that those small cacao beans, which the Aztecs considered to be the "food of the gods," would eventually become a popular luxury unparalleled in the consumer history of the world?

Fortunately, Columbus and many of the other Spanish conquistadors who followed him were aware of chocolate's value and recognized that this product, which was so highly valued in Aztec society, held great trade possibilities.

The Spaniards were obsessively protective of their vast New World empire that covered almost all of Central and South America, and they kept their discovery of the cacao bean as one of their most closely guarded secrets.

Cocoa powder—the most important ingredient in chocolate—is made by grinding dried cacao beans.

Food of the Gods

The Aztec and Mayan Indians of central and southern Mexico highly prized the cacao bean. They used cacao beans as currency when trading, since these small but treasured beans were a common and definitely easier medium of exchange than bartering. Aztec rulers received cacao beans as part of the tributes they exacted from conquered peoples within their empire.

The Aztecs believed that the gods consumed chocolate in paradise and that it was, literally, the food of the gods. They believed that the gods also conferred chocolate as a divine blessing on humanity and that chocolate was a source of wisdom and knowledge. The Aztec emperor, Montezuma, was so convinced of its therapeutic and aphrodisiacal qualities that he drank some fifty jars of chocolate every day.

The traditional Aztec method of preparing xocoatl (chocolate) was to shell the cacao beans, then grind them on a warmed grinding stone, a metate, and make the ground chocolate into a drink. They poured the mixture from one jar to another ato form a frothy top on the drink.

The Aztec army, always on the move in military expeditions throughout the far-flung empire, needed instant and nourishing provisions. A standard part of their ancient "K-rations" was instant xocoatl! Soldiers poured hot water on tablets or wafers made of compressed cacao powder, and presto, there was hot chocolate, ready to drink.

This food of the gods remains a treasured object in our time. Montezuma first proclaimed its energizing properties; modern research confirmed his findings. It seems chocolate can boost energy levels and may even affect brain chemistry and promote general feelings of well-being.

Chocolate, the Rage of European Nobility

Once chocolate was introduced to the wealthy in Spain in the sixteenth century in the form of a hot chocolate drink, its fame quickly spread across Europe. Seventeenth-century Italians and French enthusiastically welcomed the drink, and chocolate soon became the beverage of choice for royalty, aristocracy, and anyone wealthy enough to afford it. At about the same time, Spanish nuns in Mexico began producing chocolate in a different form, solid-chocolate bars intended to be eaten. Chocolate confections from these convent factories found their way to Europe, where they became featured attractions at elegant banquets.

Chocolate had its rivals in England, however. About 1650, tea and coffee were being introduced to England—roughly the same time that chocolate appeared there. Coffeehouses began offering all three beverages, soon establishing themselves as the predominant social, commercial, and political meeting places of the day.

Chocolate within Everyone's Reach

The Industrial Revolution inaugurated mass production processes that made chocolate more affordable. Mechanization replaced traditional handmade methods employed by independent chocolate makers in small shops and factories. By 1765, Dr. James Baker and John Hannon, a newly arrived Irish chocolate maker in the New World, set up an old gristmill at Milton Lower Falls, Massachusetts. In this mill, Hannon used waterpower to grind cacao beans. Their product, Hannon's Best Chocolate, was first distributed in

1772. The Baker-Hannon enterprise became what is known today as the Walter Baker Company, a familiar household name in North America.

The industrialized factory grinding of cacao beans spread to Europe. A hydraulic grinding machine processed cacao beans in France; two innovative millstones used polished steel rollers to crush them in Spain; and in England, James Watt improved a steam engine that played its part in chocolate's mechanized production.

By 1818 in the Netherlands, a chemist, Conrad Johannes van Houten, patented a machine that pressed out the "butter" content of cacao beans and thereby produced a low-fat, powdered chocolate. Thanks to this process, chocolate for drinking acquired a new and pleasant smoothness—a chocolate beverage similar to the hot chocolate we enjoy today.

Newer versions of solid chocolate also entered the scene. In 1847, the Joseph Fry and Sons Company developed a method of producing a richly smooth eating chocolate. They called it Chocolat Délicieux à Manger to highlight how delicious it was to eat. In total contrast to the dry, brittle chocolate bars produced in eighteenth-century France, the Frys Chocolat Délicieux à Manger helped make their company the largest manufacturer of chocolate in England at that time. They were so successful they even got the commission to supply eating chocolate and cacao beverages to the British Royal Navy.

Joseph Fry and Sons was not without its powerful rivals, however. In 1853, Cadbury's Chocolate, founded in Birmingham by John Cadbury, garnered a distinctive prize—appointment as purveyors of chocolate to Queen Victoria's royal household. In 1869, two brothers, Joseph and Henry Rowntree, set up a chocolate factory in York, thereby establishing that long-lasting dynasty of chocolate makers.

This chocolate-as-big-business story was echoed in Switzerland by men whose names we still recognize today—Rudolphe Lindt, Jacques Tobler, and Henry Nestlé.

Chocolate Returns to the Americas

Across the Atlantic from Europe, Ghirardelli Chocolate was founded in the United States in 1852 as a subsidiary of the Swiss Lindt-Sprüngli Company. The biggest name in chocolate in the United States, however, is Hershey's Chocolate. Hershey's founder, Milton Hershey, purchased a farm in Pennsylvania and in 1903 built a chocolate factory on it. Over time his farm-factory became the nucleus of the Hershey chocolate empire. The main thoroughfares of the town of Hershey, familiarly known as "Chocolate Town," are Chocolate and Cocoa avenues. Side streets radiating off these avenues are named after Caracas, Granada, Aruba, Trinidad, Java, Para and Ceylon (Sri Lanka)—all places where Hershey obtained cacao beans in his innovative approach to reduce costs. Hershey has often been called the "Henry Ford of the American chocolate industry," since he capitalized on many mass production techniques in his factory.

Bars of plain baking chocolate are packed at the Guittard Chocolate Company in California.

Varieties of Chocolate

Chocolate comes in many forms, depending on what is added to the liquor derived from the cacao beans. Each form of chocolate has a specific use.

Baking chocolate

Baking chocolate is pure chocolate liquor with no additives. Usually, it contains equal parts of cocoa butter and cocoa solids. It can be bought in liquid form or in dried bars. Baking chocolate is always combined with sugar and normally used to make cakes, brownies, fudge, and frosting.

Bittersweet chocolate and semisweet chocolate

Bittersweet chocolate and semisweet chocolate are made of a mixture of chocolate liquor, cocoa butter, sugar, vanilla, lecithin, and milk solids. It can be bought in the form of bars or chips. Bittersweet chocolate often has a deeper chocolate flavor than semisweet chocolate, but the two can be used interchangeably in recipes, although the final flavor and color may differ.

Milk chocolate

Milk chocolate contains more milk solids and less chocolate liquor than bittersweet or semisweet chocolate and is a very popular variety of eating chocolate. You won't find milk chocolate listed in many recipes for baked goods because the high proportion of milk solids makes it very heat sensitive.

White chocolate

White chocolate is made from cocoa butter and milk solids. Available in both bars and chips, it is very creamy and mild tasting.

Chocolate chips

Chocolate chips can be made from bittersweet, semisweet, or milk chocolates. Chocolate intended for chips is specially formulated to hold its shape when baked.

Unsweetened cocoa powder

Unsweetened cocoa powder is made from pulverized and partially defatted chocolate liquor. It may be processed in nonalkalized (natural) or alkalized (Dutch-process) forms. Dutch-process cocoa is

Tips for Baking with Chocolate

You will find it's fairly easy to handle chocolate in recipes, but it helps to know the tricks the pros use. The tips below will help make your efforts prac-tically foolproof.

- Adding one drop of liquid to melted chocolate can cause it to "seize up" and form lumps that are difficult to break up or disperse. The solution is to stir in vegetable oil immediately and slowly remelt the chocolate. Use about 1 tablespoon of oil for every 6 ounces of chocolate.

- Be careful not to overheat chocolate. When over-heated, it will break up, and it's unlikely that you can save it. So just throw it away, and start again carefully.

- Although it may not look like it, cocoa powder and flour have a lot in common, acting the same way when used in a batter. If you want to add cocoa to a brownie or cake, decrease the flour by 1 table-spoon for every 2 tablespoons of cocoa you add. Cocoa is bitter, so it's a good idea to increase the sugar by 2 tablespoons for every 1 tablespoon of cocoa added.

darker, milder in flavor, and is less acidic than natural cocoa. In general, when your recipe calls for chocolate, it is best to use nonalkalized cocoa in recipes that use baking soda as the leavening agent and Dutch-processed cocoa in recipes that use baking powder. In recipes that have neither baking soda nor baking powder as the primary leavening agent, the two can be used interchangeably.

Storing Chocolate

Chocolate should be stored, tightly wrapped, in a cool dark place (60° to 70°F). Improperly stored chocolate (at temperatures that are too hot or that fluctuate) will develop a "bloom"—a gray coating that will disappear when the chocolate is heated. You don't have to throw such chocolate out—it is still fine to use. Stored at an ideal temperature, baking chocolate will keep for years. Milk chocolate and white chocolate have a shelf life of about nine months. Chocolate can be refrigerated, but it must be very tightly wrapped to prevent condensation from wetting the surface of the chocolate.

A chef fills a pastry bag with chocolate from a bowl in preparation for decorating a cake.

Chopping, Grating, and Shaving Chocolate

1. **Chopping**: To chop chocolate, place the chocolate on a large clean cutting board and use a large, sharp knife. Slightly chilled chocolate handles more easily.

2. **Grating**: You can grate chocolate with a box grater or in a food processor. To use the box grater, hold the chocolate with a piece of waxed paper or towel to prevent the heat of your hand from melting the chocolate. In a food processor, use the pulsing action.

3. **Shaving**: To shave chocolate, scrape the blade of a paring knife or vegetable peeler across a chocolate bar at a 45° angle.

Grated and shaved chocolate melts readily, so avoid touching the pieces with your hands. If you are planning to decorate with chocolate flakes, use a large spoon to sprinkle them over your cake. Grated and shaved chocolate can be stored in the refrigerator in a tightly sealed container.

Curled chocolate shavings are the classic topping for any chocolate cake.

How to Melt Chocolate

Chocolate scorches easily, so it must be melted slowly over low heat in a double boiler or in a microwave. Never cover chocolate when melting it because the water will condense on the lid. If it should drip back into the chocolate, it will cause the mix to "seize," the technical term for chocolate that becomes lumpy.

To melt chocolate in a double boiler, place chopped chocolate in the top of a double boiler over simmering water. Remove from the heat when the chocolate is a little more than halfway melted and stir until smooth. Or melt the chocolate in a microwave over medium heat (50 percent power). Timing will vary, depending on the size of the oven and type of chocolate, but generally, 1 ounce of chocolate will take 1½ minutes.

Chocolate will hold its shape even when melted, so test for consistency by frequently stirring the chocolate you are melting. Cool melted chocolate to room temperature before adding to a batter.

Gently melt chocolate in a double boiler.

Cakes

Nothing says "special occasion" like a homemade cake. The aroma while it's baking, the thrill of seeing it rise, and the fun of decorating it to make it uniquely yours are magical. But the best part is knowing exactly what ingredients have gone into it and the joy of eating something glorious you have created.

Baking a cake doesn't need to be daunting. There are only two simple rules: (1) make certain you have all the ingredients and (2) follow the instructions to the letter. The results will be worth it!

Chocolate-Coconut Cake

A rich chocolate icing covers this light and fudgy cake.

45 minutes preparation plus cooling, 25-30 minutes baking

Makes 12 servings

Ingredients:

2 cups all-purpose flour

¾ cup unsweetened cocoa powder

1 teaspoon baking powder

½ teaspoon baking soda

¼ teaspoon salt

2 cups granulated sugar

8 ounces (2 sticks) butter, softened

5 large eggs

1 teaspoon vanilla extract

1 cup milk

1 cup shredded sweetened coconut

Frosting:

1½ cups confectioners' sugar

4 ounces (1 stick) butter, softened

¼ cup heavy cream

2 tablespoons unsweetened cocoa

Garnish:

1 cup shredded sweetened coconut

1. Preheat oven to 350°F. Grease two 9-inch round cake pans. Dust with flour; tap out excess.

2. Mix together flour, cocoa powder, baking powder, baking soda, and salt.

3. Beat together sugar and butter at medium speed until light and fluffy. Add eggs, 1 at a time, beating well after each addition. Beat in vanilla.

4. At low speed, alternately beat flour mixture and milk into egg mixture. Stir in coconut. Spoon batter evenly into prepared pans; smooth tops.

5. Bake cakes until a toothpick inserted in the centers comes out clean, 25-30 minutes. Transfer pans to wire racks to cool slightly. Turn cakes out onto racks to cool completely.

6. To prepare frosting, combine confectioners' sugar, butter, cream, and cocoa at medium speed until light and fluffy.

7. Place 1 cake layer on a serving plate. Spread top with some frosting. Top with remaining cake layer. Spread remaining frosting over top and sides.

8. To garnish, press coconut onto top edges and sides of cake.

Chocolate-Mint Cake

This mint-flavored layer cake is a refreshing dessert for a midsummer dinner party.

30 minutes preparation plus cooling, 35-40 minutes baking

Ingredients:

- 12 chocolate-covered mint thins
- 1½ tablespoons solid vegetable shortening
- 2 tablespoons unsweetened cocoa powder
- 1 teaspoon mint extract
- 2¹/₃ cups sifted cake flour
- 2 teaspoons baking powder
- ½ teaspoon baking soda
- ¼ teaspoon salt
- 6 ounces (11½ sticks) softened butter
- 1¹/₃ cups granulated sugar
- 4 large eggs
- ½ teaspoon vanilla extract
- ¾ cup milk

Filling, Topping, and Garnish:

- 3 cups whipped cream
- 1 drop yellow food coloring
- 6 tablespoons marzipan
- 15 chocolate-covered mint thins, cut into triangles

1. Preheat oven to 350°F. Grease two 8-inch round cake pans. Line with waxed paper.

2. In a saucepan over low heat, melt together mint thins and shortening. Remove from heat. Mix in cocoa and mint extract.

3. Mix together flour, baking powder, baking soda, and salt.

4. Beat together butter and sugar at medium speed until light and fluffy. Add eggs, one at a time, beating well after each addition. Beat in chocolate mixture and vanilla. At low speed, alternately beat in flour mixture and milk until just combined. Spoon batter evenly into prepared pans; smooth tops.

5. Bake cakes until a toothpick inserted in the centers comes out clean, 35-40 minutes. Transfer pans to wire racks to cool for 10 minutes. Turn cakes out onto racks to cool completely. Remove waxed paper.

6. Slice each cake in half horizontally. Place 1 cake layer on a plate. Spread some whipped cream over layer. Top with a second and third layer, spreading more whipped cream over each layer. Top with remaining cake layer. Spread more whipped cream over the top and the sides of cake.

7. Using a pastry bag fitted with a star tip, pipe remaining whipped cream in rosettes around edges of cake.

8. To garnish, knead food coloring into marzipan. Shape marzipan into a rose. Place rose in center of cake. Arrange mints around sides and top of cake.

Cook's Tip

Use a serrated knife when slicing cake layers horizontally, and hold the top of the cake with one hand to prevent the layers from shifting. Place the top layer of the cake with the cut side against the filling and the smooth side up.

Chocolate-Orange Dessert

A stunning gateau with layers of enticing flavor to impress your family and friends.

40 minutes preparation, 8-10 minutes baking plus chilling   Makes 8-10 Servings

Ingredients:

²/₃ cup all-purpose flour

1 teaspoon baking powder

½ teaspoon salt

6 tablespoons unsweetened cocoa
  powder

3 eggs

½ cup superfine sugar

2 teaspoons grated orange peel

Filling, Frosting, and Garnish:

1 package (8 ounces) cream
  cheese, softened

½ teaspoon finely grated orange
  peel

2 tablespoons superfine sugar

1¼ cups heavy cream

1 orange, peeled and chopped

1 tablespoon orange juice

2 tablespoons orange-flavored
  liqueur

4 ounces (4 squares) semisweet
  chocolate, coarsely chopped

Chocolate leaves and fine strips of
  orange peel, to garnish

1. Preheat oven to 400°F. Grease 15 x 10-inch jelly roll pan and line with waxed paper.

2. Sift together the flour, baking powder, salt, and cocoa into a mixing bowl.

3. Using an electric beater, beat together the eggs and sugar until pale and foamy and the beaters leave a trail when lifted. Beat in the orange peel, then fold in the flour mixture. Pour into the pan and level the surface.

4. Bake for 8-10 minutes, or until firm and springy to the touch. Turn out onto a wire rack, remove the paper and let cool.

5. To prepare the filling, beat together the cream cheese and orange peel until softened. Add the sugar and 6 tablespoons heavy cream. Beat until soft peaks form. Fold in the chopped orange. In a measuring cup, mix together the orange juice and liqueur.

6. Grease a 9 x 5-inch loaf pan and line with plastic wrap. Trim the edges of the cake, then slice from the long side into 3 pieces that will fit snugly into the pan.

7. Put one piece of cake in the base of the pan. Sprinkle with 2 tablespoons orange juice mixture, then spread with half the orange cream. Repeat once more, ending with a piece of cake on top. Cover with plastic wrap and chill for 30 minutes.

8. For the frosting, reserve 4 tablespoons of the remaining cream. Put the rest into a heatproof bowl with the chocolate and heat over a pan of gently simmering water, stirring, until melted and glossy. Cool for 10 minutes, stirring occasionally.

9. Turn the cake onto a serving plate and remove the plastic wrap. Cover the cake with the frosting, reserving 1 tablespoon.

10. Whip the remaining cream until thick, then mix in the reserved chocolate mixture. Spoon into a pastry bag fitted with a star tip. Pipe rosettes onto the cake and decorate with chocolate leaves and orange peel. Chill until ready to serve.

Raspberry-Chocolate Cake

This cake is the perfect pairing of rich, delectable chocolate and a hint of raspberry flavor.

45 minutes preparation plus cooling, 25-30 minutes baking   Makes 12 servings

Ingredients:

- 2 cups all-purpose flour
- 1 teaspoon baking soda
- 1 teaspoon baking powder
- 1/8 teaspoon salt
- 2 cups granulated sugar
- 2 large eggs
- 4 ounces (1 stick) butter, melted
- 4 ounces (4 squares) unsweetened chocolate, melted
- 1½ cups milk
- 1 teaspoon vanilla extract

Frosting, Filling, and Garnish:

- 1 package (16 ounces) confectioners' sugar
- 4 ounces (1 stick) butter, softened
- 6 tablespoons unsweetened cocoa powder
- 5 tablespoons milk
- 1 teaspoon vanilla extract
- 1 cup raspberry jelly, melted
- Fresh raspberries
- Sprigs of fresh mint

1. Preheat oven to 350°F. Grease two 9-inch round cake pans. Dust with flour; tap out excess.

2. Mix together flour, baking soda, baking powder, and salt.

3. Beat together sugar and eggs at medium speed until light and fluffy. Beat in melted butter and melted chocolate until blended.

4. At low speed, alternately beat in flour mixture and milk until smooth. Beat in vanilla.

5. Spread batter evenly in prepared pans; smooth tops.

6. Bake cakes until a toothpick inserted in the centers comes out clean, 25-30 minutes.

7. Transfer pans to wire racks to cool slightly. Turn cakes out onto racks to cool completely.

8. To prepare frosting, beat together confectioners' sugar, butter, cocoa, milk, and vanilla at medium speed until smooth.

9. Slice each cake in half horizontally. Spread one layer with half of jelly. Top with a second layer. Spread top with some frosting. Top with a third layer. Spread with remaining jelly. Place remaining layer on top. Spread remaining frosting on top and sides of cake.

10. Garnish with raspberries and mint sprigs.

Cocoa-Yogurt Cake

Smooth semisweet chocolate and plain yogurt combine to make an irresistible cake.

40 minutes preparation, 30 minutes baking plus cooling

Ingredients

⅔ cup plain yogurt
6 tablespoons milk
½ tablespoon lemon juice
2 cups all-purpose flour
1 tablespoon baking powder
1 tablespoon baking soda
1 teaspoon salt
½ cup unsweetened cocoa powder
4 ounces (1 stick) butter, softened
1 cup light brown sugar
3 large eggs

Filling and Frosting:

⅔ cup soft dried apricots
4 tablespoons orange juice
⅔ cup heavy cream
3 tablespoons maple syrup
4 tablespoons apricot jelly
8 ounces (8 squares) semisweet chocolate,
    coarsely chopped
1¼ cups sour cream

Garnish:

Chocolate curls (see page 185)
Confectioners' sugar

1. Preheat oven to 350°F. Grease two 8-inch round cake pans. Dust with flour; tap out excess.

2. In a bowl, beat together the yogurt, milk, and lemon juice. In another bowl, sift together the flour, baking powder, baking soda, salt, and cocoa.

3. In a large bowl, beat together the butter and brown sugar until pale and fluffy. Gradually beat in the eggs, 1 at a time, beating well after each addition. Alternately fold in the flour and yogurt mixtures.

4. Divide the batter evenly between the pans. Bake until a toothpick inserted in the centers comes out clean, 30 minutes. Cool completely in the pans.

5. To prepare filling, heat the apricots and orange juice in a saucepan until the apricots swell. Cool completely, then drain.

6. Whip the heavy cream until soft peaks form. Slice each cake in half horizontally to make 4 layers.

7. Spread the whipped cream over 2 cake layers. Sprinkle with the apricots and maple syrup. Spread the apricot jelly over the remaining 2 cakes. Put one cream-topped cake on a serving plate. Top with a jelly layer, then another cream layer and finally, the remaining jelly layer.

8. To prepare the frosting, melt the chocolate in a heatproof bowl set over a pan of simmering water. Fold in the sour cream. Spread over the top and sides of the cake. Garnish with the chocolate curls and dust with confectioners' sugar.

Creamy Chocolate Layer Cake

This cake is the ultimate dessert for the chocolate lovers in your life.

30 minutes preparation plus cooling, 40 minutes baking

Makes 8-10 servings

Ingredients

3 cups granulated sugar

2¾ cups sifted all-purpose flour

1 cup unsweetened cocoa powder

½ teaspoon baking powder

1¾ teaspoons salt

¾ teaspoon baking soda

1½ cups black coffee

1¼ cups buttermilk

⅓ cup vegetable oil

1 teaspoon vanilla extract

3 large eggs

Filling, Frosting, and Garnish:

4 cups heavy cream

½ cup confectioners' sugar

3 tablespoons raspberry liqueur or
1 teaspoon vanilla extract

¾ cup raspberry jelly

Garnish:

3 ounces (3 squares) semisweet
chocolate, shaved

1. Preheat oven to 350°F. Grease two 9-inch round cake pans. Line with waxed paper.

2. In a bowl, sift together sugar, flour, cocoa, baking powder, salt, and baking soda.

3. In another bowl, mix together coffee, buttermilk, oil, and vanilla.

4. At low speed, beat half of buttermilk mixture into flour mixture until blended and smooth. Add eggs, 1 at a time, beating well after each addition. Beat in remaining buttermilk mixture. (Batter will be thin.) Pour evenly into prepared pans.

5. Bake cakes until a toothpick inserted in the centers comes out clean, 40 minutes.

6. Transfer pans to wire racks to cool for 5 minutes. Loosen cakes by running a metal spatula around sides of pans. Turn cakes out onto racks to cool completely. Remove wax paper.

7. Meanwhile, prepare filling. In a medium bowl, beat together cream, confectioners' sugar, and liqueur at medium speed until soft peaks form.

8. Slice each cake layer in half horizontally. Place 1 cake layer on a serving plate. Spread with ¼ cup jelly, then spread with 1 cup whipped cream. Repeat this sequence with 2 more layers, stacking layers. Top with remaining layer. Spread sides and top with more whipped cream.

9. Using a pastry bag fitted with a star tip, pipe remaining whipped cream into rosettes around edges of cake. To garnish, sprinkle chocolate shavings over top.

Chocolate Cream Cookie Cake

Crisp cookies and rich chocolate make this the simplest cake to make and to eat.

30 minutes preparation, 2-3 hours chilling

Ingredients:

- 1¼ cups heavy cream
- 9 ounces (9 squares) semisweet chocolate, coarsely chopped
- 1 teaspoon vanilla extract
- 15 sugar cookies, broken into pieces (5 ounces)

1. Heat the cream in a saucepan over low heat until almost boiling, then add the chocolate and remove from the heat. Cover the pan and let stand for 5 minutes.

2. Add the vanilla extract to the mixture and stir until smooth. Pour the mixture into a large bowl and chill until it begins to thicken.

3. Line a 8 x 4-inch loaf pan with plastic wrap. Leave some excess hanging over the edge of the pan.

4. Spread one-sixth of the chocolate mixture over the base of the pan. Put a layer of cookies on top. Repeat the layering, finishing with a layer of chocolate.

5. Fold the excess plastic wrap over the top of the cake. Chill for at least 2 hours, preferably overnight, until the chocolate is set firmly.

6. Unwrap the plastic wrap from the top of the cake and turn out onto a serving plate. Carefully peel off the plastic wrap. Cut into slices to serve.

Cook's Tip

You can use graham crackers to give a crunchier texture. When layering the crackers in the pan, break them into small pieces to help cover the chocolate mixture completely.

Rich Chocolate Truffle Cake

A rich rum-soaked cake and heavy cream chocolate mousse.

45 minutes preparation, 30-40 minutes baking plus chilling

Makes 12-14 servings

Ingredients:

2 tablespoons butter

⅓ cup all-purpose flour

1 tablespoon unsweetened cocoa powder

2 large eggs, beaten

¼ cup superfine sugar

4 tablespoons rum

Filling and Frosting:

1 pound semisweet chocolate, coarsely chopped

2½ cups heavy cream

1 teaspoon unsweetened cocoa, to dust

1. Preheat oven to 375°F. Grease an 8–9 inch springform cake pan. Line with waxed paper. Melt the butter and let cool. Sift together the flour and cocoa 3 times.

2. Put the eggs and superfine sugar into a heatproof bowl set over a pan of hot water. Beat together with an electric beater for 10 minutes, or until the beater leaves a trail on the surface when lifted.

3. Remove from the heat and beat until cool. Fold in half the flour mixture. Slowly pour in the melted butter and fold in. Fold in the remaining flour mixture, then pour into the pan.

4. Bake until a toothpick inserted in the center comes out clean, 30-40 minutes. Cool for 10 minutes. Turn out onto a wire rack to cool completely.

5. Wash and dry the cake pan. Put the cake back in the pan and brush the rum on top. To prepare the filling, melt the chocolate in a heatproof bowl set over a pan of barely simmering water. Cool to room temperature.

6. In a large bowl, whip 2 cups cream until just starting to thicken. Beat in half the chocolate, then fold in the remainder. Spoon over the cake and spread level. Chill for 30 minutes, or until set.

7. Carefully turn out the cake onto a serving plate. Whip the remaining cream until soft peaks form. Spoon into a pastry bag fitted with a star tip. Pipe rosettes around the edge of the cake. Dust with cocoa and serve.

Chocolate Fudge Layer Cake

Chocolate fans will surely applaud this to-die-for fudge cake.

45 minutes preparation, 25-30 minutes baking

Makes 12 servings

Ingredients:

- 1¾ cups all-purpose flour
- ½ cup unsweetened cocoa powder
- 1¼ teaspoons baking soda
- ⅛ teaspoon salt
- 6 ounces (1½ sticks) butter, softened
- ⅔ cup granulated sugar
- ⅔ cup firmly packed brown sugar
- 2 large eggs
- 2 teaspoons vanilla extract
- 1½ cups buttermilk

Frosting and Garnish:

- 4 ounces (1 stick) butter, softened
- 1 cup confectioners' sugar, sifted
- 3 ounces (3 squares) unsweetened chocolate, melted
- 2 teaspoons vanilla extract
- Chocolate shavings (optional)

1. Preheat oven to 350°F. Line bottoms of two 9-inch round cake pans with waxed paper. Grease paper and sides of pans. Dust with flour; tap out excess.

2. Mix flour, cocoa, baking soda, and salt. In another bowl, beat butter, granulated sugar, and brown sugar at medium speed until light and fluffy. Add eggs, 1 at a time, beating well after each addition. Add vanilla.

3. At low speed, alternately beat flour mixture and buttermilk into butter mixture just until blended. Divide batter equally between prepared pans.

4. Bake cakes until a toothpick inserted in the centers comes out clean, 25-30 minutes. Transfer pans to wire racks to cool for 10 minutes. Turn out onto racks. Remove waxed paper. Turn layers top-side up and cool completely.

5. To prepare frosting, beat butter and confectioners' sugar at medium speed until light and fluffy. Add melted chocolate and vanilla; continue beating until shiny and smooth.

6. Place 1 cake layer on a serving plate; spread with frosting. Top with remaining cake layer. Spread frosting on top and sides of cake. Let cake stand for at least 30 minutes before sprinkling with chocolate shavings and slicing.

Peanut Butter-Chocolate Cake

Sweet and moist, this is the perfect cake for peanut butter and chocolate lovers.

30 minutes preparation plus cooling, 30-35 minutes baking

Ingredients:

2 cups all-purpose flour

¼ cup sifted unsweetened cocoa powder

1 tablespoon baking powder

1 teaspoon salt

2 cups firmly packed brown sugar

1 cup peanut butter, softened

⅔ cup (1¼ sticks) butter, softened

6 large eggs

2 teaspoons vanilla extract

¾ cup milk

Frosting and Garnish:

1½ cups peanut butter, softened

¾ cup honey, at room temperature

2/3 cup confectioners' sugar

3 ounces (¾ stick) butter, softened

1 cup chopped peanuts (4 ounces)

1. Preheat oven to 350°F. Grease two 9-inch round cake pans. Dust with flour; tap out excess.

2. Sift together flour, cocoa powder, baking powder, and salt.

3. Beat together brown sugar, peanut butter, and butter at medium speed until light and fluffy. Add eggs, 1 at a time, beating well after each addition. Stir in vanilla.

4. At low speed, alternately beat flour mixture and milk into batter. Pour batter into prepared pans; smooth tops.

5. Bake cakes until tops spring back when lightly pressed and a toothpick inserted in the center comes out clean, 30-35 minutes. Transfer pans to wire racks to cool for 10 minutes.

6. Loosen cakes by running a metal spatula around sides of pans. Turn cakes out onto racks to cool completely.

7. To make the frosting, beat together peanut butter, honey, confectioners' sugar, and butter until blended and smooth. Reserve about 1 cup frosting.

8. Place 1 cake layer on a serving plate. Spread top with one-quarter of remaining frosting. Top with second cake layer. Spread remaining frosting on top and sides of cake.

9. Using a pastry bag fitted with a star tip, pipe reserved frosting into rosettes on top of cake.

10. Arrange nuts on rosettes and around bottom of cake.

Rum Chocolate Cake

Make this cake the day before serving to let the rich flavors develop.

45 minutes preparation, 30-35 minutes baking plus cooling

Makes 8-10 servings

Ingredients:

6 tablespoons unsweetened cocoa powder, sifted

2 tablespoons rum

6 tablespoons warm water

4 ounces (1 stick) butter, softened

1 cup superfine sugar

2 large eggs, beaten

½ cup (2 ounces) ground almonds

1 cup all-purpose flour

½ teaspoon baking soda

1½ teaspoons baking powder

½ teaspoon salt

Filling and Frosting:

1 tablespoon rum

6 tablespoons apricot jam, warmed and sieved

8 ounces semisweet chocolate, coarsely chopped

4 ounces (1 stick) butter, cut into small pieces

Garnish:

6 ounces (6 squares) semisweet chocolate,
coarsely chopped

4 tablespoons light cream

2 ounces (½ stick) butter, softened

2 large egg yolks

1 tablespoon rum

1. Preheat oven to 325°F. Grease two 8-inch round cake pans. Line with waxed paper. Blend the cocoa powder and rum with 6 tablespoons warm water.

2. In a mixing bowl, beat the butter and sugar until pale and fluffy. Gradually beat in the eggs. Fold in the almonds, flour, baking powder, salt, baking soda, and the cocoa mixture. Spoon the mixture into the pan.

3. Bake for 30-35 minutes, or until a toothpick inserted into the centers comes out clean. Cool completely on a wire rack. Wrap in foil and keep in an airtight container for 1 day.

4. To prepare the filling and frosting, sprinkle the rum over the 2 cake layers. Spread half the warmed jam over 1 cake layer. Put the chocolate and butter into a bowl set over a pan of simmering water. Let melt, then spread a third over the plain cake layer.

5. Sandwich together the cake halves with the chocolate and jam layers touching. Brush the remaining jam over the cake. Pour over the remaining chocolate mixture and spread evenly over the top and sides. Let set.

6. For the garnish, melt the chocolate in a bowl over a pan of simmering water. Cool slightly, then gradually beat in the cream, butter, egg yolks, and rum. Cool until firm. Put into a pastry bag fitted with a star tip and pipe around the edge of the cake.

Gooey Chocolate Cake

Chocolate cake and a sumptuous frosting make this a chocolate treat to remember.

30 minutes preparation, 30-35 minutes baking plus chilling   Makes 8-10 servings

Ingredients:
- 4 ounces (4 squares) semisweet chocolate, coarsely chopped
- 1 cup milk
- 1¼ cups light brown sugar
- 4 ounces (1 stick) butter, softened
- 3 large eggs, lightly beaten
- 2 cups all-purpose flour
- 1 teaspoon baking soda

Frosting:
- 2 cups confectioners' sugar
- 4 tablespoons unsweetened cocoa powder
- 2 tablespoons light corn syrup
- 3 ounces (¾ stick) butter
- ½ teaspoon vanilla extract
- 3 tablespoons apricot jam

1. Preheat oven to 350°F. Grease two 8-inch round cake pans. Line with waxed paper.

2. Put the chocolate in a saucepan with the milk and a third of the brown sugar. Heat gently, stirring, until the chocolate melts. Cool.

3. In a large mixing bowl, beat together the butter and remaining brown sugar until pale and fluffy. Beat in the eggs and then the cooled chocolate mixture.

4. Sift the flour and baking soda into the chocolate mixture and fold in. Pour into the prepared pans.

5. Bake for 30-35 minutes, or until a toothpick inserted into the centers comes out clean. Let stand in the pans for 5 minutes. Turn out onto a wire rack to cool.

6. For the frosting, sift the confectioners' sugar and cocoa into a bowl.

7. Put the syrup, butter, and vanilla into a pan and stir over low heat until the butter melts and the mixture is simmering. Pour onto the sugar and cocoa powder and beat until smooth. Let cool.

8. Spread the top of 1 cake layer with jam and the other with a quarter of the frosting. Sandwich together with the jam and frosting layers touching and then put onto a serving plate. Beat the remaining frosting until soft, then spread over the cake, making swirls with a spatula. Chill for 1 hour before serving.

Decadent Chocolate-Jelly Cake

This chocolate sponge is filled with raspberry jelly for a truly sweet sensation.

50 minutes preparation, 30 minutes baking plus cooling   Makes 10-12 servings

Ingredients:

- 6 tablespoons unsweetened cocoa powder
- 1 teaspoon instant coffee powder
- ½ cup sour cream
- 2½ cups all-purpose flour
- 1½ teaspoons baking powder
- ½ teaspoon salt
- 4 ounces (1 stick) butter
- ¾ cup superfine sugar
- 2 large eggs
- 1 teaspoon vanilla extract
- 1 tablespoon brandy or rum
- 6 tablespoons raspberry jelly

Frosting:

- 1 cup confectioners' sugar, sifted
- 3 ounces (3 squares) bittersweet chocolate, melted
- 3 tablespoons milk
- 3 tablespoons chocolate sprinkles

Buttercream:

- 2 ounces (½ stick) butter
- ¾ cup confectioners' sugar, sifted
- 1 ounce semisweet chocolate
- 1-2 teaspoons silver balls, to garnish

1. Preheat oven to 350°F. Grease two 9-inch round cake pans and line the bases with waxed paper.

2. Put the cocoa powder and coffee into a bowl and dissolve in ½ cup boiling water. Let cool. Stir in the sour cream.

3. Sift the flour, baking powder, and salt into a bowl. In another bowl, beat together the butter and sugar until pale and fluffy. Gradually beat in the eggs, vanilla, and brandy or rum, if using.

4. Alternately fold in the sour cream and flour mixtures a little at a time. Divide the mixture between the prepared pans and smooth the tops.

5. Bake for 30 minutes, or until a toothpick inserted into the centers of the cakes comes out clean. Turn out onto a wire rack to cool. When cool, sandwich the cakes with the jelly and put onto a serving plate.

6. For the frosting, mix the confectioners' sugar, chocolate, and enough milk to form a soft frosting. Spread over the top of the cake. Press chocolate sprinkles around the edge. Let set.

7. For the buttercream, beat the butter until soft. Beat in the confectioners' sugar and chocolate.

8. Spoon into a pastry bag fitted with a star tip and pipe a ring of rosettes on top of the cake. Decorate with the silver balls.

Chocolate Espresso Roll

Moist chocolate sponge cake combines with mocha mousse to create a truly decadent experience.

45 minutes preparation, plus cooling, 12-15 minutes baking

Makes 8 servings

Ingredients:
- 4 ounces (4 squares) semisweet chocolate, coarsely chopped
- ½ cup water
- 1 teaspoon instant espresso powder
- ¾ cup cake flour
- ½ cup granulated sugar
- 4 large eggs
- Unsweetened cocoa powder

Filling:
- 4 ounces (4 squares) milk chocolate, coarsely chopped
- 2 tablespoons water
- 2 teaspoons espresso powder
- 1 teaspoon vanilla extract
- ¾ cup heavy cream
- 1 tablespoon granulated sugar
- Milk chocolate shavings

Garnish:
- Confectioners' sugar

1. Preheat oven to 350°F. Grease a 15 x 10-inch jelly-roll pan. Line with waxed paper.

2. In a saucepan, bring chocolate, water, and espresso to a boil over low heat. Boil until mixture thickens to pudding consistency, 5 minutes. Cool completely.

3. Sift together flour and ¼ cup of sugar 4 times.

4. Beat eggs at high speed for 1 minute. Gradually beat in remaining sugar until thick ribbons form when beaters are lifted.

5. Sift flour mixture over egg mixture. Gently and quickly fold in until almost combined. Add chocolate mixture all at once; fold in quickly. Immediately pour into prepared pan. Smooth top.

6. Bake cake until center springs back when lightly pressed, 12-15 minutes. Dust a clean cloth with cocoa powder. Turn cake out onto prepared cloth. Remove waxed paper. Trim cake edges. Do not let cake cool.

7. Starting with a long side, tightly roll up cake, jelly-roll style, with cloth. Transfer cake, seam-side down, to a wire rack to cool for 30 minutes.

8. To prepare filling, in a small saucepan, bring chocolate, water, espresso powder, and vanilla to a boil over low heat. Boil for 5 minutes. Cool completely.

9. Beat together cream and sugar at medium speed until soft peaks form. Fold in chocolate mixture.

10. Unroll cake; remove cloth. Spread filling over cake to within 1 inch of edges. Sprinkle with chocolate shavings.

11. Re-roll cake. Place, seam-side down, on a serving plate. Dust with confectioners' sugar.

Mocha-Glazed Coffee Cake

Pick yourself up from the four-o'clock blues with this sweet and sticky coffee cake.

25 minutes preparation plus rising and cooling, 25 minutes baking   Makes 12 servings

Ingredients:

    1 package active dry yeast

    ½ cup warm milk (105°–115°F)

    2 ounces (½ stick) butter, softened

    ¼ cup granulated sugar

    ¼ teaspoon salt

    2 cups all-purpose flour

Filling:

    3 tablespoons butter, softened

    2 tablespoons granulated sugar

    1½ ounces (1½ squares) semisweet chocolate,
       coarsely chopped

Glaze:

    1¼ cups confectioners' sugar

    3 tablespoons black coffee

    3 tablespoons unsweetened cocoa powder

1. In a medium bowl, dissolve yeast in warm milk. Let stand until foamy, 5-10 minutes.

2. Stir butter, sugar, and salt into yeast mixture. Using a heavy-duty electric mixer fitted with the paddle attachment and set on low speed, beat in flour, ½ cup at a time, until a soft dough forms.

3. On a floured surface, knead dough until smooth and elastic, 5-10 minutes, adding more flour to prevent sticking. Place dough in a large greased bowl, turning to coat. Cover loosely with a damp cloth; let rise in a warm place until almost doubled, 45 minutes.

4. Grease a 10-inch baking sheet. To prepare filling, mix together butter, sugar, and chocolate.

5. Punch down dough. On a floured surface, using a floured rolling pin, roll dough into a 20 x 12-inch rectangle. Spread filling over dough to within ½ inch of edges. Starting with a long side, roll up dough, jelly-roll style. Shape into a ring; pinch to seal.

6. Place dough, seam-side down, in prepared pan. Cover again; let rise in a warm place until almost doubled, 30 minutes.

7. Preheat oven to 400°F. Bake cake until golden, 25 minutes. Transfer pan to a wire rack to cool for 10 minutes. Turn cake out onto rack to cool completely.

8. To prepare glaze, mix together confectioners' sugar, coffee, and cocoa powder until smooth. Spread glaze over cake.

Raspberry-Chocolate Roll

Bring out this great-looking dessert at your next dinner party—it's sure to dazzle guests.

25 minutes preparation plus cooling, 12-15 minutes baking

Makes 10 servings

Ingredients:

½ cup sifted cake flour
¼ cup unsweetened cocoa powder
1 teaspoon baking powder
¼ teaspoon salt
3 large eggs, separated
½ cup granulated sugar
3 tablespoons water
1 teaspoon vanilla extract
confectioners' sugar

Filling:

½ cup heavy cream
2 tablespoons confectioners' sugar
1 tablespoon raspberry liqueur or 1
   teaspoon vanilla extract
1 cup fresh raspberries

Garnish:

Confectioners' sugar
Fresh raspberries

1. Preheat oven to 375°F.

2. Spray a 15 x 10-inch jelly-roll pan with vegetable cooking spray. Line bottom with waxed paper. Do not let paper come up sides of pan. Spray paper with vegetable cooking spray.

3. Sift together flour, cocoa powder, baking powder, and salt.

4. Beat egg yolks at high speed until foamy, 1-2 minutes. Gradually beat in sugar until thick ribbons form when beaters are lifted. Add water and vanilla; beat until well blended.

5. Sift flour mixture over egg mixture. Gently and quickly fold in until almost combined.

6. Using clean beaters, beat egg whites at high speed until stiff peaks form. Fold one-third of egg whites into batter. Fold in remaining egg whites until no white streaks remain. Pour batter into prepared pan; smooth top.

7. Bake cake until center springs back when lightly pressed, 12-15 minutes. Loosen cake around edges using a metal spatula.

8. Dust a clean cloth with confectioners' sugar. Turn cake out onto prepared cloth. Remove waxed paper. Trim cake edges. Do not let cake cool.

9. Starting with a long side, tightly roll up cake, jelly-roll style, with cloth. Transfer cake, seam-side down, to a wire rack to cool for 30 minutes.

10. To prepare filling, beat together cream, confectioners' sugar, and liqueur at medium speed until soft peaks form. Fold in raspberries. Unroll cake; remove cloth. Spread filling over cake to within 1 inch of edges.

11. Re-roll cake. Place, seam-side down, on a serving plate. Dust with confectioners' sugar. Garnish with raspberries.

Chocolate-Mint Roll

This rich, mint-flavored cream cake makes a luscious ending to a special meal.

30 minutes preparation plus cooling, 15 minutes baking

Ingredients:

- 1/3 cup cake flour
- 1/3 cup unsweetened cocoa powder
- 2 tablespoons cornstarch
- 1/2 teaspoon baking soda
- 1/2 teaspoon baking powder
- 1/8 teaspoon salt
- 4 large eggs, separated
- 3/4 cup granulated sugar

Filling and Topping:

- Granulated sugar
- 16 chocolate mint patties
  (8 ounces)
- 2 tablespoons heavy cream

Garnish:

- Whipped cream
- Sprigs of fresh mint

1. Preheat oven to 350°F. Grease a 15 x 10-inch jelly roll pan. Line with waxed paper. Grease paper. Dust with flour; tap out excess.

2. Mix together flour, cocoa powder, cornstarch, baking soda, baking powder, and salt. Beat together egg yolks and 1/4 cup sugar until light and fluffy.

3. Using clean beaters, beat egg whites at high speed until foamy. Gradually add remaining sugar, beating until stiff, but not dry, peaks form.

4. Fold one-third beaten egg whites into egg yolk mixture. Alternately fold in remaining whites and flour mixture until well blended. Spread batter in prepared pan; smooth top.

5. Bake cake until center springs back when lightly pressed, 15 minutes.

6. Dust a clean cloth with granulated sugar. Turn cake out onto prepared cloth. Remove waxed paper. Trim cake edges. Starting with a long side, tightly roll up cake with cloth. Transfer cake, seam-side down, to a wire rack to cool completely.

7. To prepare filling, in a small saucepan, melt mint patties and cream until smooth.

8. Unroll cake; remove cloth. Spread filling over cake to within 1/2 inch of edges. Re-roll cake; place, seam-side down, on a serving plate. Garnish with whipped cream and mint sprigs.

Rich Chocolate-Cheese Cake

Brown sugar and cream cheese give this chocolate cake an unusual richness and flavor.

45 minutes preparation plus cooling, 45-50 minutes baking

Makes 8 servings

Ingredients:

- 4 tablespoons unsweetened cocoa powder
- ⅔ cup milk
- 2 packages (8 ounces each) cream cheese, softened
- 2 ½ ounces (⅝ stick) butter, softened
- 1¼ cups light brown sugar
- 2 large eggs
- 1 teaspoon vanilla extract
- 1¼ cups all-purpose flour
- 2 teaspoons baking powder
- ½ teaspoon salt

Garnish:

Confectioners' sugar

1. Preheat oven to 350°F. Grease a decorative 6-cup cake mold.

2. In a saucepan, mix together cocoa powder and milk over low heat, stirring occasionally, until mixture is smooth and bubbles appear around edges of pan. Cool completely.

3. Beat together cream cheese and butter at medium speed until blended and smooth. At high speed, beat in brown sugar until light and fluffy. Add eggs, 1 at a time, beating well after each addition. Stir in vanilla.

4. Mix together flour, baking powder and salt. At low speed, alternately beat flour mixture and cocoa mixture into cream cheese mixture. Spoon batter into prepared pan; smooth top.

5. Bake cake until a toothpick inserted in the center comes out clean, 45-50 minutes.

6. Transfer pan to a wire rack to cool for 10 minutes. Turn cake out onto rack to cool completely. Dust with confectioners' sugar.

Cook's Tip

This cake can also be baked in a 6-cup Bundt pan for 40 –45 minutes.

Cakes   31

Chocolate Surprise Cake

Better than a box of chocolates, this heavenly cake has a creamy truffle center.

45 minutes preparation plus cooling, 45 minutes baking

Makes 12 servings

Filling:
- 6 ounces (6 squares) semisweet chocolate, coarsely chopped
- 1 ounce (1 square) unsweetened chocolate, coarsely chopped
- 3 tablespoons black coffee
- 3 tablespoons heavy cream
- 2 tablespoons light corn syrup

Cake:
- 2 cups whole almonds or hazelnuts, toasted and skins removed (about 8 ounces)
- 1 cup granulated sugar
- 1¾ cups all-purpose flour
- 1¼ teaspoons baking powder
- ½ teaspoon salt
- ¾ cup sour cream
- 1 tablespoon dark rum or rum extract
- 2 teaspoons vanilla extract or almond extract
- 6 ounces (1½ sticks) butter, softened
- 2 large egg yolks
- 1 large egg

Garnish:
- Confectioners' sugar

1. Preheat oven to 350°F. Grease a 10-inch tube pan.

2. To prepare filling, in a small saucepan, heat chocolate, coffee, cream, and corn syrup over low heat, stirring frequently, until chocolate melts and mixture is smooth. Remove pan from heat.

3. To prepare cake, in a blender or food processor fitted with the metal blade, process ½ cup nuts until coarsely chopped.

4. Process remaining nuts and ½ cup sugar until pastelike.

5. Sift together flour, baking powder, and salt.

6. Mix together sour cream, rum, and vanilla.

7. Beat together butter and remaining sugar at high speed until light and fluffy. Beat in nut paste. At medium speed, beat in egg yolks and egg, 1 at a time, beating well after each addition.

8. At low speed, alternately beat flour mixture and sour cream mixture into egg mixture until combined. Fold in chopped nuts.

9. Spread three-quarters of the batter in prepared pan; smooth top. Using a large spoon, make a trench, ½ inch deep and 1½ inches wide, in middle of batter. Spoon filling into trench. Cover with remaining batter.

10. Bake cake until a toothpick inserted near the center comes out clean, 45 minutes. Transfer pan to a wire rack to cool for 30 minutes. Loosen cake by running a metal spatula around sides of pan. Turn cake out onto a wire rack to cool completely. Dust with confectioners' sugar.

Cook's Tip

For best results, take care that filling does not touch the tube or sides of the pan.

Cocoa-Mocha Sponge Cake

Cocoa and espresso powders bring this festive cake to life.

20 minutes preparation, 35 minutes baking, 1½-2 hours cooling

Makes 12 servings

Ingredients:

4 large eggs, separated

⅔ cup plus 1 tablespoon granulated sugar

2 tablespoons unsweetened cocoa powder

2 tablespoons hot water

1 teaspoon instant espresso powder

1 teaspoon vanilla extract

¼ teaspoon cream of tartar

⅛ teaspoon salt

1 cup cake flour

1. Preheat oven to 350°F.

2. Beat together egg yolks and 2/3 cup of sugar at medium speed until thick, and ribbons form when beaters are lifted.

3. Mix together cocoa powder, hot water, and espresso powder until smooth. Stir in vanilla. At low speed, beat cocoa mixture into yolk mixture until well blended.

4. Using clean beaters, beat egg whites at high speed until foamy. Beat in cream of tartar and salt until soft peaks form. Beat in remaining sugar until stiff, but not dry, peaks form.

5. Sprinkle flour over cocoa mixture and fold in gently. Stir 1 cup of egg white mixture into cocoa mixture. Gently fold in remaining whites.

6. Spoon batter into an ungreased 8-cup Bundt pan; smooth top.

7. Bake cake until just set and top springs back when lightly pressed, 35 minutes. Invert pan over neck of a bottle; let cool for 1½-2 hours.

8. Loosen cake by running a metal spatula around sides of pan and tube. Invert onto a serving plate.

Brown Sugar Chocolate Delight

Light and moist, with a hint of coffee flavor, this cake is terrific on its own or with ice cream.

20 minutes preparation plus cooling, 40-45 minutes baking   Makes 12 servings

Ingredients:

- 1½ cups all-purpose flour
- ¾ cup whole-wheat flour
- 1 teaspoon baking soda
- ½ teaspoon baking powder
- ½ teaspoon salt
- 4 ounces (4 squares) semisweet chocolate, coarsely chopped
- 1 ounce (1 square) unsweetened baking chocolate, coarsely chopped
- ½ cup boiling water
- 1 teaspoon instant coffee powder
- 8 ounces (2 sticks) butter, softened
- 2 cups firmly packed dark brown sugar
- 2 large eggs
- ¾ teaspoon vanilla extract
- 1 cup milk

Topping:

- Confectioners' sugar

1. Preheat oven to 350°F. Grease a 10-inch springform tube pan. Dust with flour; tap out excess.

2. Mix together all-purpose flour, whole-wheat flour, baking soda, baking powder, and salt. Mix both types of chocolate in boiling water until chocolate melts. Dissolve coffee powder in chocolate mixture. Stir until smooth.

3. Beat together butter and sugar at medium speed until light and fluffy. Beat in eggs, 1 at a time, beating well after each addition. Beat in vanilla.

4. At low speed, alternately beat flour mixture and milk into butter mixture. Beat in chocolate mixture until combined. Pour batter evenly into prepared pan.

5. Bake cake until a toothpick inserted near the center comes out clean, 40-45 minutes. Transfer pan to a wire rack to cool for 10 minutes. Loosen cake by running a metal spatula around sides of pan. Remove sides of pan. Dust with confectioners' sugar.

Chocolate Marble Cake

Slice into this light cake to reveal the swirly pattern

25 minutes preparation, 45-50 minutes baking plus cooling

Makes 6-8 servings

Ingredients:

1½ cups all-purpose flour
1½ teaspoons baking powder
¼ teaspoon salt
4 ounces (1 stick) butter, softened
1 cup superfine sugar
3 large eggs, beaten
⅔ cup sour cream
½ teaspoon vanilla extract
2 tablespoons unsweetened cocoa
  powder, sifted
Finely grated peel of 1 orange

1. Preheat oven to 350°F. Grease an 8½-inch kugelhopf or deep fluted ring pan. Dust the pan with flour and tap out the excess. Sift the flour, baking powder, and salt into a mixing bowl and set aside.

2. In a separate bowl, beat together the butter and sugar with an electric beater or wooden spoon until pale and fluffy. Gradually add the eggs and beat well after each addition.

3. Alternately fold in the flour mixture and sour cream. Add a little at a time until the ingredients are incorporated and the mixture is smooth.

4. Put a third of the mixture into a separate bowl and stir in the vanilla. Stir the cocoa powder and orange peel into the remaining mixture.

5. Spoon half the vanilla mixture into the prepared pan. Spoon over the chocolate and orange mixture. Spoon the remaining vanilla mixture on top. Swirl through a few times with a round-bladed knife to create a marbled effect.

6. Bake for 45-50 minutes, or until a toothpick inserted into the center of the cake comes out clean.

7. Let the cake cool in the pan for 5 minutes. Turn out onto a wire rack and let cool completely.

Cook's Tip

You can also bake this cake in a larger shallow ring pan. It will take 35-40 minutes.

Banana-Chocolate Bundt Cake

Mashed bananas make this attractive ring cake temptingly moist.

20 minutes preparation, 45 minutes baking plus cooling

Ingredients:

- 1¾ cups all-purpose flour
- 2 teaspoons baking powder
- ½ teaspoon salt
- 2 ripe bananas
- 1 tablespoon lemon juice
- 5 ounces (1¼ sticks) butter, softened
- ⅔ cup light brown sugar
- 2 large eggs
- ½ cup chopped walnuts (2 ounces)

Frosting:

- 4 ounces semisweet chocolate
- 2 ounces (½ stick) butter, softened
- Walnut halves, to garnish

1. Preheat oven to 350°F. Grease an 8-cup Bundt pan. Dust with a little flour, tapping out the excess.

2. Sift together the flour, baking powder, and salt. In a separate mixing bowl, mash the bananas with the lemon juice and set aside.

3. In a mixing bowl, beat together the butter and sugar with an electric beater or wooden spoon until pale and fluffy. Beat in the eggs, 1 at a time, until blended.

4. Fold half the flour mixture into the creamed mixture. Fold in the bananas and then the remaining flour and the chopped walnuts.

5. Transfer the mixture to the prepared pan. Bake for 45 minutes, or until a toothpick inserted into the center of the cake comes out clean.

6. Let the cake cool in the pan for 10 minutes, then turn out onto a wire rack and let cool completely.

7. For the frosting, break the chocolate into squares and melt in a small bowl set over a pan of simmering water. Remove from the heat and beat in the butter until the mixture begins to thicken. Set aside to cool.

8. Spread the frosting over the cake and let set. Decorate with the walnut halves and slice to serve.

Chocolate Chip Ring

When the chips are down, there's nothing quite like a family chocolate cake.

35 minutes preparation, 30-35 minutes baking plus cooling

Ingredients:

3 ounces (¾ stick) butter, softened
⅔ cup superfine sugar
½ tsp vanilla extract
2 large eggs
2 cups all-purpose flour, sifted
1 tablespoon baking powder
1 teaspoon salt
⅔ cup sour cream

Filling and Topping:

½ cup chopped walnuts
¼ cup unsweetened cocoa powder
6 tablespoons semisweet chocolate chips
Confectioners' sugar, to dust
Strawberries, to garnish

1. Preheat oven to 350°F. Grease a 9-inch ring pan. For the filling and topping, mix together the walnuts, cocoa, and chocolate chips in a bowl. Set aside.

2. In a separate bowl, beat together the butter and superfine sugar with a large wooden spoon until pale and fluffy. Mix in the vanilla.

3. Gradually beat in the eggs, beating well after each addition. Alternately fold in the flour and sour cream, a little at a time, until smooth.

4. Spoon half the mixture into the pan. Sprinkle with half the chocolate chip mixture. Spread the remaining cake mixture over the top and cover with the remaining chocolate chip mixture. Cut through the mixture a few times with a knife to give a marbled effect.

5. Bake for 30-35 minutes, or until a toothpick inserted into the center of the cake comes out clean.

6. Let cool in the pan for 10 minutes. Run a knife around the edge of the cake and invert onto a wire rack. Remove the pan and let cool completely. Dust all over with the confectioners' sugar and garnish with the strawberries.

Chocolate-Nut Coffee Cake

This family-pleasing cake makes a fitting finale to a special celebration breakfast.

40 minutes preparation, 1 hour rising, 25 minutes baking   Makes 16 servings

Ingredients:

- 1 package active dry yeast
- ¾ cup warm milk (105°-115°F)
- ¼ cup granulated sugar
- ½ teaspoon salt
- 2½ ounces (⅔ stick) butter,
  softened
- 2 cups all-purpose flour

Filling:

- ⅓ cup walnuts or pecans
  (about 1¼ ounces)
- 2 tablespoons granulated sugar
- 1½ ounces semisweet chocolate

Glaze:

- 1 large egg, lightly beaten

1. In a large bowl, dissolve yeast in warm milk. Let stand until foamy, 5-10 minutes.

2. Stir sugar and salt into yeast mixture. Beat in butter at medium speed. At low speed, beat in flour, a little at a time, until a soft dough forms.

3. On a floured surface, knead dough until smooth and elastic, 5-10 minutes, adding more flour to prevent sticking. Place dough in a large greased bowl, turning to coat. Cover loosely with a damp cloth; let rise in a warm place until doubled, 30 minutes.

4. Meanwhile, prepare filling. In a food processor fitted with a metal blade, pulse together nuts, sugar, and chocolate until coarsely ground. Do not overprocess.

5. Punch down dough. On a floured surface, knead dough until smooth and elastic, 5-10 minutes, adding more flour to prevent sticking. Divide dough in half. Knead filling into one-half until nuts are evenly distributed. Roll into a 12-inch rope.

6. Grease a 10-inch tube pan. On a floured surface, using a floured rolling pin, roll plain dough half into a 13 x 5-inch rectangle. Place dough rope with filling lengthwise down center of rectangle. Fold sides over to enclose. Place dough, seam-side down, in prepared pan. Cover loosely with a damp cloth; let rise in a warm place until doubled, 30 minutes.

7. Preheat oven to 400°F. Brush cake with glaze.

8. Bake cake until golden brown, 25 minutes. Transfer pan to a wire rack to cool completely.

Peanut-Chocolate Chip Cake

This buttery, fragrant cake is chock-full of peanuts and chocolate.

40 minutes preparation, 45 minutes baking   Makes one 10-inch cake

Peanut Batter:

3 tablespoons butter, softened
½ cup firmly packed brown sugar
1 large egg
¼ cup molasses
1 cup all-purpose flour
1½ teaspoons ground cinnamon
1 teaspoon baking powder
½ teaspoon baking soda
¼ cup buttermilk
½ cup chopped peanuts

Chocolate Batter:

3 tablespoons butter, softened
½ cup granulated sugar
1 large egg
1 cup all-purpose flour
1 teaspoon baking powder
½ cup milk
1 cup semisweet chocolate chips

Topping:

2 tablespoons butter, softened
2 tablespoons molasses
¼ cup chopped peanuts

1. Preheat oven to 350°F. Grease a 10-inch tube pan.

2. To prepare peanut batter, in a large bowl, beat together butter and brown sugar at medium speed until fluffy. Beat in egg and molasses.

3. Mix together flour, cinnamon, baking powder, and baking soda.

4. At low speed, alternately beat flour mixture and buttermilk into egg mixture. Stir in nuts.

5. To prepare chocolate batter, in another large bowl, beat together butter and sugar at medium speed until fluffy. Beat in egg.

6. In a small bowl, mix together flour and baking powder.

7. Alternately beat flour mixture and milk into egg mixture at low speed. Stir in chocolate chips.

8. To prepare topping, mix together butter and molasses. Spread topping evenly in prepared pan. Sprinkle with nuts.

9. Alternately spoon peanut and chocolate batters into pan. Twist a knife through batters to create a marbled effect.

10. Bake until a toothpick inserted near center of cake comes out clean, 45 minutes. Transfer pan to a wire rack to cool slightly. Turn cake out onto rack. Serve warm.

Cook's Tip

Try substituting peanut butter chips for chopped peanuts in the cake topping.

Chocolate Angel Food Cake

Light, tender, and not too sweet—this chocolate-drizzled cake is truly heavenly.

25 minutes preparation, 40 minutes baking, 1½-2 hours cooling   Makes 10 servings

Ingredients:

- ¼ cup plus 2 tablespoons unsweetened cocoa powder
- ¼ cup boiling water
- 2 teaspoons vanilla extract
- ½ teaspoon instant espresso powder
- ½ teaspoon rum extract
- 12 large egg whites
- 2 teaspoons cream of tartar
- 1¾ cups granulated sugar
- 1 cup cake flour
- ¼ teaspoon salt

Glaze:

- 6 ounces (6 squares) semisweet chocolate, coarsely chopped

1. Preheat oven to 350°F.

2. Mix together cocoa powder, boiling water, vanilla, espresso powder, and rum extract.

3. Beat 6 egg whites at high speed until foamy. Beat in 1 teaspoon cream of tartar until soft peaks form. Gradually beat in ½ cup of sugar until stiff, but not dry, peaks form. Scrape into a large bowl. Repeat with remaining egg whites, cream of tartar, and another ½ cup of sugar. Add to bowl.

4. Fold 1 cup of egg white mixture into cocoa mixture.

5. Sift together flour, salt, and remaining sugar. Sift flour mixture over egg white mixture in 3 batches, folding until almost incorporated. Add cocoa mixture; gently but thoroughly fold in until no white streaks remain.

6. Immediately pour batter into an ungreased 10-inch tube pan. Wipe any batter from inside edge of pan. Gently smooth top.

7. Bake cake until top springs back when lightly pressed, 40 minutes. Invert pan over neck of a bottle. Let cool, 1½-2 hours.

8. Loosen cake by running a metal spatula around sides of pan and tube. Transfer to a serving plate.

9. To prepare glaze, in top of a double boiler set over simmering (not boiling) water, melt chocolate, stirring until smooth. Remove from over water. Drizzle glaze over cake. Let stand until set.

Frosted Chocolate Cheesecake

Impressive to look at, this dessert will surely please cheesecake and chocolate lovers alike!

20 minutes preparation, 50 minutes baking, 2 hours chilling

Makes one 9-inch cheesecake

Crust:
  2 cups chocolate wafer crumbs
  5 tablespoons melted butter
Filling:
  3 packages (8 ounces each) cream
    cheese, at room temperature
  1 cup granulated sugar
  5 large eggs
  2 ounces (2 squares) semisweet
    chocolate, melted
Frosting:
  6 ounces (6 squares) semisweet
    chocolate, melted
  ½ cup sour cream

1. To prepare crust, in a medium bowl, mix together chocolate crumbs and melted butter until well blended. Press into a 9-inch springform pan.

2. Preheat oven to 300°F.

3. To prepare filling, in a large bowl, beat together cream cheese, sugar, and eggs at medium speed until smooth and fluffy. Spoon half of cream cheese mixture into crust.

4. Stir chocolate into remaining cream cheese mixture until well blended. Drizzle over batter in crust to make swirls.

5. Bake cheesecake for 50 minutes. Transfer pan to a wire rack. Cool completely. Transfer cheesecake to a serving plate, cover with plastic wrap, and chill for 2 hours.

6. Uncover cheesecake; carefully remove the sides of the pan.

7. To prepare frosting, in a small bowl, mix together chocolate and sour cream. Spread over top of cheesecake. Pipe some frosting around edge of cake if desired. Chill briefly until frosting is set.

Cook's Tip

Cheesecake can be made 2-3 days in advance and kept, covered with plastic wrap, in the refrigerator. Or, the cake can be frozen for up to 3 weeks. Defrost before serving.

Chocolate Espresso Cheesecake

A mocha cheesecake enriched with silky-smooth sour cream.

1 hour preparation, 50-55 minutes baking plus cooling

Makes 10-12 servings

Ingredients:

- 12 graham crackers, crushed
- ½ teaspoon ground cinnamon
- 1 tablespoon unsweetened cocoa powder
- 1 tablespoon superfine sugar
- 3 ounces (¾ stick) butter, melted

Filling:

- 6 tablespoons superfine sugar
- 8 ounces (8 squares) semisweet chocolate, broken into squares
- 3 tablespoons butter
- 1 tablespoon instant espresso powder
- 4 large eggs, separated
- 2 packages (8 ounces each) cream cheese
- 1¼ cups sour cream
- 6 tablespoons unsweetened cocoa powder
- 2 tablespoons cornstarch
- Chocolate leaves, raspberries, and sifted confectioners' sugar, to garnish

1. Preheat oven to 350°F. Grease a 9-inch springform cake pan. In a large bowl, mix the crushed crackers with the cinnamon, cocoa powder, superfine sugar, and butter until evenly mixed. Press onto the base and sides of the pan.

2. To prepare filling, reserve 1 tablespoon superfine sugar. Melt together the chocolate, butter, and espresso powder in a bowl set over a pan of barely simmering water. Transfer to a large bowl. Beat in the egg yolks, remaining superfine sugar, cream cheese, sour cream, cocoa powder, and cornstarch.

3. Beat the egg whites until soft peaks form. Beat in the reserved sugar until stiff peaks form. Fold into the cheese mixture, then pour into the pan.

4. Bake for 50-55 minutes, or until the edge of the cheescake is set firm. Cool completely in the pan. Turn out and garnish with the chocolate leaves and rasp-berries. Dust with confectioners' sugar and serve.

Cook's Tip

The cake continues to set as it cools down, so bake only until the edge is firm. Store the cheesecake at room temperature—do not chill.

Chocolate-Orange Cheesecake

This chocolate cheesecake has a crunchy oat base and a creamy orange frosting.

40 minutes preparation, 1 hour baking plus cooling and chilling   Makes 8 servings

Ingredients:
- 1 cup crushed oatmeal cookies
- 6 tablespoons (¾ stick) melted butter

Filling:
- 2 packages (16 ounces) cream cheese
- 1¼ cups superfine sugar
- 4 tablespoons all-purpose flour
- 4 large eggs, beaten
- 4 ounces (4 squares) white chocolate, coarsely chopped
- 3 ounces (3 squares) milk chocolate, coarsely chopped
- grated peel of ½ orange
- 1 tablespoon orange juice
- 1 tablespoon unsweetened cocoa powder

Frosting:
- 3 tablespoons orange juice
- 1 tablespoon superfine sugar
- 2 ounces milk chocolate, chopped
- 1 package (8 ounces) cream cheese
- Chocolate curls, to garnish

1. Crush the cookies and mix with the melted butter. Grease an 8-inch springform cake pan. Press the crumb mixture over the base of the pan and chill for 1 hour.

2. Preheat oven to 350°F. Beat together the cream cheese, sugar, flour, and eggs until smooth. Divide the mixture between 2 bowls.

3. Melt the white chocolate in a bowl set over a saucepan of simmering water. Melt the milk chocolate in the same way.

4. Stir the melted white chocolate into one of the bowls of cheesecake mixture and beat until smooth. Stir in the orange peel and juice. Stir the melted milk chocolate into the remaining cheesecake mixture and beat until smooth, then beat in the cocoa powder.

5. Spoon the white chocolate mixture over the cookie base. Spoon the milk chocolate mixture on top and gently swirl the 2 mixtures together.

6. Bake for 1 hour, or until risen and set. Put on a wire rack to cool.

7. For the frosting, bring the orange juice and sugar to a boil in a small saucepan. Remove from the heat and stir in the chocolate until melted. Set aside to cool.

8. Beat the cream cheese until smooth, then gradually beat in the melted chocolate mixture until smooth. Spread over the cheesecake and chill overnight.

9. Remove the sides of the pan and put the cheesecake on a serving plate. Garnish with the chocolate curls.

Chocolate Velvet Cheesecake

Not for the diet-conscious, this makes a glorious dessert cake.

25 minutes preparation, 1 hour baking plus chilling and cooling

Makes 8-10 servings

Ingredients:

- 12 chocolate-covered graham crackers, crushed
- 4-5 tablespoons (½ stick) butter, melted

Filling and Garnish:

- 3½ packages (8 ounces each) cream cheese
- 1 cup superfine sugar
- 1 teaspoon vanilla extract
- 4 large eggs, beaten
- 4 tablespoons unsweetened cocoa powder
- 4 tablespoons warm water
- Chocolate curls
- Confectioners' sugar, to dust

1. Preheat oven to 350°F. Line the base of a springform cake pan with waxed paper.

2. In a bowl, mix together the crackers and melted butter. Spoon into the pan and press evenly over the base. Chill.

3. For the filling, put the cheese and superfine sugar into a bowl. Beat together with an electric beater or wooden spoon until smooth. Beat in the vanilla extract. Gradually beat in the eggs until fully incorporated.

4. In a small bowl, mix the cocoa powder with warm water to make a paste. Beat into the cheese mixture until well combined.

5. Spoon the mixture into the pan and level the surface. Put the pan on a baking sheet. Bake for 1 hour, or until the cake feels spongy to the touch in the center and the side shrinks away from the pan. Put the pan on a wire rack and let cool completely. Chill in the pan overnight.

6. To serve, run a knife around the edge of the cake. Remove the sides of the pan and transfer the cake to a serving plate. Put the chocolate curls on top and dust with confectioner's sugar.

Cook's Tip

This cheesecake keeps for up to 3 days in the refrigerator. If preferred, make the base with shortbread, chocolate chip cookies, or oatmeal cookies. Dust the top of the cake with confectioners' sugar, cocoa powder, or chocolate milk powder instead of the chocolate curls.

Luscious Chocolate Cheesecake

Decadent, yet light and fluffy, this cheesecake is the perfect treat for real chocoholics.

20 minutes preparation, 1¼ hours baking plus standing and chilling   Makes 10 servings

Ingredients:

1¾ cups (7 ounces) chocolate wafer crumbs

7 tablespoons melted butter

Filling:

3 packages (8 ounces each) cream cheese

1⅓ cups granulated sugar

4 large eggs

1½ teaspoons vanilla extract

1 cup sour cream

8 ounces (8 squares) semisweet chocolate, coarsely chopped

½ cup heavy cream

Glaze and Garnish:

4 ounces (4 squares) semisweet chocolate, coarsely chopped

2 tablespoons (¼ stick) butter

½ cup heavy cream

2 teaspoons light corn syrup

Confectioners' sugar

Chocolate leaves (optional)

Fresh strawberries or raspberries

1. Preheat oven to 300°F. Grease bottom and sides of a 9-inch springform pan.

2. Combine cookie crumbs and melted butter. Press crumb mixture evenly over bottom and up sides of prepared pan.

3. To prepare filling, in a large bowl, beat cream cheese at medium speed until smooth. Beat in sugar until well blended. Beat in eggs, 1 at a time, beating for 2-3 minutes after each addition. Beat in vanilla and sour cream.

4. In the top of a double boiler set over simmering (not boiling) water, melt chocolate, stirring until smooth. Remove from heat. Stir in cream until blended.

5. Stir chocolate mixture into cream cheese mixture. Pour filling into prepared base; smooth top.

6. Bake cake until edges are slightly puffed and lightly browned, 1¼ hours. Turn off oven. Let cake stand in oven with door slightly open for 1 hour.

7. Transfer pan to a wire rack to cool. While cake is still warm, gently run a knife around edges. When cool, carefully remove sides of pan and transfer to a serving plate.

8. To prepare glaze, in the top of a double boiler set over simmering (not boiling) water, melt chocolate and butter, stirring until smooth. Stir in cream until well blended. Remove from heat; stir in corn syrup. Let cool until thickened, 10-15 minutes.

9. Using a metal spatula, spread top of cheesecake with chocolate glaze. Chill for at least 5 hours.

10. Dust with confectioners' sugar. Garnish with chocolate leaves and strawberries.

Raspberry-Brownie Cheesecake

This dessert combines chocolate brownies with a rich, creamy cheesecake.

45 minutes preparation, 75-80 minutes baking plus chilling

Makes 8-10 servings

Ingredients:

- 6 ounces double chocolate chip cookies
- ½ cup finely chopped walnuts
- 2 ounces semisweet chocolate
- 2 ounces (½ stick) butter

Brownies:

- ½ cup superfine sugar
- 2 large eggs
- ¾ cup all-purpose flour, sifted
- ½ teaspoon baking powder
- ½ teaspoon salt
- 1 teaspoon vanilla extract
- ½ cup unsweetened cocoa powder, sifted
- 2 tablespoons seedless raspberry jelly
- 3 ounces (¾ stick) butter, melted

Filling and Topping:

- 2 packages (8 ounces each) cream cheese
- ¾ cup superfine sugar
- 1 teaspoon vanilla extract
- 3 large eggs
- ⅔ cup sour cream
- 5 tablespoons seedless raspberry jelly, warmed

1. Put the chocolate in a bowl with the butter. Stand over a pan of simmering water until melted.

2. Mix the melted chocolate and butter with the cookie crumb mixture. Spoon into a deep 8-inch springform cake pan and press evenly over the base and up the sides of the pan. Set aside.

3. For the brownies, preheat oven to 350°F. Grease and line an 8-inch square cake pan. Beat together the sugar and eggs until light and fluffy. Gradually beat in the rest of the brownie ingredients. Spoon the mixture into the pan and spread level.

4. Bake for 20 minutes, or until a toothpick inserted into the center comes out almost clean. Do not bake the brownies completely. Leave the oven on and transfer the pan to a wire rack to cool. Cut the the cake into small squares.

5. For the cheesecake, beat together the cream cheese, sugar, and vanilla until smooth. Gradually add the eggs, beating well after each addition. Stir in the sour cream and beat until smooth. Gently fold in the brownies.

6. Spoon the cheesecake mixture over the prepared base, smoothing the surface. Put the pan on a baking sheet and bake for 55-60 minutes, or until set. Turn the oven off and let the cheesecake cool gradually in the oven for an additional 20 minutes.

7. Transfer the cake pan to a wire rack to cool slightly. While the cake is still warm, run a knife around the edge of the pan. Chill the cheesecake for 2 hours. When cool, carefully remove sides of pan and transfer to a serving plate.

8. Spread the jelly over the top of the cheesecake and chill for 20 minutes before serving.

Chocolate & Vanilla Cupcakes

Dark chocolate cases filled with a rich mousse and topped with a swirl of cream.

35 minutes preparation plus cooling

Casing:
  8 ounces (8 squares) semisweet
    chocolate

Filling:
  3 ounces (3 squares) semisweet
    chocolate
  ½ cup heavy cream
  1 tablespoon superfine sugar
  Drops of vanilla extract

1. Put 8 ounces (8 squares) of chocolate into a heatproof bowl and set over a saucepan of simmering water. Leave the chocolate to melt, stirring occasionally.

2. Put 8 paper liners into muffin pans. Brush with the melted chocolate over the inside of the cases and leave to set.

3. For the filling, melt 2 ounces (2 squares) of semisweet chocolate in a heatproof bowl over a pan of barely simmering water.

4. Put cream, sugar, and vanilla extract into a mixing bowl and whip until soft peaks form.

5. Beat 2 tablespoons of cream mixture into the melted chocolate until smooth and combined. Put the remainder into a large star-shaped nozzle and chill.

6. Spoon the chocolate-cream mixture into each chocolate case and level the surface. Chill until firm. Using a potato peeler, scrape the remaining chocolate squares to form flakes.

7. Pipe rosettes of cream on top of each dessert. Carefully peel away the paper liners and transfer them onto a serving plate.

8. Decorate with the chocolate flakes and serve at once with raspberries.

Cakes   47

Little Sacher Tortes

These luscious chocolate-glazed cakes are the perfect ending to a formal sit-down dinner.

20 minutes preparation plus cooling and standing, 15 minutes baking   Makes 1 dozen cakes

Ingredients:

1¼ cups all-purpose flour

1/3 cup granulated sugar

1/3 cup ground almonds (about 1½ ounces)

½ teaspoon baking powder

½ teaspoon baking soda

¼ teaspoon salt

3 ounces (¾ stick) butter, softened

⅔ cup firmly packed light brown sugar

2 large eggs

½ cup milk

2 ounces (2 squares) unsweetened chocolate, melted

1 tablespoon rum or 1 teaspoon rum extract

½ cup apricot preserves, melted

Glaze:

⅔ cup heavy cream

6 ounces (6 squares) semisweet chocolate, coarsely
   chopped

2 tablespoons butter

2 tablespoons light corn syrup

Topping and Garnish:

Whipped cream

Candied violets

1. Preheat oven to 350°F. Grease 12 standard size muffin-pan cups or line with paper liners. Dust with flour; tap out excess.

2. Mix together flour, granulated sugar, nuts, baking powder, baking soda, and salt.

3. Beat together butter and brown sugar at medium speed until light and fluffy. Add eggs, 1 at a time, beating well after each addition.

4. At low speed, beat in milk, melted chocolate, and rum. Beat flour mixture into milk mixture until combined. Spoon batter into prepared pan, filling cups three-quarters full.

5. Bake cakes until a toothpick inserted in the center comes out clean, 15 minutes. Transfer pan to a wire rack to cool for 10 minutes. Turn cakes out onto rack to cool completely.

6. Brush melted preserves over cakes. Let stand until set, 30 minutes.

7. To prepare glaze, in a medium saucepan, heat cream, chocolate, butter, and corn syrup over medium heat, stirring constantly, until chocolate melts and mixture boils. Remove from heat; let stand for 1 minute. Stir vigorously until mixture thickens.

8. Spread glaze evenly over cakes. Let stand until set.

9. Using a pastry bag fitted with a star tip, pipe whipped cream rosettes on top. Garnish with a candied violet in the center of each rosette.

Chocolate Fudge Cups

Deep, dense, and fudgy, these small cakes look enchanting garnished with cream and fruit.

15 minutes preparation, 25-30 minutes baking

Makes 6 cakes

Cakes:
- 1 cup all-purpose flour
- ⅔ cup granulated sugar
- 3 tablespoons unsweetened cocoa powder
- 2 teaspoons baking powder
- ¼ teaspoon salt
- ½ cup milk
- 2 ounces (½ stick) butter, melted
- 1 teaspoon vanilla extract
- ½ cup chopped pecans (2 ounces)

Topping:
- ⅔ cup firmly packed brown sugar
- 3 tablespoons unsweetened cocoa powder
- 12 tablespoons warm water

Garnish:
- Whipped cream
- Fresh raspberries

1. Preheat the oven to 350°F. Grease six 6-ounce custard cups.

2. To prepare the cakes, in a medium bowl, mix together the flour, sugar, cocoa powder, baking powder, and salt.

3. In a small bowl, mix together the milk, melted butter, and vanilla. Stir into the flour mixture. Fold in the nuts. Spoon batter into the prepared custard cups, dividing evenly. Place the cups on a baking sheet.

4. To prepare the topping, in a small bowl, mix together the brown sugar and cocoa powder. Sprinkle each cup of batter with some topping, then sprinkle each cup with 2 tablespoons of the warm water.

5. Bake until a toothpick inserted in the center comes out clean, 25-30 minutes.

6. Cool the cakes in the cups for about 20 minutes. Loosen sides of the cakes and invert onto serving dishes. Garnish with whipped cream and raspberries.

Cook's Tip

Sprinkling each batter-filled cup with 2 tablespoons of warm water before baking dissolves the topping so it melts into the cakes, creating an extra-moist result.

Double Chocolate Cupcakes

With an intense chocolatey flavor, these cupcakes will entice both kids and adults alike.

20 minutes preparation, 20 minutes baking

Makes 2 dozen cupcakes

Ingredients:

- 1 cup plus 1 tablespoon all-purpose flour
- 1 teaspoon baking soda
- ¼ teaspoon salt
- 4 ounces (1 stick) butter, softened
- 1 cup granulated sugar
- 2 large eggs
- ⅔ cup buttermilk
- 2 ounces (2 squares) unsweetened chocolate, melted and cooled slightly
- 1 teaspoon vanilla extract
- 1½ cups semisweet mini chocolate chips

Frosting:

- 1½ cups confectioners' sugar
- 2 tablespoons butter, softened
- 2 tablespoons unsweetened cocoa powder
- 2½ tablespoons milk

1. Preheat oven to 325°F. Line 24 standard size muffin-pan cups with paper liners.

2. Mix together 1 cup of flour, baking soda, and salt.

3. Beat together butter and sugar at medium speed until light and fluffy. Add eggs, 1 at a time, beating well after each addition.

4. Alternately beat flour mixture and buttermilk into butter mixture. Stir in melted chocolate and vanilla.

5. Toss 1 cup chocolate chips with remaining 1 tablespoon of flour; stir into batter. Spoon batter into prepared pans, filling cups two-thirds full.

6. Bake cupcakes until tops are firm, 20 minutes. Transfer to a wire rack to cool completely.

7. To prepare frosting, mix together confectioners' sugar, butter, cocoa powder, and milk. If frosting is too thick, add a little more milk. If too thin, add a little more confectioners' sugar.

8. Spread frosting over cupcakes. Sprinkle with remaining chocolate morsels, if desired.

Cook's Tip

Buttermilk adds moistness and flavor to these cupcakes. If there's none on hand, mix 2/3 cup milk with 1 teaspoon lemon juice as an alternative. Let the mixture stand for 5 minutes before using as recipe directs.

The cupcakes keep well if covered with plastic wrap and refrigerated. Or, they can be wrapped tightly in plastic wrap and frozen for up to 3 months.

White Chocolate-Almond Cupcakes

These cupcakes, topped with a creamy, light frosting, are irresistible.

30 minutes preparation plus cooling and chilling, 20 minutes baking   Makes 1 dozen cupcakes

Ingredients:

$1/3$ cup all-purpose flour

$1/2$ teaspoon baking powder

$1/8$ teaspoon salt

$2/3$ cup granulated sugar

4 ounces (1 stick) butter, softened

1 package (7 ounces) marzipan

4 large eggs

1 tablespoon kirsch liqueur or
   orange juice

$1/4$ teaspoon almond extract

Frosting:

$1/2$ cup heavy cream

6 ounces (6 squares) white
   chocolate, coarsely chopped

2 ounces ($1/2$ stick) butter

Garnish:

$1/2$ cup slivered, blanched almonds
   (about 2 ounces), toasted

1. Preheat oven to 350°F. Grease 12 standard size muffin-pan cups. Dust with flour; tap out excess.

2. Mix together flour, baking powder, and salt.

3. Beat together sugar, butter, and marzipan at medium speed until blended and smooth.

4. Add eggs, 1 at a time, beating well after each addition. Beat in liqueur and almond extract.

5. At low speed, beat in flour mixture until just blended.

6. Spoon batter evenly into prepared pan, filling cups two-thirds full.

7. Bake cupcakes until tops are golden, 20 minutes. Transfer pan to a wire rack to cool slightly. Turn cupcakes out onto rack to cool completely.

8. To prepare frosting, in a small saucepan, heat cream over medium heat until bubbles appear around edges of pan.

9. Add white chocolate and butter, stirring constantly until melted and smooth. Remove from heat; cool completely.

10. Beat white chocolate mixture at low speed until just thickened.

11. Spread frosting over cupcakes. Sprinkle with nuts. Chill until frosting is set.

Cook's Tip

Overbeating the frosting will cause it to separate. If it does, chill mixture until just set, then gradually beat in a small amount of heavy cream and some additional melted white chocolate. Use the best quality white chocolate possible.

Cakes   51

Mocha-Almond Cakes

Bake-shop perfect, these yummy cakes have a surprise jelly and chocolate cream filling.

1 hour preparation plus cooling, 15 minutes baking

Makes 10 cakes

Ingredients:

1 package (18½ ounces) chocolate
    cake mix

Filling and Garnish:

1½ tablespoons instant espresso
    powder

1 teaspoon water

4 cups heavy cream

½ cup confectioners' sugar

2-3 tablespoons coffee liqueur or 1
    teaspoon almond extract

2 tablespoons raspberry jelly

3 ounces (3 squares) semisweet
    chocolate, shaved

3 cups blanched, slivered almonds,
    toasted (about 12 ounces)

5 maraschino cherries, drained
    and halved

1. Preheat oven to 350°F. Grease a 15 x 10-inch jelly roll pan. Line with waxed paper.

2. Prepare cake mix according to package directions. Spread batter into prepared pan; smooth top.

3. Bake cake until top springs back when lightly pressed, 15 minutes. Transfer baking pan to a wire rack to cool for 5 minutes. Turn cake out onto rack. Remove waxed paper. Cool completely.

4. Using a 3-inch round cookie cutter, cut out 20 circles from chocolate cake.

5. To prepare filling, dissolve espresso powder in water.

6. Beat together cream, confectioners' sugar, liqueur, and espresso mixture until soft peaks form.

7. Spread jelly evenly over 10 cake circles. Spread 2 tablespoons whipped cream mixture on top of jelly. Sprinkle chocolate shavings evenly over cream mixture. Place remaining circles on top of cakes, pressing down slightly.

8. Spread sides and top with more whipped cream mixture. Press nuts onto sides of each cake.

9. Using a pastry bag fitted with a star tip, pipe remaining cream mixture into rosettes on top of cakes. Garnish each with a cherry.

Banana-Chocolate Coconut Loaf

This sweet treat is guaranteed to be popular with the whole family.

45 minutes preparation plus cooling, 50-60 minutes baking   Makes 8 servings

Ingredients:

2 cups all-purpose flour
1 teaspoon baking powder
1 teaspoon baking soda
4 ounces (1 stick) butter, softened
½ cup firmly packed brown sugar
2 large eggs
2 medium ripe bananas, mashed
½ cup sour cream
½ cup shredded sweetened
   coconut, toasted
⅔ cup semisweet chocolate chips

Frosting:

1½ cups confectioners' sugar
2 tablespoons fresh lemon juice
1½ teaspoons butter, softened

Garnish:

1 cup shredded sweetened coconut,
   toasted

1. Preheat oven to 350°F. Grease a 9 x 5-inch loaf pan. Dust with flour; tap out excess.

2. Mix together flour, baking powder, and baking soda.

3. Beat together butter and brown sugar at medium speed until light and fluffy. Add eggs, 1 at a time, beating well after each addition. Stir in mashed bananas and sour cream.

4. At low speed, beat flour mixture into banana mixture, ½ cup at a time, until combined. Stir in coconut. Fold in chocolate chips. Spread batter in prepared pan; smooth top.

5. Bake cake until golden and a toothpick inserted in the center comes out clean, 50-60 minutes. Transfer pan to a wire rack to cool slightly.

6. Loosen cake by running a metal spatula around sides of pan. Turn cake out onto rack to cool completely.

7. To prepare frosting, mix together confectioners' sugar, lemon juice, and butter until smooth.

8. Spread frosting over top of cake. To garnish, sprinkle with coconut.

Chocolate-Buttercream Loaf Cake

Serve this intriguing buttercream-filled dessert with fresh fruit or berries in season.

1 hour preparation plus cooling, 65-70 minutes baking   Makes 12 servings

Ingredients:
- 2 ounces (2 squares) unsweetened chocolate, finely chopped
- 1 cup boiling water
- 2 cups all-purpose flour
- 1 teaspoon ground cinnamon
- ¾ teaspoon baking soda
- ¼ teaspoon salt
- 1½ cups firmly packed light brown sugar
- 4 ounces (1 stick) butter, softened
- 2 large eggs
- ½ cup sour cream

Filling and Topping:
- ½ cup confectioners' sugar
- 2 ounces (½ stick) butter, softened
- 1½ tablespoons heavy cream
- 1 tablespoon light corn syrup
- ½ teaspoon ground cinnamon
- Confectioners' sugar

1. Preheat oven to 350°F. Grease a 9 x 5-inch loaf pan. Dust with flour; tap out excess.

2. Mix together chocolate and boiling water until chocolate melts. Cool completely.

3. Mix together flour, cinnamon, baking soda, and salt.

4. Beat together brown sugar and butter at medium speed until light and fluffy. Add eggs, 1 at a time, beating well after each addition. Beat in sour cream.

5. At low speed, alternately beat chocolate mixture and flour mixture into butter mixture until blended. Spread batter in prepared pan; smooth top.

6. Bake cake until a toothpick inserted in the center comes out clean, 65-70 minutes. Transfer pan to a wire rack to cool for 10 minutes. Loosen cake by running a metal spatula around sides of pan. Turn cake out onto rack to cool completely.

7. To prepare filling, beat together confectioners' sugar and butter at medium speed until light and fluffy. Beat in cream, corn syrup, and cinnamon.

8. Cut a 1-inch slice from top of cake; reserve slice. Cut out center of cake in 1 piece, leaving a ½-inch shell.

9. Trim ⅛ inch from sides and bottom of cake center and from bottom of reserved top. Spread filling evenly over sides and bottom of cake center.

10. Replace center in cake shell. Spread remaining filling over top of cake center. Replace reserved top.

11. Dust top of cake with confectioners' sugar.

Zucchini-Chocolate Cake

Zucchini keeps this delectable cake moist enough to last for days.

30 minutes preparation, 20-25 minutes baking

Makes 8 servings

Ingredients:

- 2 cups (8 ounces) grated zucchini
- ½ teaspoon salt
- 1 cup all-purpose flour
- ⅓ cup unsweetened cocoa powder
- 1 teaspoon baking soda
- 1 teaspoon ground cinnamon
- 2 large eggs
- 1 cup granulated sugar
- 1 tablespoon grated orange peel
- ¾ cup vegetable oil

Frosting:

- 2 cups confectioners' sugar
- 2 ounces (½ stick) butter, softened
- 2 tablespoons orange juice
- 1 teaspoon grated orange peel

1. Preheat oven to 350°F. Grease a 13 x 9-inch baking pan. Dust with flour; tap out excess.

2. Place grated zucchini in a colander; sprinkle with salt. Set aside to drain.

3. Mix together flour, cocoa powder, baking soda, and cinnamon.

4. Mix together eggs, sugar, and orange peel. Stir in oil.

5. Stir flour mixture into egg mixture until dry ingredients are just moistened.

6. Press down on zucchini with paper towels to extract all moisture. Stir zucchini into batter. Spread into prepared pan.

7. Bake cake until a toothpick inserted in the center comes out clean, 20-25 minutes. Transfer pan to a wire rack to cool completely.

8. To prepare frosting, mix together all ingredients.

9. Invert cake onto a serving plate. Spread with frosting.

Iced Chocolate Slices

Another scrumptious brownie loaf variation topped with sweetened soft cheese.

30 minutes preparation, 30 minutes baking, plus cooling

Makes 20 slices

Ingredients:

3 eggs

1 cup granulated sugar

¾ cup vegetable oil

¾ cup light cream

1 tsp baking powder

½ tsp baking soda

1 cup all-purpose flour

⅓ cup unsweetened cocoa powder

1 tsp ground cinnamon

1½ cups (8 ounces) grated zucchini

½ cup chopped walnuts

Pinch of salt

Frosting:

8 ounces cream cheese

4 ounces (1 stick) butter, softened

1 tablespoon heavy cream

2 cups confectioners' sugar, sifted

Garnish:

Candied orange peel strips

1. Preheat oven to 350°F. Lightly grease a 12 x 8-in baking pan.

2. Using an electric mixer, beat together the eggs and sugar until pale and fluffy. Beat in the oil and cream.

3. In a bowl, mix together the baking powder, baking soda, flour, cocoa, salt, and cinnamon. Set the mixer at a low speed and add the flour mixture. Stir in the zucchini and nuts. Pour the mixture into the pan and level the surface.

4. Bake for 30 minutes, or until the center of the cake springs back when lightly pressed. Transfer the pan to a wire rack. Turn out after 5 minutes. Let cool completely.

5. Meanwhile, make the frosting. Beat together the cream cheese, butter, cream, and orange rind. Gradually add the sugar, beating until the mixture is smooth and creamy.

6. Spread the frosting over the top of cake. Decorate with strips of orange rind.

Nutty Cocoa-Carrot Cake

This easy-to-make cake is a delightful variation of a family favorite.

25 minutes preparation plus cooling, 30 minutes baking

Makes 20 servings

Ingredients:

2 cups all-purpose flour

⅓ cup unsweetened cocoa powder

1 teaspoon baking powder

1 teaspoon ground cinnamon

¾ teaspoon baking soda

¼ teaspoon salt

3 large eggs

1¼ cups granulated sugar

⅓ cup vegetable oil

¾ cup buttermilk

2 cups (8 ounces) grated carrots

1 cup chopped walnuts
    (about 4 ounces)

Frosting:

8 ounces cream cheese

4 ounces (1 stick) butter, softened

1 tablespoon heavy cream

1 tablespoon grated orange peel

2 cups confectioners' sugar, sifted

Garnish:

Candied orange peel strips

1. Preheat oven to 350°F. Line a 13 x 9-inch baking pan with waxed paper. Spray paper with vegetable cooking spray.

2. Mix together flour, cocoa powder, baking powder, cinnamon, baking soda, and salt.

3. Beat together eggs and sugar at medium speed until light and fluffy. Beat in oil. At low speed, alternately beat in cocoa mixture and buttermilk. Stir in carrots and nuts. Spread batter in prepared pan; smooth top.

4. Bake cake until the center springs back when lightly pressed, 30 minutes. Transfer pan to a wire rack to cool completely.

5. To prepare frosting, beat together cream cheese, butter, cream, and orange peel at medium speed until blended. At low speed, beat in confectioners' sugar until smooth.

6. Spread frosting over top of cake. Garnish with candied orange peel strips.

Cook's Tip

For a moist, lower-fat cake, omit the frosting. If desired, make the unfrosted cake a day ahead and store it, wrapped in plastic wrap, at room temperature.

Iced Pear-Chocolate Cake

Slices of soft pear are captured inside this chocolate-flecked cake.

40 minutes preparation, 35-40 minutes baking plus cooling   Makes 8-10 servings

Ingredients:

6 ounces (1½ sticks) butter,
   softened

¾ cup superfine sugar

3 large eggs

1½ cups all-purpose flour

1 teaspoon vanilla extract

2 teaspoons baking powder

¾ teaspoon salt

4 ounces (4 squares) semisweet
   chocolate, finely grated

1 can (14-ounce) pear halves in
   syrup

1 cup confectioners' sugar, sifted

2-3 teaspoons lemon juice

Chocolate sprinkles, to garnish

1. Preheat oven to 375°F. Lightly grease an 8-inch springform cake pan. Line the base and side with waxed paper.

2. Put the butter and superfine sugar into a mixing bowl. Beat with a wooden spoon or electric beater until pale and fluffy. Gradually beat in the eggs, 1 at a time, with 1 teaspoon flour, beating well after each addition.

3. Mix the vanilla extract with 1 tablespoon cold water and beat into the creamed mixture. Gradually fold in the remaining flour, baking powder, salt, and the grated chocolate until blended.

4. Spoon half the batter into the pan and spread level. Drain the pears and dry on paper towels. Cut into slices and arrange on top of the batter in the pan. Spoon the remaining batter over the top and spread level.

5. Bake for 35-40 minutes, or until a toothpick inserted into the center of the cake comes out clean. Turn out onto a wire rack and let cool.

6. Mix the confectioners' sugar with the lemon juice until smooth, then spread on top of the cake. Sprinkle the chocolate on top. Let frosting set about 2 hours, then serve.

Chocolate-Apple Cake

Very moist and with a rich chocolate taste, this cake makes a great afternoon snack or dessert.

20 minutes preparation, 45-55 minutes baking

Makes 10 servings

Ingredients:

2 cups all-purpose flour

⅓ cup unsweetened cocoa powder

1 teaspoon baking powder

1 teaspoon baking soda

¼ teaspoon salt

5 ounces (1¼ sticks) butter, softened

1¼ cups granulated sugar

2 large eggs

1 teaspoon vanilla extract

⅔ cup milk

2 medium Granny Smith apples, pared, cored, and finely chopped

Frosting:

3 cups confectioners' sugar

2 ounces (½ stick) butter, softened

¼ cup unsweetened cocoa powder

⅓ cup milk

1. Preheat oven to 350°F. Grease an 8-inch square deep cake pan. Dust with flour; tap out excess.

2. Mix together flour, cocoa powder, baking powder, salt, and baking soda.

3. Beat together butter and sugar at medium speed until light and fluffy. Add eggs, 1 at a time, beating well after each addition. Beat in vanilla.

4. At low speed, alternately beat flour mixture and milk into butter mixture. Stir in apples. Pour into prepared pan.

5. Bake cake until a toothpick inserted in center comes out clean, 45-55 minutes. Transfer pan to a wire rack to cool for 10 minutes. Turn cake out onto rack to cool completely.

6. To prepare frosting, beat together confectioners' sugar, butter, and cocoa powder at low speed. Beat in milk. Spread frosting over top and sides of cake.

Cook's Tip

To test if baking powder is still fresh, combine 1 teaspoon of it with ¹/₃ cup hot water. If the mixture bubbles vigorously, the powder is fine to use. McIntosh or Cortland apples can be substituted for the Granny Smith apples. This cake can also be baked in a 9-inch springform cake pan. Allow for a few minutes less baking time.

Chocolate Brownie Cake

Serve this brownie-style cake with vanilla ice cream or a flavored whipped cream.

15 minutes preparation plus cooling, 30-35 minutes baking — Makes 6 servings

Ingredients:

- ¾ cup all-purpose flour
- ½ teaspoon baking soda
- ½ teaspoon salt
- ¼ teaspoon ground cinnamon
- 1½ tablespoons unsweetened cocoa powder
- ⅓ cup hot water
- 3 ounces (3 squares) semisweet chocolate, coarsely chopped
- 3 ounces (¾ stick) butter
- ¾ cup granulated sugar
- ⅓ cup light corn syrup
- 1 large egg
- 1 large egg yolk

Garnish:

- Sprigs of fresh mint

1. Preheat oven to 350°F. Grease a 9-inch quiche pan or 9-inch round cake pan. Dust with flour; tap out excess.

2. Mix together flour, baking soda, salt, and cinnamon.

3. Dissolve cocoa powder in hot water.

4. In a medium saucepan, heat chocolate and butter over low heat, stirring until melted and smooth. Stir in sugar and corn syrup. Remove from heat. Cool slightly.

5. Beat together egg and egg yolk at medium speed until light and fluffy. Beat chocolate mixture and cocoa mixture into egg mixture.

6. At low speed, beat in flour mixture until blended and smooth. Spread batter in prepared pan.

7. Bake cake until a toothpick inserted in the center comes out almost clean, 30-35 minutes. Transfer pan to a wire rack to cool completely. Garnish each slice with a mint sprig.

Cook's Tip

Don't overbake this cake. The toothpick should be moist with a few crumbs sticking to it.

Crunchy Chocolate-Bran Cake

Chocolate chips and bran flakes are baked onto the top of this cake.

25 minutes preparation, 25-30 minutes baking plus cooling   Makes 8-10 servings

Ingredients:

- 2 ounces (½ stick) butter, melted
- 3 large eggs
- ½ cup superfine sugar
- 1 cup all-purpose flour
- 1½ teaspoons baking powder
- ½ teaspoon salt
- 1 tablespoon unsweetened cocoa powder

Topping:

- 4 ounces (1 stick) butter
- 6 tablespoons superfine sugar
- 6 tablespoons honey
- ⅓ cup (2 ounces) plain chocolate chips
- 1½ cups bran flakes or cornflakes

1. Preheat oven to 375°F. Lightly grease a 9-inch springform cake pan. Line the base with greased waxed paper.

2. Put the eggs and sugar into a large bowl set over a pan of hot water. Beat with an electric beater for 5-10 minutes, or until the beaters leave a trail on the surface when lifted. Stir in the melted butter.

3. Sift in the flour, baking powder, salt and cocoa powder and fold in gently. Spoon the mixture into the pan and spread level. Bake for 15 minutes.

4. Meanwhile, prepare the topping. Put the butter, sugar, and honey into a heavy-based saucepan. Heat gently, stirring, until smooth and blended.

5. Using a wooden spoon, stir in the chocolate chips and bran flakes or cornflakes until evenly coated in the mixture.

6. Spread the topping mixture over the top of the cake. Bake for an additional 10-15 minutes, or until the cake feels firm to the touch on top.

7. Let the cake cool in the pan for 5 minutes. Turn out onto a wire rack and let cool completely. Cut into slices with a sharp, serrated knife and serve.

Chocolate-Nut Cake

This cake's delicious combination of chocolate and almonds is a dessert lover's joy.

20 minutes preparation plus cooling, 30-35 minutes baking

Makes 8 servings

Ingredients:

⅓ cup solid vegetable shortening

2 ounces (2 squares) unsweetened chocolate, coarsely chopped

¾ cup all-purpose flour

½ teaspoon baking powder

½ teaspoon salt

1 cup granulated sugar

2 large eggs

½ cup coarsely chopped almonds, hazelnuts, or pecans (about 2 ounces)

Garnish:

Whipped cream

1. Preheat oven to 350°F. Grease a 9-inch round cake pan. Dust with flour; tap out excess.

2. In a small saucepan, heat shortening and chocolate over low heat, stirring constantly, until melted and smooth. Cool slightly.

3. Mix together flour, baking powder, and salt.

4. Beat together sugar and eggs at medium speed until light and fluffy. Stir in chocolate mixture. At low speed, beat in flour mixture until well blended. Stir in ¼ cup nuts.

5. Spread batter in prepared pan; smooth top. Sprinkle with remaining nuts; press into batter.

6. Bake cake until a toothpick inserted in the center comes out clean, 30-35 minutes. Transfer pan to a wire rack to cool slightly.

7. Loosen cake by running a metal spatula around sides of pan. Transfer cake to rack to cool completely. Serve cake with a dollop of whipped cream.

Cook's Tip

For a special occasion, bake 2 cakes. Spread 1 cake layer with chocolate frosting. Top with the second cake layer. Decorate with whipped cream rosettes and strawberry slices.

Chocolate-Strawberry Shortcake

Chocolate shortcake adds a delicious new twist to everyone's favorite dessert.

15 minutes preparation, 20-25 minutes baking

Ingredients:

- 2 cups all-purpose flour
- 4 teaspoons baking powder
- ¼ teaspoon salt
- ¾ cup plus 1 tablespoon granulated sugar
- ⅓ cup unsweetened cocoa powder
- 4 ounces (1 stick) chilled butter
- ½ cup milk
- 2 large eggs
- 1 teaspoon vanilla extract
- 2 cups heavy cream
- 1 pint fresh strawberries, coarsely chopped and sweetened

1. Preheat oven to 425°F. Grease a baking sheet.

2. Mix together flour, baking powder, salt, ½ cup sugar, and cocoa powder.

3. Using a pastry blender or 2 knives, cut butter into flour mixture until coarse crumbs form.

4. Mix together milk, eggs, and vanilla.

5. Make a well in the center of flour mixture. Add milk mixture, tossing with a fork until a soft dough forms. (Do not knead.)

6. Pat dough out into a 1-inch-thick square on baking sheet. Sprinkle with 1 tablespoon sugar.

7. Bake dough until firm to the touch, 20-25 minutes. Transfer pan to a wire rack to cool slightly. Transfer shortcake to rack to cool completely.

8. Beat cream and remaining sugar until soft peaks form.

9. Cut cooled shortcake into 8 squares. Using a knife, slice each square in half horizontally.

10. Place 8 shortcake squares on serving plates. Top with ¾ of strawberries and ¾ of whipped cream. Put remaining shortcake squares on top.

Italian Chocolate Dessert

Slice into this dessert to reveal a tiramisu-style filling made with mascarpone cheese.

40 minutes preparation, 8-10 minutes baking plus cooling   Makes 8 servings

Ingredients:

3 large eggs

½ cup firmly packed brown sugar

¾ cup all-purpose flour

1½ tablespoons unsweetened cocoa powder

Filling:

2 large egg yolks

4 tablespoons confectioners' sugar

3 tablespoons almond liqueur

9 ounces mascarpone or cream cheese

1 tablespoon instant coffee powder, dissolved in 6 tablespoons warm water

2 ounces amaretti or ratafia biscuits, crushed

Confectioners' sugar, unsweetened cocoa powder and grated chocolate, to garnish

1. Preheat oven to 425°F.

2. Spray a 15 x 10-inch jelly-roll pan with vegetable cooking spray. Line bottom with waxed paper. Spray paper with vegetable cooking spray.

3. Beat egg yolks at high speed until foamy, 1-2 minutes. Slowly beat in sugar until thick ribbons form when beaters are lifted.

4. Sift together the flour and cocoa powder. Fold half into the egg mixture. Mix in 1 tablespoon hot water, then fold in the remaining flour mixture. Pour into the pan, tipping it from side to side to level the surface.

5. Bake for 8-10 minutes, or until springy to the touch. Turn out onto a wire rack and let cool. Carefully remove the waxed paper. Trim cake edges.

6. Line a 1-quart bombe mold with plastic wrap. Use two-thirds of the chocolate sponge to line the mold.

7. To prepare the filling, beat the egg yolks and confectioners' sugar until pale and thick. Gradually beat in 2 tablespoons liqueur, then the mascarpone cheese, beating until thick and smooth.

8. Combine the coffee with the remaining liqueur. Drizzle over the sponge in the mold. Spoon in the mascarpone mixture, then sprinkle over the biscuits. Spoon in the rest of the mascarpone mixture.

9. Cut pieces of the remaining sponge to fit the top. Cover with plastic wrap and chill for 2 hours.

10. Turn out the dessert onto a plate. Sprinkle with confectioners' sugar, cocoa, and grated chocolate.

Luscious Mocha Fudge Cake

A bittersweet glaze and a swirl of whipped cream complement this densely rich chocolate cake.

30 minutes preparation plus cooling and standing, 35 minutes baking   Makes 12 servings

Ingredients:

1 cup all-purpose flour
1 teaspoon baking soda
⅛ teaspoon salt
1 cup firmly packed light brown sugar
2 ounces (½ stick) butter, softened
2 large eggs
2 ounces (2 squares) semisweet
   chocolate, melted
1 teaspoon vanilla extract
½ cup plain yogurt
1 tablespoon instant coffee powder
½ cup boiling water

Glaze:

2 tablespoons instant coffee powder
¼ cup boiling water
1½ cups confectioners' sugar
5 tablespoons unsweetened cocoa
   powder
2 tablespoons butter, melted
1 teaspoon vanilla extract

1. Preheat oven to 350°F. Grease a 9-inch round cake pan. Dust with flour; tap out excess.

2. Mix together flour, baking soda, and salt.

3. Beat together brown sugar and butter at medium speed until light and fluffy. Add eggs, 1 at a time, beating well after each addition. Beat in melted chocolate and vanilla. Alternately beat flour mixture and yogurt into chocolate mixture.

4. Dissolve coffee powder in boiling water. Stir coffee mixture into batter. Pour batter evenly into prepared pan; smooth top.

5. Bake cake until a toothpick inserted in the center comes out clean, 35 minutes. Transfer pan to a wire rack to cool slightly. Turn cake out onto rack to cool completely.

6. Dissolve coffee powder in boiling water. Mix together confectioners' sugar, coffee mixture, cocoa powder, melted butter, and vanilla until smooth. Pour glaze over cake. Let stand until set.

Cook's Tip

To garnish, using a pastry bag fitted with a star tip, pipe a whipped cream rosette on each slice and add a chocolate fan.

Cookies, Brownies & Candies

Cookies provide instant gratification–an immediate and appreciative "mmmm." There are so many different varieties, you could bake a different one every day. Cookies are great with milk, with coffee or tea, or just grabbed from the cookie jar to be eaten en route somewhere.

Brownies are a wonderful fusion of cookies and cake, rich and satisfying as a snack or as a dessert.

Candymaking produces truly professional and delicious results and is easier to do than you may think. And any one of these recipes will make a wonderful, thoughtful gift.

Best-Ever Chocolate Chip Cookies

These are about as good as cookies get, so make several batches and watch them disappear fast.

15 minutes preparation plus chilling, 10-12 minutes baking per batch   Makes 4 dozen cookies

Ingredients:

- 1½ cups sifted all-purpose flour
- 1 teaspoon baking soda
- 1 teaspoon ground cinnamon
- 8 ounces (2 sticks) butter, softened
- ½ cup firmly packed light brown sugar
- 1 cup granulated sugar
- 1 large egg
- 1 teaspoon vanilla extract
- 1½ cups old-fashioned rolled oats
- 1 cup semisweet chocolate chips (6 ounces)

1. Mix together flour, baking soda, and cinnamon.

2. Beat together butter, brown sugar, and granulated sugar at medium speed until light and fluffy. Beat in egg and vanilla.

3. At low speed, beat in flour mixture until blended. Fold in oats and chocolate chips. Cover with plastic wrap; chill for 1 hour.

4. Preheat oven to 350°F. Grease 2 baking sheets.

5. Shape dough into 1-inch balls. Place cookies, 2 inches apart, on prepared baking sheets. Flatten each cookie slightly.

6. Bake cookies until lightly browned around edges, 10-12 minutes. Transfer baking sheets to wire racks to cool slightly. Transfer cookies to racks to cool completely.

Cook's Tip

Make dough ahead of time and freeze it. Later, use defrosted dough to make homemade cookies in minutes.

Chocolate Chip Oatmeal Cookies

One bite of these cookies and they'll soar to the top of your hit list.

20 minutes preparation, 8-10 minutes baking per batch   Makes 3 dozen cookies

Ingredients:

¾ cup all-purpose flour

½ teaspoon baking soda

½ teaspoon salt

4 ounces (1 stick) butter, softened

½ cup firmly packed light brown sugar

¼ teaspoon granulated sugar

1 large egg

½ teaspoon vanilla extract or almond extract

1 cup old-fashioned rolled oats

1¼ cups semisweet chocolate chips (8 ounces)

½ cup chopped pecans (2 ounces)

⅛ cup golden raisins

1. Preheat oven to 375°F. Spray 2 baking sheets with vegetable cooking spray.

2. Mix together flour, baking soda, and salt.

3. Beat together butter, brown sugar, and granulated sugar at medium speed until light and fluffy. Beat in egg and vanilla until well blended.

4. At low speed, beat in flour mixture and oats until combined. Stir in chocolate chips, nuts, and raisins.

5. Drop dough onto prepared baking sheets by rounded tablespoons, 2 inches apart.

6. Bake cookies until golden, 8-10 minutes. Transfer baking sheets to wire racks to cool for 2 minutes. Transfer cookies to racks to cool completely.

Cook's Tip

Vary this recipe by substituting white chocolate chips for the semisweet chocolate, macadamia nuts for the pecans, and finely chopped, pitted prunes for the raisins.

Chocolate Almond Cookies

Beware of cookie thieves after baking a batch of these nut-filled chocolate delights.

20 minutes preparation, 10-12 minutes baking per batch   Makes 5 dozen cookies

Ingredients:

   2 cups all-purpose flour
   ⅛ cup unsweetened cocoa powder
   1 teaspoon baking powder
   Pinch of salt
   12 ounces (3 sticks) butter,
      softened
   1 cup firmly packed light brown
      sugar
   1 cup granulated sugar
   2 large eggs
   1 teaspoon vanilla extract
   1½ cups finely chopped almonds
      (about 6 ounces)

1. Preheat oven to 350°F. Grease 2 baking sheets.

2. Sift together flour, cocoa powder, baking powder, and salt.

3. Beat together butter, brown sugar, and granulated sugar at medium speed until light and fluffy. Add eggs, 1 at a time, beating well after each addition. Beat in vanilla.

4. At low speed, gradually beat flour mixture into egg mixture until well blended. Stir in nuts.

5. Drop dough onto prepared baking sheets by rounded tablespoons, 2 inches apart.

6. Bake cookies until just set, 10-12 minutes. (Cookies should not change color.)

7. Transfer baking sheets to wire racks to cool slightly. Transfer to racks to cool completely.

Cook's Tip

When using 2 cookie sheets, position racks to divide oven into thirds. Place 1 sheet on the upper rack and 1 on the lower rack. Reverse the baking sheet positions, and rotate front to back halfway through baking.

Chocolate Chunk Granola Cookies

A variation on an all-time favorite, these cookies will disappear like hotcakes.

20 minutes preparation, 12 minutes baking per batch

Makes 7 dozen cookies

Ingredients

2½ cups old-fashioned rolled oats

2 cups all-purpose flour

4 ounces (4 squares) milk chocolate, grated

1 teaspoon baking powder

½ teaspoon salt

8 ounces (2 sticks) butter, softened

1 cup firmly packed dark brown sugar

1 cup granulated sugar

2 large eggs

1 teaspoon vanilla extract

1 cup shredded sweetened coconut

1. Preheat oven to 350°F. Grease 2 large baking sheets.

2. In a food processor fitted with the metal blade, process oats until finely ground.

3. Mix together oats, flour, chocolate, baking powder, and salt.

4. Beat together butter, brown sugar, and granulated sugar at medium speed until light and fluffy. Beat in eggs and vanilla. At low speed, gradually beat in flour mixture. Stir in coconut.

5. Drop dough by rounded teaspoonfuls, 2 inches apart, on prepared baking sheets. Bake cookies until just set, 12 minutes. Transfer to wire racks to cool.

Cook's Tip

Use a box grater to grate the chocolate; alternatively, chop it in a food processor fitted with the metal blade.

Chocolate Coconut Buttons

Studded with crunchy coconut, these rich chocolate cookies go great with a glass of milk.

20 minutes preparation, 12 minutes baking per batch   Makes 7 dozen cookies

Ingredients:

- 2½ cups old-fashioned rolled oats
- 2 cups all-purpose flour
- 4 ounces (4 squares) milk chocolate, grated
- 1 teaspoon baking powder
- ½ teaspoon salt
- 8 ounces (2 sticks) butter, softened
- 1 cup firmly packed dark brown sugar
- 1 cup granulated sugar
- 2 large eggs
- 1 teaspoon vanilla extract
- 1 cup shredded sweetened coconut

1. Preheat oven to 350°F. Grease 2 large baking sheets.

2. In a food processor fitted with the metal blade, process oats until finely ground.

3. Mix together oats, flour, chocolate, baking powder, and salt.

4. Beat together butter, brown sugar, and granulated sugar at medium speed until light and fluffy. Beat in eggs and vanilla. At low speed, gradually beat in flour mixture. Stir in coconut.

5. Drop dough by rounded teaspoonfuls, 2 inches apart, on prepared baking sheets. Bake cookies until just set, 12 minutes. Transfer to wire racks to cool.

Cook's Tip

Use a box grater to grate the chocolate; alternatively, chop it in a food processor fitted with the metal blade.

Chocolate Nut Fingers

For the perfect impromptu dessert, dress up a dish of ice cream with these luscious cookies.

30 minutes preparation plus chilling, 10 minutes baking per batch   Makes 6 dozen cookies

Ingredients:
- 30 minutes preparation plus chilling, 10 minutes baking per batch
- 1½ cups all-purpose flour
- ¾ cup unsweetened cocoa powder
- ⅛ teaspoon salt
- 1¼ cups granulated sugar
- 8 ounces (2 sticks) butter, softened
- 1 large egg
- 1½ teaspoons almond extract

Topping:
- ½ cup coarsely chopped almonds (about 2 ounces)

1. Mix together flour, cocoa powder, and salt.

2. Beat together sugar and butter at medium speed until light and fluffy. Beat in egg and almond extract.

3. At low speed, beat flour mixture into butter mixture, ½ cup at a time, until a soft dough forms. Shape dough into a disk, wrap in plastic wrap, and chill for 1 hour.

4. Preheat oven to 375°F.

5. On a floured surface, using a floured rolling pin, roll dough to a ¼-inch thickness. Cut dough into 1½-inch-wide strips. Using a fork, press lengthwise down strips to form ridges.

6. Cut dough strips into desired lengths.

7. Place cookies, 1 inch apart, on 2 ungreased baking sheets. Sprinkle with nuts.

8. Bake cookies until firm, 10 minutes. Transfer cookies to racks to cool completely.

Cook's Tip
For variety, cut cookies into different lengths; dip one end in melted chocolate.

Chocolate Dream Cookies

These tantalizing cookies are crunchy on the outside and soft on the inside.

15 minutes preparation, 12-14 minutes baking plus cooling   Makes about 25 cookies

Ingredients:

- 2 ounces (2 squares) semisweet chocolate
- 1 ounce (¼ stick) butter, diced
- 1 cup superfine sugar
- 1 large egg, lightly beaten
- 1 teaspoon vanilla extract
- 1¼ cups all-purpose flour
- 1 teaspoon baking powder
- ½ cup (2 ounces) chopped pecan nuts or walnuts (optional)

1. Preheat oven to 350°F. Grease 2 baking sheets. Break the chocolate into squares and put in a heatproof bowl. Add the butter and put the bowl over a pan of barely simmering water. Let the mixture melt, stirring occasionally. Remove the bowl from the heat.

2. Beat the sugar into the melted mixture with a wooden spoon. Beat in the egg and vanilla.

3. Sift the flour and baking powder into the mixture and stir until well combined. Add the nuts, if using, and mix until a smooth dough forms.

4. Shape the dough into balls, about ¾-inch in diameter. Divide the balls between the prepared baking sheets, 2 inches apart.

5. Bake for 12-14 minutes, or until just firm on the outside. Let cool competely on the baking sheets.

Cook's Tip

You can store the baked cookies in an airtight container for up to 1 week. The cookies can be frozen in freezer bags for up to 3 months. Thaw at room temperature for 2 hours.

Chocolate-Pecan Oatmeal Cookies

Chewy and bursting with bits of chocolate, these cookies are a perfect after-school treat.

45 minutes preparation, 10-12 minutes baking per batch   Makes 3½ dozen cookies

Ingredients:

3 cups old-fashioned rolled oats

⅔ cup all-purpose flour

⅔ cup coarsely chopped walnuts
   or pecans (about 2½ ounces)

1 teaspoon baking powder

4 ounces (1 stick) butter, softened

⅛ cup packed dark brown sugar

⅛ cup granulated sugar

1 large egg, lightly beaten

2½ ounces (2½ squares) semisweet
   chocolate, chopped

1. Mix together oats, flour, nuts, and baking powder.

2. In a saucepan, heat butter, brown sugar, and granulated sugar over medium heat, stirring occasionally, until butter has melted and mixture is smooth. Remove from heat.

3. Stir half of oat mixture into butter mixture. Stir in egg, mixing well, then stir in remaining oat mixture. Cool for 20 minutes. Stir in chocolate.

4. Preheat oven to 350°F. Shape dough into 1½-inch balls. Place balls, 2 inches apart, on ungreased baking sheets. Flatten each ball slightly.

5. Bake cookies until lightly browned, 10-12 minutes. Transfer to a wire rack to cool.

Cook's Tip

This cookie dough lends itself to endless variations. Add raisins, chopped dates, dried apricots, or a bit of grated orange peel. Omit nuts, or prepare them plain without chocolate.

Almond-Chocolate Chippers

Everyone loves chocolate chip cookies, and this version is a hands-down favorite.

30 minutes preparation, 7 minutes baking per batch

Makes 4 dozen cookies

Ingredients:

- 1 cup all-purpose flour
- 1 cup ground almonds (about 4 ounces)
- ½ teaspoon baking soda
- ½ teaspoon salt
- 4 ounces (1 stick) butter, softened
- ⅛ cup granulated sugar
- ⅛ cup firmly packed light brown sugar
- 1 large egg
- 1½ teaspoons vanilla extract
- ½ teaspoon hot water
- 1 cup semisweet chocolate chips (6 ounces)

Topping:

- ½ cup coarsely chopped almonds

1. Preheat oven to 375°F. Grease 2 baking sheets.

2. Mix together flour, ground nuts, baking soda, and salt.

3. Beat together butter, granulated sugar, and brown sugar at medium speed until light and fluffy. Beat in egg, vanilla, and water.

4. At low speed, beat flour mixture into butter mixture, ½ cup at a time, until a soft dough forms. Fold in chocolate chips.

5. Drop batter by rounded teaspoonfuls onto prepared baking sheets, 2 inches apart. Press chopped nuts on top.

6. Bake cookies until set and browned, 7 minutes. Transfer baking sheets to wire racks to cool for 2 minutes. Transfer cookies to racks to cool completely.

Cook's Tip

If you don't have a baking sheet, make a simple substitute by doubling a piece of heavy-duty aluminum foil to standard baking pan size.

Try substituting milk chocolate or peanut butter chips for the semisweet chocolate chips.

Chocolate Coconut Cookies

Chocoholics get a double dose of their favorite food in these light-as-a-cloud cookies.

25 minutes preparation, 45 minutes baking, 3 hours standing   Makes 3 dozen cookies

Ingredients:

¾ cup confectioners' sugar

½ cup shredded sweetened coconut, finely chopped

1½ ounces (1½ squares) semisweet chocolate, grated

2 large egg whites

½ teaspoon coconut extract

¼ teaspoon cream of tartar

¼ cup granulated sugar

Glaze:

8 ounces (8 squares) semisweet chocolate, coarsely chopped

2 teaspoons vegetable oil

1. Preheat oven to 275°F. Line a baking sheet with aluminum foil; spray foil with vegetable cooking spray.

2. Mix together confectioners' sugar, coconut, and chocolate.

3. Beat together egg whites, coconut extract, and cream of tartar at high speed until soft peaks form. Gradually beat in granulated sugar until stiff, but not dry, peaks form. Fold in coconut mixture.

4. Place mixture in a pastry bag fitted with a large star tip. Pipe mixture into 1½-inch mounds, ½ inch apart, on prepared baking sheet.

5. Bake cookies for 45 minutes. Turn off oven; let stand with door closed to dry for at least 3 hours or overnight. Carefully remove foil.

6. To prepare glaze, in the top of a double boiler set over simmering (not boiling) water, melt chocolate with oil, stirring constantly. Remove from heat.

7. Dip base of each cookie into melted chocolate. Place on waxed paper until chocolate sets.

Cook's Tip

Grate chocolate with a hand-held grater or in a food processor fitted with the shredding disk.

Double Chocolate Macadamias

This unbeatable cookie features chocolate chips, white chocolate, and macadamia nuts.

15 minutes preparation, 10-12 minutes baking per batch Makes 2½ dozen cookies

Ingredients:

- ½ cup (2 ounces) macadamia nuts
- 4 ounces (1 stick) butter
- ⅛ cup firmly packed brown sugar
- ⅛ cup granulated sugar
- ½ teaspoon vanilla extract
- 1 large egg
- 1¼ cups all-purpose flour
- ½ teaspoon baking soda
- ½ teaspoon salt
- 4 tablespoons unsweetened cocoa powder
- ¾ cup semisweet chocolate chips
- ¾ cup white chocolate chips

1. In a blender or food processor fitted with the metal blade, chop the macadamia nuts coarsely.

2. Preheat oven to 375°F. Grease 2 baking sheets.

3. Beat together butter, brown sugar, and granulated sugar at medium speed until light and fluffy. Beat in vanilla and egg.

4. Mix together flour, baking soda, salt, and cocoa powder.

5. At low speed, beat flour mixture into sugar mixture, ½ cup at a time, until a soft dough forms. Fold in semisweet chocolate chips, white chocolate chips, and macadamia nuts.

6. Drop dough by rounded teaspoonfuls onto prepared baking sheets, 2 inches apart.

7. Bake cookies until firm, 10-12 minutes.

8. Transfer baking sheets to wire racks to cool slightly. Transfer cookies to racks to cool completely.

Cook's Tip

The macadamia nuts can be replaced by coarsely chopped pecans, walnuts, almonds, or peanuts if you prefer.

Refrigerator Cookie Duo

Fill up the cookie jar with these two great-tasting, easy-to-make cookies.

20 minutes preparation, 1 hour chilling, 10 minutes baking per batch   Makes 4 dozen cookies

Ingredients:

3 cups all-purpose flour

¼ teaspoon salt

8 ounces (2 sticks) butter, softened

1 cup granulated sugar

2 large eggs

1 teaspoon vanilla extract

2 tablespoons unsweetened cocoa powder

1. Mix together flour and salt.

2. Beat together butter and sugar at medium speed until light and fluffy. Add eggs, 1 at a time, beating well after each addition.

3. Add vanilla. Beat in flour mixture at low speed until blended. Reserve one-third of the dough.

4. Divide remaining dough in half. Place each dough piece between 2 sheets of plastic wrap. Roll out each dough piece into an 8 x 4-inch rectangle. Remove top sheets of plastic wrap.

5. Mix together reserved dough and cocoa powder. Sprinkle bits of cocoa dough on top of dough rectangles, dividing evenly. Starting with a long side and using plastic wrap as an aid, roll each rectangle into a 6-inch log.

6. Wrap tightly in plastic wrap; chill until firm, 1 hour. Preheat oven to 350°F. Grease 2 baking sheets. Cut each log into ¼-inch-thick slices. Place slices, 1 inch apart, on prepared sheets.

7. Bake cookies until just firm, 10 minutes. Transfer baking sheets to a wire rack to cool slightly. Transfer cookies to rack to cool completely.

Cook's Tip

To prepare Chocolate–Almond Cookies, beat 2 tablespoons unsweetened cocoa powder into dough when adding vanilla. Shape dough into two 6-inch logs, wrap, chill, and slice as directed. Garnish with almonds. Bake as directed.

Chocolate Pecan Drops

Serve these soft cookies on their own or as an accompaniment to ice cream.

20 minutes preparation, 10-12 minutes baking, plus cooling

Makes about 30 cookies

Ingredients:

- 2 tablespoons milk
- 1 teaspoon instant coffee powder
- 1 cup all-purpose flour
- ½ teaspoon baking soda
- Pinch of salt
- 2 ounces (½ stick) butter, softened
- ½ cup firmly packed brown sugar
- 1 tablespoon clear honey
- 1 large egg, beaten
- ½ teaspoon vanilla extract
- ¼ cup unsweetened cocoa powder
- ½ cup pecans, finely chopped (2 ounces)
- 2 ounces (2 squares) bittersweet chocolate

1. Preheat oven to 375°F. Line 2 baking sheets with waxed paper. Heat the milk and coffee in a small pan until the coffee dissolves. Let cool.

2. Sift the flour, baking soda, and salt into a large mixing bowl. Set aside.

3. Put the butter and sugar into a separate bowl. Beat together with an electric beater until pale and fluffy. Beat in the honey, egg, vanilla, cocoa, and nuts.

4. Alternately fold in the flour and milk mixture. Add a little at a time and fold in with a wooden spoon.

5. Melt the chocolate in a heatproof bowl set over a pan of barely simmering water. Stir into the dough mixture until well combined. Put teaspoonfuls of the mixture onto the prepared baking sheets, 2 inches apart.

6. Bake for 10-12 minutes, or until the cookies are set and firm. Leave to cool completely on the baking sheets.

Cook's Tip

When measuring the honey, dip the tablespoon in hot water first. This will help the honey drop off the spoon easily. Be sure to use only a level tablespoon of honey, as too much will make the cookie mixture runny.

Chopped walnuts, hazelnuts, and almonds are all suitable alternatives to pecans.

Butterscotch Chocolate Chippers

Offer these melt-in-the-mouth cookies to the kids and they'll quickly ask for seconds.

25 minutes preparation, 7 minutes baking per batch   Makes 4 dozen cookies

Ingredients:

1¼ cups sifted all-purpose flour
½ teaspoon baking soda
½ teaspoon salt
4 ounces (1 stick) butter, softened
½ cup firmly packed brown sugar
⅛ cup granulated sugar
1 large egg
1 teaspoon vanilla extract
¼ teaspoon water
1 cup semisweet mini chocolate
  chips (6 ounces)
1 cup butterscotch chips
  (6 ounces)
¾ cup coarsely chopped pecans,
  toasted (about 3 ounces)

1. Preheat oven to 375°F.

2. Mix together flour, baking soda, and salt.

3. Beat together butter, brown sugar, and granulated sugar at medium speed until light and fluffy. Beat in egg, vanilla, and water.

4. At low speed, beat in flour mixture, ½ cup at a time, until a soft dough forms. Fold in chocolate chips, butterscotch chips, and nuts.

5. Drop batter by rounded teaspoonfuls onto 2 ungreased baking sheets, 2 inches apart.

6. Bake cookies until golden, 7 minutes. Transfer baking sheets to wire racks to cool slightly. Transfer cookies to racks to cool completely.

Cook's Tip

To add tartness, fold ¼ cup chopped dried cherries into dough.

Almond Chocolate Macaroons

An orange buttercream filling gives these macaroons extra flavor and flair.

30 minutes preparation, 15 minutes baking

Makes 2½ dozen macaroons

Macaroons:
- 4 large egg whites
- 1 cup granulated sugar
- 2 cups finely ground almonds
- 5 tablespoons (about 8 ounces) unsweetened cocoa powder

Filling:
- ½ cup confectioners' sugar
- 2 tablespoons (¼ stick) butter, softened
- 2 tablespoons orange marmalade

Glaze:
- ½ cup semisweet chocolate chips
- 2 tablespoons butter
- 1 teaspoon vegetable oil

1. Preheat the oven to 350°F. Line 2 baking sheets with foil.

2. To prepare macaroons, in a large bowl, using an electric mixer set on medium speed, beat the egg whites until soft peaks form. Increase the mixer speed to high. Gradually beat in the sugar until stiff glossy peaks form.

3. In a small bowl, mix together nuts and cocoa powder. Gently fold into the egg whites. Drop the batter by tablespoonfuls onto prepared baking sheets, 2 inches apart.

4. Bake until just firm, 15 minutes. Transfer to wire racks to cool.

5. To prepare filling, in a small bowl, mix together confectioners' sugar, butter, and marmalade until smooth. Spread flat sides of half the macaroons with a little filling. Sandwich with remaining macaroons, flat-side down.

6. To prepare glaze, in a small saucepan, combine chocolate chips, butter, and oil. Heat over very low heat, stirring the mixture constantly, until smooth. Remove from the heat. Dip the macaroon sandwiches in glaze. Place on waxed paper until set.

Cook's Tip

For a varied presentation, sprinkle some sandwiches with confectioners' sugar instead of dipping in chocolate. For a different filling, substitute lemon marmalade.

Chocolate Buttercream Macaroons

Serve these light, buttery, chocolate-glazed cookies to very special people.

45 minutes preparation plus cooling, freezing, and chilling, 12-15 minutes baking   Makes 2 dozen macaroons

Ingredients:

2 large egg whites
½ cup granulated sugar
2½ cups finely ground almonds
   (about 10 ounces)

Filling:

8 ounces (2 sticks) butter, softened
2 cups confectioners' sugar
2 large egg yolks
1 teaspoon vanilla extract

Glaze:

5 ounces (5 squares) semisweet
   chocolate, coarsely chopped
1½ tablespoons vegetable oil

1. Preheat oven to 350°F. Line 2 baking sheets with waxed paper.

2. Beat egg whites at high speed until foamy. Gradually add sugar, beating until stiff, but not dry, peaks form. Fold in nuts.

3. Drop batter by rounded teaspoonfuls onto prepared baking sheets, 2 inches apart.

4. Bake macaroons until golden, 12-15 minutes. Transfer baking sheets to wire racks to cool for 5 minutes. Transfer macaroons to racks to cool completely.

5. To prepare filling, beat butter at medium speed until light and fluffy. Beat in confectioners' sugar, egg yolks, and vanilla until smooth.

6. Mound 1½ tablespoons filling over bottom of each macaroon. Freeze until filling sets, 15 minutes.

7. Meanwhile, prepare glaze. In the top of a double boiler set over simmering (not boiling) water, heat chocolate and oil, stirring frequently, until melted and smooth. Cool slightly.

8. Holding macaroon by cookie bottom, dip into melted chocolate.

9. Transfer macaroons to wire racks. Let stand until glaze sets. Chill until ready to serve.

Chocolate Truffle Macaroons

These cookies have a luscious, rich filling and a smooth chocolate glaze.

45 minutes preparation plus cooling, chilling, freezing, and standing, 12-15 minutes baking Makes 2 dozen macaroons

Ingredients:

2 large egg whites

½ cup granulated sugar

2½ cups ground almonds
(about 10 ounces)

Filling:

¾ cup heavy cream

6 ounces (6 squares) semisweet
chocolate, coarsely chopped

Glaze:

5 ounces (5 squares) semisweet
chocolate, coarsely chopped

1½ teaspoons vegetable oil

1. Preheat oven to 350°F. Line 2 baking sheets with aluminum foil.

2. Beat egg whites at high speed until foamy. Gradually add sugar, beating until stiff, but not dry, peaks form. Fold in nuts.

3. Drop batter by rounded tablespoonfuls, onto prepared baking sheets, 2 inches apart.

4. Bake macaroons until browned, 12-15 minutes. Transfer baking sheets to wire racks to cool slightly. Transfer macaroons to racks to cool completely.

5. To prepare filling, in a small saucepan, heat cream over medium heat until bubbles appear around edges of pan. Remove from heat. Add chocolate;

stir constantly until melted and smooth. Cover with plastic wrap; chill for 30 minutes.

6. Spread 1½ tablespoons filling over flat side of each macaroon; smooth filling into a mound. Freeze for 15 minutes.

7. To prepare glaze, in the top of a double boiler set over simmering (not boiling) water, heat together chocolate and oil, stirring frequently, until melted and smooth. Remove from the heat. Cool slightly.

8. Line 2 baking sheets with waxed paper.

9. Dip filled sides of macaroons into glaze, letting any excess to drip back into pan. Place cookies on prepared baking sheets. Let stand until set. Chill macaroons until just before serving.

Fancy Chocolate Macaroons

Crumbly cookies filled with buttercream and topped with glacé icing.

50 minutes preparation, 10 minutes baking plus cooling

Makes 15 macaroons

Ingredients:

4 ounces (1 stick) butter, softened

¼ cup superfine sugar

½ teaspoon vanilla extract

1 large egg, beaten

1 cup all-purpose flour

½ teaspoon baking powder

¼ teaspoon salt

6 tablespoons unsweetened cocoa powder

Chocolate chips

½ cup mixed nuts or walnuts (about 2 ounces)

Filling and Garnish:

2 ounces (½ stick) butter, softened

1½ cups confectioners' sugar, sifted

5 ounces (5 squares) semisweet chocolate, broken into squares

1 tablespoon fine-cut orange marmalade

1. Preheat oven to 375°F. Grease 2 baking sheets. Put the butter, superfine sugar, and vanilla extract into a large mixing bowl. Beat together until pale and creamy.

2. Beat in the egg. Sift in the flour, baking powder, salt, and cocoa powder. Fold in with a wooden spoon, then fold in the chocolate chips and nuts.

3. Drop 30 teaspoonfuls of the mixture onto the baking sheets and flatten slightly.

4. Bake for 10 minutes. Let cool slightly until firm, then transfer to a wire rack with a palette knife. Cool completely.

5. Meanwhile, make the filling. Put the butter and 1 cup confectioners' sugar into a bowl and beat until pale and creamy.

6. Put the chocolate into a heatproof bowl set over a pan of simmering water. Let melt, then cool. Stir into the creamed mixture with the marmalade.

7. Mix the remaining confectioners' sugar with 2 teaspoons water. Drizzle over the macaroons, then sandwich them together with the filling.

Cook's Tip

You can freeze the undecorated macaroons for up to 2 months. Pack loosely into freezer bags or an airtight container and seal.

Best Chocolate Syrup Brownies

These tempting brownies are very easy to prepare and have a delicious mild chocolate flavor.

20 minutes preparation, 35 minutes baking

Makes 1½ dozen brownies

Ingredients:

- 1 cup all-purpose flour
- ⅛ teaspoon salt
- 4 ounces (1 stick) butter, softened
- 1 cup granulated sugar
- 3 large eggs
- ¾ cup chocolate syrup
- 1 teaspoon vanilla extract
- ¾ cup chopped pecans or walnuts (3 ounces)

Garnish:

- Confectioners' sugar
- Pecan halves

1. Preheat oven to 350°F. Grease a 9-inch square baking pan. Dust with flour; tap out excess.

2. Mix together flour and salt.

3. Beat together butter and sugar at medium speed until light and fluffy. Add eggs, 1 at a time, beating well after each addition.

4. At low speed, beat in flour mixture until combined. Stir in chocolate syrup, vanilla, and nuts.

5. Spoon batter into prepared pan. Smooth top.

6. Bake brownies until a toothpick inserted in the center comes out almost clean, 35 minutes.

7. Transfer pan to a wire rack to cool completely. Cut brownies into squares.

8. Dust tops of brownies with confectioners' sugar. Garnish each brownie with a pecan half.

Cook's Tip

Shelled nuts can be stored in the freezer for up to 1 year.

Brown Sugar Blondies

These little "cakes" are the lighter-colored version of brownies, and they're just as delicious.

15 minutes preparation, 25 minutes baking   Makes 2 dozen blondies

Ingredients:

2¼ cups sifted all-purpose flour

1 teaspoon baking powder

1 teaspoon ground cinnamon

½ teaspoon salt

8 ounces (2 sticks) butter, softened

⅔ cup firmly packed light brown sugar

⅔ cup granulated sugar

2 large eggs

⅔ cup light cream

2 teaspoons vanilla extract

1 cup semisweet chocolate chips (6 ounces)

1 cup peanut butter chips or butterscotch chips (6 ounces)

¾ cup coarsely chopped walnuts, toasted (about 3 ounces)

1. Preheat oven to 375°F. Grease a 13 x 9-inch baking pan.

2. Mix together flour, baking powder, cinnamon, and salt.

3. Beat together butter, brown sugar, and granulated sugar at medium speed until light and fluffy. Add eggs, 1 at a time, beating well after each addition. Beat in cream and vanilla.

4. At low speed, beat in flour mixture, ½ cup at a time, until blended and smooth. Fold in chocolate chips, peanut butter chips, and nuts. Spread batter in prepared pan; smooth top.

5. Bake blondies until golden brown and a toothpick inserted in the center comes out almost clean, 25 minutes. Transfer pan to a wire rack to cool completely. Using a sharp knife, cut blondies into squares.

Cook's Tip

When testing to see if cakes and brownies are done, you can use a stick of uncooked spaghetti if you don't have any toothpicks on hand.

If you leave a greased pan sitting in a warm kitchen, the butter may melt and slide down the sides, causing the cake to stick to the unbuttered areas. To prevent this, place the pan in the freezer after greasing, and remove it just before pouring in the batter.

Black and White Brownies

Sinfully delicious, these rich brownies are loaded with nuts and white chocolate.

15 minutes preparation, 30-35 minutes baking   Makes 2 dozen brownies

Ingredients:

- 1½ cups all-purpose flour
- 1 cup unsweetened cocoa powder
- ¼ teaspoon salt
- 12 ounces (3 sticks) butter, melted and cooled
- 3 cups granulated sugar
- 6 large eggs
- 2 tablespoons bourbon (optional)
- 1 cup coarsely chopped almonds (about 4 ounces)
- 6 ounces (6 squares) white chocolate, coarsely chopped

1. Preheat oven to 350°F. Grease a 13 x 9-inch baking pan.

2. Mix together flour, cocoa powder, and salt.

3. Beat together butter and sugar at medium speed until light and fluffy. Add eggs, 1 at a time, beating well after each addition. Beat in bourbon, if using.

4. At low speed, beat in flour mixture until combined. Stir in nuts and white chocolate. Spoon batter into prepared pan; smooth top.

5. Bake brownies until a toothpick inserted in the center comes out almost clean, 30-35 minutes. Transfer pan to a wire rack to cool completely. Cut into 24 rectangles.

Cook's Tip

For a variation, add ¼ cup dark raisins or mint chocolate mini-chips to batter instead of white chocolate pieces.
For a festive garnish, drizzle top of brownies with melted white or dark chocolate, or dust with confectioners' sugar.

Chocolate Cake Brownies

These delicious brownies have a light, fudgelike consistency that will please chocolate fans.

15 minutes preparation, 35 minutes baking

Makes 24 brownies

Brownies:

1½ cups all-purpose flour

1½ teaspoons baking powder

¼ teaspoon salt

4 ounces (1 stick) butter, softened

1 cup granulated sugar

3 large eggs

1 teaspoon vanilla extract

1½ cups chocolate syrup

Garnish:

Confectioners' sugar

1. Preheat the oven to 350°F. Grease an 8-inch square cake pan.

2. To prepare the brownies, in a small bowl, mix together the flour, baking powder, and salt.

3. In a large bowl, using an electric mixer set on medium speed, beat together the butter and sugar until light and fluffy. Add the eggs, 1 at a time, beating well after each addition. Beat in the vanilla.

4. Reduce the mixer speed to low. Gradually beat in the flour mixture. Beat in the chocolate syrup. Pour into prepared pan.

5. Bake the brownies until a toothpick inserted in the center comes out clean, 35 minutes.

6. Transfer the pan to a wire rack to cool completely. Cut brownies into squares. Just before serving, sprinkle the brownies with the confectioners' sugar.

Cook's Tip

Brownies can be prepared up to 4 days ahead. They will remain fresh if they are covered with plastic wrap and kept in the refrigerator.

Chocolate Cheesecake Brownies

Chocolate and cheesecake—a heavenly match of textures and flavors.

30 minutes preparation, 35-40 minutes baking

Makes 1 dozen brownies

Ingredients:

- 4 ounces (4 squares) semisweet chocolate, coarsely chopped
- 4 ounces (1 stick) butter, softened
- 1½ cups plus 1 tablespoon granulated sugar
- 1 teaspoon vanilla extract
- 4 large eggs
- ¾ cup plus 1½ tablespoons all-purpose flour
- 1 package (8 ounces) cream cheese, softened

Drop chocolate batter in mounds on top of cream cheese layer.

1. Preheat oven to 325°F. Grease an 8-inch square baking pan.

2. In a small saucepan, heat chocolate and butter over low heat, stirring constantly, until melted and smooth. Remove from heat.

3. Beat together 1½ cups sugar, melted chocolate mixture, and ½ teaspoon vanilla at medium speed until blended. Beat in 3 eggs, 1 at a time, beating well after each addition. At low speed, beat in ¾ cup flour until blended and smooth.

4. In a separate bowl, beat together cream cheese, remaining flour, remaining sugar, remaining egg, and remaining vanilla at medium speed until blended and smooth.

5. Spread two-thirds of chocolate batter in prepared pan. Spread cream cheese batter over chocolate batter. Drop remaining chocolate batter in mounds on top. Run a knife through batter to create a marble pattern.

6. Bake brownies until a toothpick inserted in the center comes out almost clean, 35-40 minutes. Transfer pan to a wire rack to cool completely.

Cook's Tip

Chocolate lovers can drizzle 2 ounces (2 squares) melted semisweet chocolate on top. Let stand until set.

Chocolate Pecan Brownies

Ready in less than an hour, these fudgy treats are delightfully sweet and rich.

15 minutes preparation, 30-35 minutes baking — Makes about 16 brownies

Ingredients:

½ cup all-purpose flour
¼ teaspoon baking soda
¾ cup granulated sugar
2½ ounces (2/3 stick) butter
2 tablespoons water
9 ounces semisweet chocolate
  chips
1 teaspoon vanilla extract
2 large eggs
½ cup chopped pecans
  (2 ounces)

1. Preheat oven to 325°F. Grease a 9-inch square baking pan.

2. In a small bowl, mix together flour and baking soda.

3. In a small saucepan, combine sugar, butter, and water. Bring to a boil over medium heat; remove immediately from heat.

4. Stir in ½ cup of chocolate chips and vanilla extract until chocolate is melted and mixture is smooth.

5. Transfer mixture to a medium bowl. Cool completely.

6. Stir in eggs, 1 at a time, beating well after each addition. Gradually stir in flour mixture until smooth.

7. Stir remaining chocolate chips and nuts into batter. Pour batter into prepared pan.

8. Bake until a toothpick inserted in center comes out almost clean, 30-35 minutes. Transfer pan to a wire rack to cool completely. Cut into squares.

Cook's Tip

For light, moist brownies, cool chocolate mixture completely before combining it with other ingredients; test for doneness 2-3 minutes before the suggested baking time.

Fudge Brownies

Offer these brownies at a party and watch them disappear in the blink of an eye.

15 minutes preparation, 30-35 minutes baking   Makes 2 dozen brownies

Ingredients:

- 8 ounces (2 sticks) butter
- 4 ounces (4 squares) unsweetened chocolate
- 5 large eggs
- 2 cups granulated sugar
- 2 teaspoons vanilla extract
- 1½ cups all-purpose flour
- 1 teaspoon salt
- 1 cup coarsely chopped walnuts or pecans (about 4 ounces)
- 24 walnut or pecan halves

1. Preheat oven to 325°F. Grease a 13 x 9-inch baking pan.

2. In a saucepan, melt butter and chocolate over low heat. Remove from heat; cool.

3. Beat eggs at high speed until foamy. Gradually add sugar, beating until pale yellow and slightly thickened. Beat in cooled chocolate mixture, then vanilla.

4. Sift together flour and salt. Add nuts, tossing to coat. Stir flour mixture into chocolate mixture just until flour is incorporated.

5. Spoon batter into prepared pan. Decorate top with nut halves.

6. Bake until a toothpick inserted in center comes out almost clean, 30-35 minutes. Do not overbake. Cool brownies in pan for 15 minutes.

Cook's Tip

The top "crust" may crack or separate slightly from these brownies. This does not affect the taste.

Iced Chocolate Brownies

These fabulously fudgy treats are heavenly with a cup of coffee.2

5 minutes preparation plus cooling and standing, 30-35 minutes baking

Makes 20 brownies

Ingredients:

12 ounces (3 sticks) plus 1 tablespoon butter, melted

1 cup unsweetened cocoa powder

2 cups granulated sugar

5 large eggs

1 tablespoon vanilla extract

1 cup all-purpose flour

Pinch of salt

1 cup coarsely chopped pecans or walnuts (about 4 ounces)

Frosting:

4 ounces (4 squares) semisweet chocolate, coarsely chopped

1 teaspoon vegetable oil

1. Preheat oven to 325°F. Line a 13 x 9-inch baking pan with aluminum foil. Brush foil with 1 tablespoon melted butter.

2. Mix together remaining melted butter and cocoa powder.

3. At medium speed, beat sugar, eggs, and vanilla into cocoa mixture until well combined. Stir in flour and salt until well blended. Stir in nuts. Spoon batter into prepared pan.

4. Bake brownies until a toothpick inserted in the center comes out almost clean, 30-35 minutes. Transfer pan to a wire rack to cool completely.

5. Invert brownies onto a board. Remove foil. Turn right-side-up.

6. To prepare frosting, in a small saucepan, melt chocolate and oil over low heat, stirring until smooth. Spread frosting over brownies. Let stand until set, 30 minutes. Cut into squares.

Cook's Tip

For more cakelike brownies, use an 8-inch square baking pan. The key to great brownies is not to overbake them. Remove them from the oven before the tooth-pick is clean. Small crumbs on the toothpick means they are done.

Chocolate Nut Snaps

Crisp and crunchy, these chocolate squares really are a snap to prepare.

30 minutes preparation, 15 minutes baking

Ingredients:

- ¾ cup all-purpose flour
- ¼ cup unsweetened cocoa powder
- ½ teaspoon baking powder
- ¼ teaspoon salt
- 4 ounces (1 stick) butter, softened
- ¾ cup granulated sugar
- 1 large egg, lightly beaten
- ½ teaspoon vanilla extract
- ¾ cup (about 3 ounces) chopped walnuts or pecans

1. Preheat the oven to 375°F. Grease and flour a 12 x 18-inch baking sheet.

2. In a medium bowl, mix together the flour, cocoa powder, baking powder, and salt.

3. In a large bowl, using an electric mixer set on medium speed, beat together the butter and sugar until light and fluffy. Beat in the egg and vanilla.

4. Stir the flour mixture into the butter mixture until well blended.

5. Using a rubber spatula, spread the batter evenly over the prepared baking sheet. Sprinkle evenly with the nuts, gently patting them in with fingertips.

6. Bake the snaps until just set, 15 minutes. While still hot, cut into squares. Transfer the pan to a wire rack to cool.

Cook's Tip

For a tasty variation, try a combination of chopped almonds and hazelnuts.

Chocolate Oat Squares

In no time at all, you'll be able to bake a pan of these rich chocolate treats.

15 minutes preparation, 15 minutes baking   Makes 16 squares

Ingredients:

- 1½ cups all-purpose flour
- 1½ cups old-fashioned rolled oats
- 1¼ cups firmly packed light brown sugar
- 1 teaspoon baking soda
- ¼ teaspoon salt
- 6 ounces (1½ sticks) butter, melted

Frosting:

- 9 ounces (9 squares) semisweet chocolate, cut into small pieces
- 5 tablespoons heavy cream

1. Preheat oven to 350°F. Grease a 9-inch square baking pan.

2. Mix together flour, oats, brown sugar, baking soda, and salt.

3. Pour melted butter over flour mixture; stir until well combined. Spread oat mixture in prepared pan. Pat into an even layer.

4. Bake until lightly browned, 15 minutes. Transfer pan to a wire rack to cool completely.

5. Meanwhile, prepare frosting. In top of a double boiler set over simmering (not boiling) water, melt chocolate. Stir in heavy cream. Spread frosting over cooled oat mixture.

6. Chill until chocolate is set, 30 minutes. Cut into 2-inch squares.

Cook's Tip

For delicious variations, sprinkle chopped nuts or toasted coconut over bars while frosting is still soft. Substitute milk or bittersweet chocolate for semisweet chocolate in frosting.

Chocolate-Peanut Butter Bars

Chopped peanuts and peanut butter make these chocolate-studded bars absolutely irresistible.

20 minutes preparation plus cooling, 18-20 minutes baking   Makes 2 dozen bars

Ingredients:

- 4 ounces (1 stick) butter, softened
- ½ cup chunky peanut butter
- 1 cup firmly packed brown sugar
- 1 large egg
- 1 tablespoon water
- 1 teaspoon vanilla extract
- 1¼ cups all-purpose flour
- ¾ teaspoon baking soda
- ½ teaspoon baking powder
- 1 package (12 ounces) semisweet chocolate chips
- ½ cup chopped unsalted peanuts

1. Preheat oven to 375°F. Grease a 13 x 9-inch baking pan.

2. Beat together butter, peanut butter, and sugar at medium speed until light and fluffy.

3. Beat egg, water, and vanilla into butter mixture.

4. Mix together flour, baking soda, and baking powder. At low speed, beat flour mixture into peanut butter mixture. Stir in half of chocolate chips.

5. Spread batter in prepared pan. Bake until brown and a toothpick inserted in the center comes out clean, 18-20 minutes.

6. Turn off oven. Sprinkle remaining chocolate chips over top of cookie base. Return to oven until chocolate melts, 1 minute.

7. Spread chocolate evenly over top of cookie base. Sprinkle with chopped nuts.

8. Transfer pan to a wire rack to cool completely. Cut cookies into 24 bars.

Cook's Tip

If you prefer, replace half of the semisweet chocolate chips with peanut butter chips.

Chocolate Almond Shortbread

This is a crunchy, rich version of a true-blue favorite.

10 minutes preparation plus cooling and standing, 30 minutes baking   Makes 16 squares

Ingredients:

1 cup blanched slivered almonds
  (about 4 ounces)
1/8 cup granulated sugar
1½ cups all-purpose flour
½ cup confectioners' sugar
½ cup cornstarch
½ cup unsweetened cocoa powder
8 ounces (2 sticks) butter, melted
  and cooled

Glaze and Garnish:

4 ounces (4 squares) semisweet
  chocolate, coarsely chopped
2 tablespoons butter
1/8 cup blanched slivered almonds,
  toasted (about 1½ ounces)

1. Preheat oven to 300°F. Grease a 13 x 9-inch baking pan.

2. In a blender or food processor fitted with a metal blade, process nuts and granulated sugar until finely ground.

3. Mix together flour, confectioners' sugar, cornstarch, and cocoa powder. Stir in nut mixture and melted butter until just combined. Press dough evenly into prepared pan.

4. Bake shortbread until just set, 30 minutes. Transfer pan to a wire rack to cool slightly.

5. To prepare glaze, in a small saucepan, heat together chocolate and butter over low heat until melted and smooth.

6. Spread glaze over warm shortbread in pan. To garnish, arrange nuts on top. Let stand until set. Cut into bars.

Chocolate Oat Walnut Bites

These chewy, chocolate-topped treats are a cake version of oatmeal cookies.

25 minutes preparation plus cooling and standing, 25 minutes baking

Makes 16 servings

Ingredients:
- 1¼ cups old-fashioned rolled oats
- 1 cup all-purpose flour
- 1 teaspoon baking soda
- ⅛ teaspoon salt
- 1 cup firmly packed light brown sugar
- 4 ounces (1 stick) butter, softened
- 1 large egg
- 1 teaspoon vanilla extract
- ½ cup finely chopped walnuts (about 2 ounces)

Topping and Garnish:
- 4 ounces (4 squares) semisweet chocolate, melted
- 1 teaspoon vegetable oil
- 16 walnut halves

1. Preheat oven to 325°F. Grease an 8-inch square baking pan.

2. Mix together oats, flour, baking soda, and salt.

3. Beat together brown sugar and butter at medium speed until light and fluffy. Beat in egg and vanilla. At low speed, beat in flour mixture, ½ cup at a time, until combined. Stir in nuts.

4. Spread batter evenly in prepared pan; smooth top.

5. Bake cake until a toothpick inserted in the center comes out clean, 25 minutes. Transfer pan to a wire rack to cool completely.

6. Cut cake into squares. Transfer squares to a wire rack set over a sheet of waxed paper.

7. To prepare topping, mix together melted chocolate and oil. Spoon topping evenly over each square.

8. Garnish squares with walnut halves. Let stand until set.

Chocolate Caramels

You won't be able to keep your hands off these chewy chocolate caramels.

30 minutes preparation, 3 hours setting   Makes about 2 dozen caramels

Ingredients:

1⅛ cups heavy cream
1⅛ cups granulated sugar
1 cup light corn syrup
⅛ teaspoon salt
2 ounces (2 squares)
   unsweetened chocolate
2½ ounces (2/3 stick) butter, cut
   into small pieces

1. Generously grease a 9-inch square baking pan.

2. In a medium heavy saucepan, combine the cream, sugar, corn syrup, and salt and bring to a boil over medium-high heat.

3. Using a wooden spoon, cook the mixture, stirring constantly, until it reaches 220°F on a candy thermometer.

4. Stir in the chocolate and butter and continue cooking, stirring constantly, until the mixture reaches 240°F (soft ball stage).

5. Pour the mixture into the prepared pan. Do not scrape the saucepan. Let the mixture stand at room temperature until firm, about 3 hours.

6. Cut into 1-inch squares and wrap each one in waxed paper. Store in an airtight container.

Cook's Tip

To test for soft ball stage, drop a little mixture into a cup of iced water. Pick up the ball that has formed and roll it between your finger and thumb. It should flatten and feel sticky.

Nutty Chocolate English Toffee

Sweet, chewy, and nutty—this is the ultimate toffee experience.

1 hour preparation plus cooling and standing

Makes about 3½ pounds candy

Ingredients:

2½ cups granulated sugar

1 pound (4 sticks) butter,
cut into small pieces

½ cup water

¼ cup light corn syrup

12 ounces (12 squares) semisweet
chocolate, coarsely chopped

1 cup blanched, slivered almonds
or chopped pecans
(about 4 ounces)

1. Line 2 baking sheets with aluminum foil.
   Grease foil.

2. In a large, heavy saucepan, mix together sugar,
   butter, water, and corn syrup. Bring to a boil over
   medium heat; boil, stirring constantly, until mixture
   is smooth and thickened.

3. Reduce heat to low. Cook without stirring until a
   candy thermometer registers 325°F (hard crack
   stage), 25 minutes.

4. Pour toffee onto prepared baking sheets. Cool to
   room temperature.

5. In the top of a double boiler set over simmering (not
   boiling) water, heat chocolate, stirring constantly,
   until melted and smooth. Remove from heat.

6. Spread melted chocolate over toffee. Sprinkle with
   nuts; gently press nuts into chocolate. Let stand
   until almost set.

7. Using a sharp knife, score toffee into approximately
   3 x 1½-inch pieces.

8. Let toffee cool completely at room temperature.
   Break toffee into pieces.

Chocolate-Coconut Petits Fours

These coconut-covered morsels are made with small squares of chocolate cake.

40 minutes preparation, 20-25 minutes baking, plus cooling   Makes 24 petits fours

Ingredients:
2½ cups all-purpose flour
1 teaspoon baking powder
½ teaspoon salt
4 ounces (1 stick) butter, softened
¾ cup superfine sugar
1 teaspoon vanilla extract
2 large eggs, beaten
⅔ cup milk

Frosting and Garnish:
3 cups confectioners' sugar
6 tablespoons unsweetened
   cocoa powder
1¾ cups sweetened coconut flakes
12 candied cherries, halved

1. Preheat oven to 350°F. Grease a 12 x 8-inch baking pan and line the base with waxed paper.

2. Sift the flour, baking powder, and salt into a mixing bowl. In a separate bowl, beat together the butter and sugar until pale and fluffy. Gradually add the vanilla and eggs, 1 at a time, beating well after each addition.

3. Alternately fold in the flour mixture and milk. Add a little at a time to form batter.

4. Put the mixture into the pan and spread level. Bake for 20-25 minutes, or until a toothpick inserted in the center comes out clean. Transfer to a wire rack and let cool completely. Cut into 1½-inch squares.

5. For the frosting, sift the confectioners' sugar and cocoa into a bowl set over a pan of hot water. Beat in 6 tablespoons boiling water until smooth.

6. Spear the cake squares on a fork and dip into the frosting. Toss in the coconut and put on a wire rack to set. Top each cake with a cherry half.

Cook's Tip
Cut and ice the cake the day after baking when it will be firmer and easier to handle.

Chocolate-Coconut Candies

Treat the kids to a little rainy day candy making.

50 minutes preparation plus cooling and chilling

Makes 10 candies

Ingredients:

- 1 cup heavy cream
- 1 2-inch cinnamon stick
- 1 vanilla bean, split lengthwise
- ¾ cup sweetened coconut flakes
- ¼ cup granulated sugar
- 1/8 teaspoon salt
- 4 ounces (4 squares) semisweet chocolate, coarsely chopped

1. In a medium saucepan, mix together cream, cinnamon stick, and vanilla bean. Bring to a boil over medium heat. Reduce heat to low; cook for 5 minutes.

2. Stir coconut, sugar, and salt into cream mixture. Cook, stirring frequently, until mixture thickens and pulls away from sides of pan, 20 minutes.

3. Remove cinnamon stick and vanilla bean.

4. Transfer pan to a wire rack; cool to room temperature, 30 minutes.

5. Line an 8-inch round or 8-inch square baking pan with waxed paper. Spoon coconut mixture into pan; smooth top. Chill until firm, 1 hour.

6. Invert coconut mixture onto a cutting board. Remove waxed paper. Cut into 10 equal pieces. Shape each piece into a 1½ x 1-inch square. Grease a wire rack.

7. In the top of a double boiler set over simmering (not boiling) water, melt chocolate, stirring until smooth. Remove from over water. Let cool until chocolate begins to set just slightly, 10 minutes.

8. Using 2 forks, dip each coconut piece into melted chocolate, turning to coat on all sides. Place on prepared rack. Chill until firm, 1 hour.

Cook's Tip

For easy clean-up, place a baking sheet lined with waxed paper under the wire rack to catch any chocolate drippings.

Chocolate-Pecan Cups

Delight the whole family with these sweet, chewy chocolate candies in pretty paper cups.

30 minutes preparation plus standing and cooling   Makes 2 dozen candies

Ingredients:

    10 ounces (10 squares) milk
        chocolate, coarsely chopped

Filling:

    1 cup heavy cream
    ¼ cup sweetened condensed milk
    2 ounces (½ stick) butter
    1 cup light corn syrup
    1 cup granulated sugar
    ¼ cup water

Topping:

    ½ cup finely chopped nuts, such as
        pecans or walnuts
    2 tablespoons vegetable oil

1. In a small saucepan, heat chocolate over low heat, stirring constantly, until smooth.

2. Using a small pastry brush, paint 24 small foil candy cups evenly with some melted chocolate (see page 185). Cool in the refrigerator until set.

3. To prepare filling, in a small heavy saucepan, heat together cream, condensed milk, and butter over low heat until melted and smooth.

4. In another heavy saucepan, stir together corn syrup, sugar, and water. Cook over medium heat, stirring occasionally, until mixture reaches 240°F on a candy thermometer (soft ball stage).

5. Stir in milk mixture. Cook until candy mixture reaches 240°F again on the thermometer, 10 minutes. Remove from heat. Cool slightly, stirring constantly.

6. Drop candy mixture by rounded tablespoonfuls into chocolate-lined cups. Let stand at room temperature until cool.

7. To prepare topping, reheat remaining chocolate in saucepan until just melted. Stir in nuts and oil. Spoon nut mixture over each cup. Let stand until set.

Cookies, Brownies & Candies   103

Chocolate Nut Fudge

There's no need to wait for a special occasion to sample these deliciously decadent candies.

20 minutes preparation plus chilling

Makes 16 candies

Ingredients:

1⅛ cups granulated sugar

1 cup marshmallow cream
(½ 7-ounce jar)

⅔ cup evaporated milk

3 tablespoons butter

¼ teaspoon salt

2 packages (12 ounces each)
    semisweet chocolate chips

¾ cup coarsely chopped peanuts
    (about 3 ounces)

1 teaspoon vanilla extract

6 tablespoons light corn syrup

1 tablespoon water

1. Line an 8-inch square baking pan with aluminum foil.

2. In a medium, heavy saucepan, mix together sugar, marshmallow cream, milk, butter, and salt. Bring mixture to a boil over medium heat. Boil, stirring constantly, for 5 minutes.

3. Remove pan from heat. Add 1 package of chocolate chips, stirring until melted and smooth. Stir in nuts and vanilla. Pour chocolate-nut mixture evenly into prepared pan. Chill for 1 hour.

4. In the top of a double boiler set over simmering (not boiling) water, heat remaining chocolate chips, corn syrup, and water, stirring constantly, until melted and smooth.

5. Pour chocolate mixture over chocolate-nut layer; smooth top. Chill until firm, 2 hours. Cut into thirty-two 2 x 1-inch rectangles.

Cook's Tip

For a pretty presentation and a different flavor, substitute pistachios for the peanuts. Reserve 2 tablespoons of nuts and use as a garnish.

Chocolate Nut Balls

A fudgy, delectable mocha center makes these yummy chocolate bonbons unforgettable.

30 minutes preparation plus cooling and standing   Makes 2½ dozen candies

Ingredients:

2 cups granulated sugar

⅔ cup cold coffee

⅛ cup heavy cream

⅛ teaspoon salt

3 tablespoons butter, softened

¼ cup chocolate chips

2 tablespoons coffee-flavored
   liqueur (optional)

½ teaspoon vanilla extract

½ cup coarsely chopped peanuts
   (about 2 ounces)

Topping:

9 ounces (9 squares) semisweet
   chocolate, melted

1. Line 2 baking sheets with waxed paper.

2. In a medium saucepan, combine sugar, coffee, cream, and salt. Cook over medium heat, stirring constantly, until mixture reaches 240°F (soft-ball stage) on a candy thermometer. Remove from heat.

3. Add butter, chocolate chips, liqueur, and vanilla to saucepan, stirring constantly until melted and smooth. Cool completely.

4. Roll chocolate mixture into 1-inch balls. Roll balls in nuts.

5. Using 2 forks, dip each candy into melted chocolate. Place candies on prepared baking sheets. Let stand until set.

Cook's Tip

For a nut-filled center, add an additional ½ cup finely chopped peanuts, walnuts, hazelnuts, or pecans to the filling.

Chocolate-Orange Truffles

These mouth-watering little chocolates are perfect after dinner with coffee.

40 minutes preparation plus chilling and cooling   Makes about 18 truffles

Ingredients:

- 2 ounces (½ stick) butter
- 3 tablespoons heavy cream
- 4 ounces (4 squares) semisweet chocolate, coarsely chopped
- 2 tablespoons orange liqueur
- 1 teaspoon grated orange peel
- 4-5 tablespoons unsweetened cocoa powder

1. Put the butter and cream into a heavy-based saucepan. Heat until the butter melts, stirring occasionally. Bring to a boil, then remove from the heat.

2. Using a large wooden spoon, stir in the chocolate until melted. Stir in the liqueur and orange peel.

3. Pour the mixture into a shallow bowl and let cool completely. Chill for about 1 hour, or until firm. Line a baking sheet with waxed paper and chill.

4. Using your hands, shape the mixture into small balls. Carefully transfer the balls to the chilled baking sheet.

5. Sprinkle a sheet of waxed paper with the cocoa. Roll the truffles in the cocoa. Chill for 1 hour, or until firm.

Cook's Tip

To make brandy-flavored truffles, replace the orange liqueur and peel with 2 tablespoons brandy. Store the truffles in an airtight container in the refrigerator for up to 3 days.

Chocolate-Pistachio Bonbons

Offer these delicious candies with creamy marshmallow centers as a lovely hostess gift.

30 minutes preparation plus chilling   Makes 30 candies

Ingredients:

⅔ cup granulated sugar

½ cup heavy cream

12 large marshmallows, halved

4 ounces (4 squares) semisweet
    chocolate, coarsely chopped

2 teaspoons rum or vanilla extract

30 whole pistachios, skins removed

Glaze:

4 ounces (4 squares) semisweet
    chocolate, coarsely chopped

Garnish:

30 whole pistachios, skins removed

1. In a medium saucepan, mix together sugar and cream. Bring to a boil over medium heat, stirring constantly, until mixture turns a light caramel color, 5 minutes. Remove from heat.

2. Stir in marshmallows, chocolate, and rum until melted and smooth. Chill for 1 hour.

3. Roll 1 level tablespoon of chocolate mixture into a ball. Press a nut into the center. Place candy on an aluminum foil-lined tray. Repeat with remaining chocolate mixture and nuts. Chill for several hours.

4. To prepare glaze, in the top of a double boiler set over simmering (not boiling) water, heat chocolate, stirring, until melted and smooth.

5. Using 2 forks, dip candies in melted chocolate; return to tray. To garnish, press a nut on top of each candy. Chill until set.

Cook's Tip

For added special flavor, after melting chocolate for the glaze, stir in 2 tablespoons of rum or 1 teaspoon rum extract.

Bittersweet Chocolate Truffles

Don't spend a fortune on store-bought truffles—they're one of the easiest candies to make.

45 minutes preparation, 2 hours chilling   Makes 3 dozen truffles

Ingredients:

- 2 ounces (½ stick) butter
- 3 tablespoons heavy cream
- 4 ounces (4 squares) semisweet chocolate, finely chopped
- 2 tablespoons rum or 1 teaspoon rum extract

Coating:

- 4 ounces (4 squares) semisweet chocolate, finely chopped
- 1 teaspoon vegetable oil
- ½ cup chocolate sprinkles

1. In a saucepan, bring butter and cream to a boil over medium-high heat. Remove pan from heat. Stir in chocolate until completely melted. Stir in rum.

2. Pour chocolate mixture into a shallow bowl. Chill until firm for 2 hours.

3. Line a baking sheet with waxed paper. Shape rounded teaspoonfuls of chocolate mixture into small balls. Place balls on prepared baking sheet. Chill until firm, 30 minutes.

4. Meanwhile, prepare coating. In the top of a double boiler set over simmering (not boiling) water, melt chocolate with oil, stirring until smooth. Remove from heat. Cool completely.

5. Place chocolate sprinkles in a shallow bowl.

6. Drop truffles, 4 or 5 at a time, into melted chocolate mixture. Using a fork, lift out truffles, tapping gently on side of pan to let excess chocolate coating drip back into pan.

7. Immediately roll truffles in sprinkles. Return to baking sheet. Repeat with remaining truffles, coating, and sprinkles. Chill until coating has set, 30 minutes.

Cook's Tip

Truffles keep beautifully for up to 3 months in the freezer, so it's an excellent idea to make a double batch. Thaw the truffles at room temperature until slightly softened, about 30 minutes.

White Chocolate Truffles

Serve these elegant candies at the end of a dinner party or give them as a gift.

30 minutes preparation plus standing, chilling, and cooling

Makes 1½ dozen truffles

Ingredients:

¼ cup blanched, slivered almonds, toasted (1 ounce)

2 tablespoons butter

3 tablespoons heavy cream

8 ounces (8 squares) white chocolate, coarsely chopped

1 teaspoon almond extract or vanilla extract

¼ cup shredded sweetened coconut

1. In a blender or food processor fitted with the metal blade, process nuts until finely ground.

2. In a small saucepan, melt butter over medium heat. Stir in cream. Bring to a boil over medium-high heat. Remove from heat. Stir in white chocolate. Let stand until softened, 2 minutes. Stir until smooth.

3. Stir in almond extract and nuts. Chill until firm, 2 hours.

4. In a skillet, toast coconut over medium heat, stirring frequently, until golden brown, 5 minutes. Let stand until cool.

5. Shape white chocolate mixture into eighteen 1-inch balls. Roll truffles in toasted coconut to coat. Chill overnight.

Cook's Tip

Store truffles, covered, in the refrigerator for up to 10 days.

For a nuttier flavor, roll the truffles in ¼ cup coarsely chopped almonds.

Making Fancy Chocolates

Bonbon-making is an artistic and economical way to create gifts for your loved ones.

Creating luscious, fancy chocolate candies from scratch may seem like a project that is simply out of a beginner's realm, but it need not be. Below are directions for making several easy and impressive confections.

The Centers

Fillings, also known as centers, are the building blocks of chocolate bonbons. Centers can range in texture from soft and satiny creams and chewy nougats to crunchy, nut-filled pralines.

Some centers are quite simple to prepare, and require no equipment other than a pan and wooden spoon. Others are trickier, and demand a candy thermometer. On these pages we have gathered some of the best center recipes, all of which are extremely easy to make, with no candy thermometer required!

Making Truffles

Chocolate truffles are probably the most delicious and luxurious candy you can prepare.

To begin, you will need ¾ cup heavy cream and 6 ounces (6 squares) semisweet chocolate. Finely chop the chocolate. Bring the cream almost to a boil, then remove it from the heat.

Stir the chocolate into the hot cream until the mixture is smooth. You can add a tablespoon of liqueur or a teaspoon of vanilla extract for flavoring. Chill the mixture until it is firm enough to shape, 2 hours. Shape the mixture into either balls or oblongs, or press it through a pastry bag into fancy swirls. Alternatively, chill the truffle mixture in a square cake pan and cut into squares or rectangles. The truffles can be served as is, or they can be dipped in chocolate. This recipe makes about 25 truffles, and can be doubled.

Making Chocolate Cups

To make these superlative treats, you will need 24 1-inch fluted foil candy cups, a small paint brush, and a pastry bag or spoon.

Melt 4 ounces (4 squares) chopped semisweet chocolate with ½ teaspoon vegetable oil. Paint the insides of each foil cup with a thick layer of chocolate, making sure that there are no gaps. Chill the cups until they are set, about 20 minutes. Using a pastry bag or spoon, fill the cups as you desire or follow one of these suggestions:

- Pipe buttercream or sweetened whipped cream into the cups and garnish with chopped nuts.
- Spoon a layer of apricot or raspberry jelly into the cups, top with a whole toasted nut, and cover with melted chocolate.

- Mix equal parts peanut butter, honey, and butter into a paste. Pipe into the cups.
- Pipe in chocolate truffle mixture.

Making Marzipan Chocolates

Chocolates filled with marzipan on its own can be wonderful, but for a delightful combination of flavors and textures, add nuts or dried fruit to the marzipan.

To fashion these tempting morsels, you will need 6 ounces of marzipan and ½ cup of nuts or dried fruit. Roll the marzipan into balls and stuff with pieces of the fruit and/or nuts. Then dip the centers into melted chocolate (see photo at right). The results are terrific!

Dipping Chocolates

To prepare chocolate for dipping, melt 8 ounces (8 squares) chopped bittersweet or milk chocolate in a double boiler or the microwave. Place the chocolate in a wide, deep bowl and mix in 1 tablespoon vegetable oil. When the chocolate is cool, in about 15 minutes, drop a center, such as a truffle or a nut, into the coating. Using a fork, retrieve the center, tapping the fork on the side of the bowl to let excess coating fall back into the bowl. Place the chocolate on a foil-lined tray. Repeat with remaining centers. Let coating set before decorating.

Decorating Chocolates

You can embellish chocolate bonbons by rolling them in chopped nuts or topping them with candied fruit morsels, sugared flowers, glacé citrus peel, or whole nuts. However, for a professional finish, you might want to enhance them with a piped chocolate design. Decorate with a contrasting color of chocolate; if you have used bittersweet chocolate, garnish with milk chocolate, for example. White chocolate also makes a stunning contrast.

Melt 4 ounces of chopped chocolate with ½ teaspoon vegetable oil. Then, using a pastry bag fitted with a writing tip, pipe swirls, twists, or stripes onto the chocolates. Let the garnish set before serving.

Small, colorful fluted foil cups can be painted with melted chocolate and filled with a variety of delectable fillings.

Creamy chocolate truffles can be formed either with a spoon or your hands, or piped from a pastry bag into ornate swirls.

For a special candy, dip marzipan centers into melted dark chocolate, then garnish the top with a piece of walnut.

Decorate the dipped bonbons with melted chocolate designs, using either a light or dark chocolate for color contrast.

Pastries

Looking at these pastries, you can almost smell the coffee brewing and imagine you are in an exclusive patisserie in Paris or Vienna. Whether you're a novice or an experienced cook, you, too, can make these delectable pastries.

Learning these straightforward techniques will enable you to produce sophisticated goodies that will fill you with satisfaction—and those who are lucky enough to eat them will admire your undeniable talent.

Classic Choux Pastry

Mastering the simple art of choux pastry will help you to prepare impressive cream puffs and eclairs, and many delicious appetizers and hors d'oeuvres.

Pâte à choux (pronounced paht-ah-shoe) is one of the fundamental French pastry doughs. The dough consists of water, butter, flour, and eggs, quickly cooked together. When it enters the oven, it springs to life, like popovers, in another of the miracles of baking. No special equipment is required, but a pastry bag with a large round tip is helpful and offers a professional look. However, teaspoons can also be used for shaping.

Sweet and Savory Creations

Pâte (French for paste or dough) à choux is so called because of the likeness of cream puffs to mini cabbages (or choux). But this versatile dough makes much more than cream puffs, including slender shapes for eclairs, and rings for elegant desserts like Paris-Brest. Even the beautiful croquembouche starts with little cream puffs which are filled with vanilla custard, then dipped in hot caramel, and formed into a pyramid.

Fillings for eclairs and cream puffs can range from a simple sweetened whipped cream flavored with vanilla or almond extract, to a pudding mix enriched with cream and egg yolk, or a pastry cream or custard filling. Top off eclairs or cream puffs with a chocolate glaze or dust with confectioners' sugar. Fill tiny puffs or eclairs with ice cream and add a sauce, and you've got profiteroles. If eclairs or cream puffs are filled with coffee ice cream, add a dollop of warm chocolate sauce; if using vanilla ice cream, pour on hot butterscotch sauce.

For hot first courses or luncheon entrées, fill puffs with creamed chicken, tuna, or mushrooms. For party hors d'oeuvres, fill tiny puffs with bits of crab, shrimp, or ham salad, or a smoked salmon spread.

For a warm treat at a cocktail party, make a few dozen savory gougères. Stir ¾ cup of Parmesan cheese, 1 teaspoon of dry mustard, and a pinch of cayenne into the basic dough. Form into tiny puffs and sprinkle with cheese before baking.

Method

To make 12 to 18 puffs, in a medium, heavy-bottom saucepan, heat ½ cup (1 stick) butter and 1 cup water over medium heat until mixture boils and butter has melted. For dessert puffs, add 1-2 tablespoons granulated sugar; for savory puffs, add ½ teaspoon salt.

Add 1 cup all-purpose flour all at once, beating vigorously with a wooden spoon until the mixture forms a ball and pulls away from the sides of the pan. Remove pan from the heat; cool slightly.

Transfer the mixture to a bowl; add 4 large eggs, 1 at a time, beating well after each addition.

Forming the Pastry

For cream puffs, use a spoon and a rubber spatula, or a pastry bag fitted with a ½-inch round tip to drop or pipe dough, 2 inches apart, onto a greased and floured baking sheet. For tiny puffs, use slightly rounded teaspoonfuls of dough. For eclairs, drop or pipe 10 mounds, 5 inches apart, onto a greased baking sheet. Spread each mound into a 4 x ¾-inch rectangle, piling dough on top and slightly rounding sides.

For a Paris-Brest, pipe two large rings of dough onto a greased baking sheet. Pipe a second ring on top of each of the two bottom rings.

Baking

Preheat oven to 400°F. For standard size puffs, bake until lightly golden, 35 minutes. (Check smaller puffs after 20 minutes.) Remove from oven; make a 1-inch-long slit on one side of each pastry. Reduce temperature to 375°F. Bake for 10 minutes. Cool in a turned-off oven with the door open. Halve pastries; remove any uncooked dough from inside.

Variations

For dessert puffs, fold ½ cup miniature chocolate chips into the finished dough, or add 1-2 teaspoons granulated sugar or vanilla sugar, a pinch of ground nutmeg or cinnamon, finely ground toasted nuts, or grated lemon or orange peel.

For savory puffs, add a pinch of cayenne pepper, ¼ teaspoon of dried herbs, dried onion flakes, coarsely ground black pepper, or grated cheese.

Storage

These pastries always taste best if they are eaten within a few hours of filling; that way, you avoid the problem of the pastry turning soggy. If you want to make cream puffs and eclairs ahead of time, store them unfilled in an airtight container. Or, wrap unfilled pastries in plastic wrap and freeze. To thaw, remove plastic wrap and reheat at 425°F for 5 minutes.

Add flour all at once to melted butter-water mixture, then continue to beat mixture over low heat. The mixture will form a ball and pull away from the sides of the pan.

After beating in the eggs, the dough should be thick and hold its shape. Cool slightly if the dough isn't firm enough to pipe immediately.

To pipe eclairs, draw pastry bag tip along baking sheet for about 4 inches. To pipe cream puffs, hold the pastry bag directly over the baking sheet; pipe dough in a circle.

To release moisture from baked eclairs and cream puffs, make a 1-inch-long slit on one side of the pastry. Return pastries to the oven for 10 minutes more.

Chocolate-Banana Cream Puffs

These light puffs encase one of the all-time favorite combinations: chocolate and bananas.

50 minutes preparation plus cooling, 25 minutes baking   Makes 6 cream puffs

Ingredients:

- 1 cup all-purpose flour
- 1 tablespoon granulated sugar
- ½ teaspoon ground nutmeg
- 1 cup water
- 2½ ounces (⅔ stick) butter
- 5 large eggs

Filling:

- 2 cups half-and-half
- ½ cup granulated sugar
- ⅓ cup all-purpose flour
- 3 large eggs, lightly beaten
- 3 tablespoons coffee-flavored liqueur or 2 teaspoons vanilla extract
- 3 ounces (3 squares) semisweet chocolate, coarsely chopped
- 2 large, ripe bananas, sliced

Topping:

- 1½ cups prepared chocolate sauce

1. Preheat oven to 400°F. Line a baking sheet with waxed paper.

2. Mix together flour, sugar, and nutmeg.

3. In a medium saucepan, heat water and butter over medium-high heat until mixture boils and butter melts. Reduce heat to low.

4. Add flour mixture all at once, stirring until mixture forms a ball and pulls away from sides of pan. Remove from heat. Cool for 5 minutes.

5. Add eggs, 1 at a time, beating well after each addition.

6. Drop dough by tablespoonfuls onto prepared baking sheet, 2 inches apart.

7. Bake puffs until golden, 25 minutes. Make a 1-inch slit on side of each puff. Turn off oven; leave oven door slightly open. Let puffs cool for 1 hour.

8. Slice puffs in half horizontally. Pull out any uncooked dough.

9. To prepare filling, in the top of a double boiler set over simmering (not boiling) water, cook together half-and-half, sugar, and flour, stirring constantly, until thickened, 7 minutes. Remove pan from over water.

10. Pour ½ cup hot filling into beaten eggs. Stir egg mixture into remaining filling mixture in pan. Return pan to double boiler. Cook, stirring frequently, 4 minutes more. Stir in liqueur. Remove from heat.

11. Pour custard into a bowl. Press plastic wrap directly onto surface of filling. Cool completely.

12. Stir chocolate into filling. Spoon filling evenly into cream puff bottoms. Place banana slices on top. Replace tops.

13. To serve, ladle some chocolate sauce over cream puffs. Ladle remaining sauce onto serving plates.

Chocolate-Glazed Napoleons

Meet your dessert "Waterloo" with these delicious, cream-filled pastries.

20 minutes preparation plus chilling and cooling, 15-20 minutes baking

Makes 8 pastries

Ingredients:

1 sheet (½ 17-ounce package) frozen
   puff pastry, thawed according to package
   directions

Filling:

1 cup milk

3 large egg yolks

⅓ cup granulated sugar

1 tablespoon cornstarch

⅛ teaspoon salt

1 tablespoon butter, softened

½ teaspoon vanilla extract

Frosting and Garnish:

4 ounces (4 squares) semisweet chocolate,
   coarsely chopped

2 tablespoons water

1½ tablespoons butter

2 teaspoons light corn syrup

8 walnut halves

Fresh strawberries

Sprigs of fresh mint

1. To prepare filling, in a saucepan over low heat, heat milk until bubbles appear around edges of pan.

2. Mix together egg yolks, sugar, cornstarch, and salt. Stir in 2 tablespoons warm milk.

3. Stir egg mixture into remaining milk in saucepan. Bring milk mixture to a boil over low heat, stirring constantly; cook for 30 seconds. Pour into a bowl. Stir in butter and vanilla. Press plastic wrap directly onto surface. Chill completely.

4. On a floured surface, unfold pastry so that it lies flat. Using a floured rolling pin, roll into a 16 x 10-inch rectangle.

5. Prick pastry several times with a fork. Cut into sixteen 4 x 2½-inch rectangles. Place pastry on an ungreased baking sheet. Chill for 1 hour.

6. Preheat oven to 375°F. Bake pastry until golden, 15-20 minutes. Transfer baking sheet to a wire rack to cool.

7. To prepare frosting, in the top of a double boiler set over simmering (not boiling) water, heat chocolate, stirring constantly, until melted and smooth. Remove from heat. Stir in water, butter, and corn syrup. Cool to room temperature, stirring occasionally.

8. Place 8 rectangles on a serving plate. Spread filling over rectangles. Spread frosting over remaining rectangles. Place frosted rectangles on top of filling. Place a nut on top of each pastry. Garnish with strawberries and mint sprigs.

Cook's Tip

Serve the assembled Napoleons as soon as possible. They will become soggy if left to sit.

Chocolate Mousse Pastry Ring

A classic, rich mousse is the filling in this light and buttery puff pastry ring.

45 minutes preparation plus cooling, standing, and chilling, 35 minutes baking   Makes 8 servings

Ingredients:

1 cup water
4 ounces (1 stick) butter
⅛ teaspoon salt
1 cup all-purpose flour
4 large eggs
Filling and Topping:
2 cups heavy cream
¾ cup granulated sugar
4 ounces (4 squares) unsweetened
    chocolate, coarsely chopped
2 tablespoons butter
3 large eggs, separated
1 package unflavored gelatin
¼ cup coffee-flavored liqueur or
    1 teaspoon strong coffee
Confectioners' sugar

1. Preheat oven to 400°F. Grease a baking sheet; line with waxed paper. Trace a 9-inch circle on waxed paper.

2. In a heavy saucepan, heat water, butter, and salt over medium-high heat until butter melts. Add flour all at once, stirring until mixture forms a ball and pulls away from sides of pan. Remove from heat. Cool for 10 minutes.

3. Add eggs to flour mixture, 1 at a time, beating well after each addition.

4. Drop dough in mounds, touching each other, in a circle over tracing on prepared baking sheet.

5. Bake pastry until golden, 35 minutes. Turn off oven. Using a small knife, cut small slits in pastry sides while still in oven.

6. Let stand in oven with the door closed for 20 minutes. Transfer pastry to a wire rack to cool completely.

7. To prepare filling, in a saucepan, heat cream, sugar, chocolate, butter, and egg yolks over low heat, stirring constantly, until smooth. Remove from heat.

8. Sprinkle gelatin over chocolate mixture. Let stand until softened, 5-10 minutes.

9. Cook chocolate mixture over low heat, stirring constantly, until thickened, 10 minutes. Remove from heat. Stir in liqueur. Cool completely.

10. Beat egg whites at high speed until stiff, but not dry, peaks form. Fold one-third of beaten egg whites into chocolate mixture. Fold in remaining whites.

11. Transfer filling to a bowl. Press plastic wrap directly onto surface. Chill for 3 hours.

12. Slice pastry in half horizontally. Remove any uncooked dough from inside pastry. Spoon filling into bottom half of pastry; replace top. Dust with confectioners' sugar.

Chocolate Profiteroles

Try these chocolate puffs filled with ice cream and served with a coffee sauce.

45 minutes preparation, 25-30 minutes baking plus cooling

Makes 12 puffs

Ingredients:

3 tablespoons butter, cut into
  small pieces

¾ cup all-purpose flour, sifted

1 tablespoon unsweetened cocoa
  powder

2 eggs, lightly beaten

Filling and Sauce:

1 tablespoon cornstarch

6 tablespoons superfine sugar

1¼ cups milk

1 tablespoon instant coffee
  powder dissolved in
  2 teaspoons hot water

⅔ cups heavy cream

12 tablespoons vanilla ice cream

1. Preheat oven to 400°F. Line a baking sheet with waxed paper.

2. Put the butter in a pan with 2/3 cup water and melt over low heat. Bring to a boil and remove the pan from the heat. Add the flour and cocoa and beat until smooth.

3. Return the pan to medium heat. Beat the dough until it forms a ball and leaves the side of the pan clean. Remove from the heat and let cool for 5 minutes.

4. Add eggs, 1 at a time, beating well after each addition. Spoon into a pastry bag fitted with a large star-shaped tip. Pipe 12 mounds onto prepared baking sheet, 2 inches apart. Bake puffs until golden, 25 minutes.

5. Cut off the top third of each puff and transfer the tops and bases to a wire rack to cool completely.

6. Meanwhile, make the sauce. Blend the cornstarch and sugar with a little of the milk until smooth. Heat the remaining milk until almost boiling. Pour onto the cornstarch mixture, then return the mixture to the pan. Bring to a boil, stirring constantly until thickened and smooth. Cover the surface with plastic wrap and set aside to cool.

7. Beat the coffee mixture and cream into the cooled sauce. Put the puffs onto individual serving plates. Spoon 1 tablespoon ice cream onto the base of each puff. Replace the tops. Serve with the coffee sauce.

Chocolate-Pecan Pastries

These half-moon confections feature a rich chocolate-pecan filling surrounded by a flaky pastry.

25 minutes preparation plus chilling, cooling, and standing, 20-25 minutes baking   Makes 1 dozen pastries

Ingredients:

1 cup all-purpose flour

¼ cup granulated sugar

1/8 teaspoon salt

2½ ounces (⅔ stick) chilled butter,
   cut into small pieces

3 tablespoons chilled solid
   vegetable shortening

1 large egg

1 tablespoon ice water

Filling:

3 ounces (3 squares) semisweet
   chocolate, melted

¼ cup ground pecans
   (about 1 ounce)

Glaze and Topping:

¾ cup confectioners' sugar

2 tablespoons milk

2 tablespoons strawberry jelly

1. In a large bowl, mix together flour, sugar, and salt. Using a pastry blender or 2 knives, cut butter and shortening into flour mixture until coarse crumbs form.

2. Mix together egg and water. Add egg mixture to flour mixture, 1 teaspoon at a time, tossing with a fork until a dough forms. Shape dough into a disk, wrap in plastic wrap, and chill for several hours or overnight.

3. Grease a baking sheet. Dust with flour; tap out excess. On a floured surface, using a floured rolling pin, roll dough into a 10 x 7-inch rectangle.

4. To prepare filling, spread melted chocolate evenly over dough to within ½ inch of edges. Sprinkle nuts over chocolate.

5. Starting with a short side, fold dough in half over filling. Roll dough to a ½-inch thickness. Using a floured 3-inch round cookie cutter, cut out 6 circles.

6. Using the back of a spoon, make a slight indentation in top of pastries. Place pastries, 1 inch apart, on prepared baking sheet. Chill for 30 minutes.

7. Preheat oven to 375°F.

8. Bake pastries until golden, 20-25 minutes. Transfer baking sheet to a wire rack to cool.

9. To prepare glaze, mix together confectioners' sugar and milk. Spread jelly evenly over pastries. Spread glaze over jelly. Let stand until set. Cut each round in half to serve.

Cook's Tip

Make a colorful presentation by using assorted jellys, such as blueberry, peach, and cherry.

Chocolate-Peach Meringues

Make good use of summer's fruit bounty in these pretty meringues.

45 minutes preparation plus cooling, 1 hour baking, and standing   Makes 6 meringues

Meringues:
- ½ cup granulated sugar
- 2 tablespoons sifted cornstarch
- 1½ tablespoons sifted unsweetened cocoa powder
- 4 large egg whites
- ¼ teaspoon cream of tartar
- ⅛ teaspoon salt
- 1 teaspoon vanilla extract

Filling:
- 1½ cups heavy cream
- 3 tablespoons confectioners' sugar
- 2 medium fresh peaches or nectarines, peeled, pitted, and finely chopped

Garnish:
- 1 medium fresh peach or nectarine, thinly sliced

1. Preheat oven to 200°F. Line a baking sheet with waxed paper. Dust with flour; tap out excess.

2. To prepare meringues, mix together ¼ cup sugar, cornstarch, and cocoa powder.

3. Beat together egg whites, cream of tartar, and salt at medium speed until foamy. Beat in remaining sugar until soft peaks form.

4. At low speed, beat cocoa mixture into egg whites until just blended. At high speed, beat meringue mixture until stiff, but not dry, peaks form. Stir in vanilla.

5. Using a 3-inch round cookie cutter, trace 12 circles, 3 inches apart, on prepared baking sheet. Spoon meringue mixture into the center of each circle; spread to cover circle.

6. Bake until crisp and dry, 1 hour. Turn oven off and let meringues stand in unopened oven until cool, about 1 hour. Transfer baking sheet to a wire rack to dry completely.

7. To prepare filling, beat cream at medium speed until soft peaks form. Beat in confectioners' sugar until stiff, but not dry, peaks form. Fold peaches into whipped cream.

8. Using a pastry bag fitted with a large star tip, pipe half of filling onto 6 meringues. Place remaining meringues on top of filling. Pipe 2 rows of cream on top of each meringue. Stand 2 peach slices in cream; pipe a rosette on top of peaches.

Cook's Tip

Substitute fresh strawberries, raspberries, or blueberries for the peaches or nectarines.

Chocolate-Dipped Palmiers

Folded puff pastry slices dipped in melted dark chocolate.

20 minutes preparation, 10-12 minutes baking plus cooling   Makes 24 palmiers

Ingredients:

- 1 pound ready-made puff pastry
- ¼ cup superfine sugar
- 3 ounces (3 squares) semisweet chocolate, broken into squares

1. Preheat oven to 425°F. Dampen 2 large baking sheets with a little water.

2. Put the pastry onto a lightly floured surface and roll out to form a 12 x 10-inch rectangle.

3. Sprinkle a thin layer of sugar evenly over the rolled-out pastry. Fold in the long edges of the pastry halfway toward the center.

4. Sprinkle the pastry again with sugar. Fold the pastry in half lengthwise to form a long strip. Press down lightly.

5. Using a sharp knife, cut the pastry into 24 slices. Transfer the slices to the baking sheets. Gently open out the folds in each pastry slice, using the end of a knife and your fingertips. Flatten each slice slightly with a palette knife.

6. Bake for 6 minutes, or until light golden. Carefully turn over the palmiers with a palette knife. Bake for an additional 4-6 minutes, or until puffed and golden.

7. Transfer the palmiers to a wire rack and let cool completely.

8. Put the chocolate into a heatproof bowl set over a pan of barely simmering water. Let the chocolate melt, stirring occasionally.

9. Dip the the palmiers into the chocolate. Transfer to a sheet of waxed paper and let set.

Cook's Tip

You can shape the palmiers up to 2 days in advance and keep in the refrigerator until ready to bake. Cover the baking sheets with foil if keeping the palmiers in the refrigerator. For a real treat, sandwich together pairs of palmiers with heavy cream.

Chocolate Palmier Sandwiches

Filled with a rich chocolate cream, these elegant pastries are quick and easy to make.

15 minutes preparation, 8-10 minutes baking plus chilling   Makes 8 palmier sandwiches

Ingredients:

13 ounces (¾ 17-ounce package) puff pastry thawed according to package directions

Filling:

1¼ cups whipping cream

1 tablespoon chocolate spread

Unsweetened cocoa powder and confectioner's sugar, to dust

1. Preheat oven to 425°F. Lightly grease 2 large baking sheets.

2. Dust a work surface with cocoa. With the long side facing toward you, roll out the pastry into a 14 x 9-inch rectangle. Brush with cold water and sprinkle with cocoa and confectioners' sugar.

3. Mark the center of the pastry. Roll up the short sides so the 2 coils meet in the middle. Brush the join with a little water and gently press the coils together to secure.

4. Using a sharp knife, cut into 16 thin slices. Carefully transfer to the prepared baking sheets, spaced 2 inches apart.

5. Bake for 8-10 minutes, or until the pastries are well risen and golden brown. Let cool completely on a wire rack.

6. Meanwhile, make the filling. Beat the cream with an electric or hand-held beater until soft peaks form. Slowly beat in the chocolate spread until just blended.

7. Spoon the mixture into a pastry bag fitted with a star-shaped tip. Pipe the cream onto half the pastries. Top with the remaining pastries.

8. Dust with cocoa and confectioners' sugar. Chill until ready to serve.

Cook's Tip

If preferred, omit the chocolate spread from the cream filling and cover the surface of the palmiers with chocolate spread instead.

Chocolate Temptations

Impress your dinner guests with these elegantly professional chocolate temptations.

1 hour preparation plus cooling and chilling, 5 minutes baking

Ingredients:

- ¼ cup all-purpose flour
- 1 tablespoon unsweetened cocoa powder
- 2 teaspoons instant coffee powder
- 1 teaspoon baking powder
- ½ cup granulated sugar
- 3 large eggs
- Confectioners' sugar

Filling:

- 3 ounces (¾ stick) butter, softened
- ½ cup confectioners' sugar
- 2 tablespoons unsweetened cocoa powder
- 1 teaspoon instant coffee powder
- 1 teaspoon vanilla extract
- 1 large egg yolk

Glaze and Frosting:

- 4 ounces (4 squares) semisweet chocolate, melted
- 1 teaspoon vegetable oil
- ½ cup confectioners' sugar
- 2 teaspoons hot water

1. Preheat oven to 450°F. Grease a 15 x 10-inch jelly roll pan. Dust with flour; tap out excess.

2. Mix together flour, cocoa powder, coffee, and baking powder. Beat together sugar and eggs at high speed until light and fluffy. Fold flour mixture into egg mixture. Spread batter evenly in prepared pan; smooth top.

3. Bake cake until set, 5 minutes. Transfer pan to a wire rack to cool, 5 minutes. Dust a cloth with confectioners' sugar. Turn cake out onto cloth; trim edges.

4. To prepare filling, beat together butter, confectioners' sugar, cocoa, powder, coffee, and vanilla at medium speed until blended and smooth. Beat in egg yolk.

5. Spread half of filling over cake. Cut cake lengthwise into 6 strips. Roll up strips; secure with a toothpick. Chill for 30 minutes.

6. To prepare glaze, mix together melted chocolate and oil. Let stand until thickened.

7. To prepare frosting, mix confectioners' sugar and water.

8. Remove toothpicks; stand cakes on wire rack. Spread glaze over sides of cakes. Spoon frosting over top. Using a pastry bag fitted with a writing tip, pipe remaining filling around edges. Chill for 1 hour.

Strawberry-Chocolate Pastries

Two firm favorites are used to fill these light, flaky pastries. 45 minutes preparation,
20 minutes baking plus cooling

Ingredients:

13 ounces (¾ 17-ounce package)
frozen puff pastry

Filling:

2 cups milk

¼ cup superfine sugar

1 cup cornstarch

3 large egg yolks

1 ounce (1 square) bittersweet
chocolate, broken into pieces

¼ teaspoon vanilla extract

1 pint strawberries, hulled and
sliced

Topping:

4 ounces (4 squares) semisweet
chocolate, broken into pieces

2 tablespoons butter

2 teaspoons light corn syrup

1. Preheat oven to 400°F. On a lightly floured surface, roll out the pastry into a 17 x 11-inch rectangle. Cut in half to make two 11 x 8½-inch rectangles.

2. Put on 2 dampened baking sheets, cover and chill for 15 minutes. Prick all over with a fork and bake for 15 minutes. Turn over and bake for 5 minutes more, or until crisp and golden. Transfer to a wire rack to cool completely.

3. Meanwhile make the filling. Heat the milk in a small saucepan until almost boiling. In a bowl, mix together the sugar, cornstarch, and egg yolks. Gradually pour on the milk, mixing thoroughly.

4. Return mixture to the pan and stir in the chocolate until melted. Cook over low heat until mixture thickens, stirring continuously.

5. Stir in the vanilla extract, pour into a bowl. Cover the surface with plastic wrap, cool completely, then chill.

6. For the topping, put the chocolate, 2 tablespoons water, butter, and syrup into a saucepan. Heat gently, stirring continuously, until the chocolate melts.

7. Cut each pastry rectangle into four 2½-inch strips. Cut each strip in half.

8. Spread the filling onto half the pastry rectangles. Arrange a layer of strawberries on top. Put the remaining pastry rectangles on top and spread with the topping. Keep chilled until ready to serve.

Chocolate Danish Pastries

Enjoy these luscious chocolate cream-filled pastries at lunchtime, teatime, or any time of day.

30 minutes preparation plus rising and freezing, 25 minutes baking   Makes 10 pastries

Ingredients:
- 1 package active dry yeast
- ½ cup warm water (105°-115°F)
- ⅓ cup granulated sugar
- ⅓ cup plus 1 tablespoon milk
- 2 ounces (½ stick) butter, melted and cooled
- 1 large egg
- ½ teaspoon salt
- 3½ cups all-purpose flour

Filling:
- ¼ cup heavy cream
- 4 ounces (4 squares) semisweet chocolate, coarsely chopped

Glaze:
- 2 tablespoons milk

1. In a large bowl, dissolve yeast in warm water. Let stand until foamy, 5-10 minutes.

2. Stir sugar, 1/3 cup milk, melted butter, egg, and salt into yeast mixture. Using a heavy-duty electric mixer fitted with the paddle attachment and set on low speed, beat in flour, ½ cup at a time, until a soft dough forms.

3. On a floured surface, knead dough until smooth and elastic, 5-10 minutes, adding more flour to prevent sticking. Place dough in a large greased bowl, turning to coat. Cover loosely with a damp cloth; let rise in a warm place until doubled, 1 hour.

4. To prepare filling, in a small saucepan, heat cream over medium heat until bubbles appear around edges of pan. Remove from heat. Add chocolate; stir until smooth.

5. 5 Press plastic wrap directly onto surface; freeze for 1 hour.

6. Grease a baking sheet. Punch down dough.

7. Roll dough into a rope; cut into 10 equal pieces. On a floured surface, using a floured rolling pin, roll each dough piece into a 7 x 3½-inch rectangle.

8. Spoon filling evenly into center of each rectangle. Brush edges with remaining milk. Fold dough over filling; press seams to seal; fold ends under.

9. Place buns, seam-sides down, on prepared baking sheet. Cover again; let rise in a warm place until almost doubled, 1 hour.

10. Preheat oven to 400°F. Brush pastries with milk.

11. Bake pastries until golden and bottoms sound hollow when tapped, 25 minutes. Transfer to a wire rack to cool.

Cook's Tip

To make frosting for these buns, mix together ½ cup confectioners' sugar and 1½ tablespoons water.

Chocolate-Almond Danish

Square off at the breakfast table with these delightful sweet pastries.

1 hour preparation plus rising and cooling, 10-12 minutes baking   Makes 10 pastries

Ingredients:

- 1 package active dry yeast
- 1 cup warm milk (105°-115°F)
- ⅓ cup granulated sugar
- 2 ounces (½ stick) butter, melted and cooled
- ⅛ teaspoon salt
- 3½ cups all-purpose flour

Filling:

- 3 tablespoons butter, softened
- 2 tablespoons granulated sugar
- 1 teaspoon ground cardamom

Glaze and Topping:

- 1 large egg, lightly beaten
- 2 ounces (2 squares) semisweet chocolate, melted
- 3 tablespoons blanched, slivered almonds

1. In a large bowl, dissolve yeast in warm milk. Let stand until foamy, 5-10 minutes.

2. Using a heavy-duty electric mixer fitted with the paddle attachment and set on medium speed, beat sugar, butter, and salt into yeast mixture. At low speed, beat in flour, ½ cup at a time, until a dough forms.

3. On a floured surface, knead dough until smooth and elastic, 5 to 10 minutes, adding more flour to prevent sticking.

4. Place dough in a large greased bowl, turning to coat. Cover loosely with a damp cloth; let rise in a warm place until doubled, 45 minutes.

5. To prepare filling, mix together butter, sugar, and cardamom.

6. Grease a baking sheet. Punch down dough.

7. Shape dough into a 20-inch-long rope. Flatten rope into a 3-inch-wide strip. Cut dough into 10 3 x 2-inch rectangles. Make an indentation in each center. Spoon filling evenly into centers.

8. Place pastries, 2 inches apart, on prepared baking sheet. Cover again; let rise in a warm place until almost doubled, 30 minutes.

9. Preheat oven to 425°F. Brush pastries with beaten egg. Bake until golden, 10-12 minutes. Transfer baking sheet to a wire rack to cool slightly. Transfer pastries to rack to cool completely.

10. For topping, spoon melted chocolate in center of each pastry. Sprinkle nuts on top.

Pain au Chocolat

Eat these French specialties warm for breakfast, dipped into a cup of coffee.

40 minutes preparation, 15-18 minutes baking plus rising

Makes 8 pastries

Ingredients:

- 2 cups bread flour
- 1 package instant yeast
- 1 teaspoon salt
- 1 teaspoon superfine sugar
- 2 ounces (½ stick) butter, cut into small pieces
- 6 tablespoons lukewarm milk
- 2 large eggs, beaten
- 4 ounces (4 squares) semisweet chocolate, cut into 8 pieces

1. Mix together the flour, yeast, salt and sugar in a large bowl. Rub in the butter with your fingertips until the mixture resembles fine bread crumbs. Mix in the milk and half the eggs to form a soft dough.

2. Knead the dough on a lightly floured surface for 10 minutes, or until smooth and elastic. Put the dough into a lightly oiled bowl and cover loosely with oiled plastic wrap. Let rise in a warm place for 40 minutes.

3. Roll out the dough to form a 12 x 8-inch rectangle. Cut the rectangle in half lengthwise. Cut each half into 4 equal pieces.

4. Brush the dough with water and put 1 piece of chocolate onto each one. Roll up each piece of dough into a tube.

5. Preheat oven to 425°F. Line a baking sheet with waxed paper. Put the pieces of dough onto the baking sheet. Brush with the remaining beaten egg. Cover the rolls with oiled plastic wrap. Let rise in a warm place for 25 minutes, or until doubled in size.

6. Bake for 15-18 minutes, or until pale golden. Serve warm with a cup of fresh coffee.

Cook's Tip

To speed up the rising process in Step 2, use a microwave oven. For a 650W oven, put the dough in a covered bowl and heat on full power for 20 seconds. Leave for 5 minutes, then repeat. The dough should double in size in about 20 minutes.

Chocolate Chip Eclairs

Chocolate chips give these deliciously decadent pastries a polka-dot effect.

1 hour preparation plus chilling, 35 minutes baking   Makes 10 eclairs

Filling:
  - 1 package (about 3½ ounces) instant chocolate pudding and pie filling
  - 2 cups milk

Pastry:
  - 1 cup water
  - 4 ounces (1 stick) butter, cut into small pieces
  - ¼ teaspoon salt
  - 1 cup all-purpose flour
  - 4 large eggs
  - 3 tablespoons miniature chocolate chips

Frosting and Garnish:
  - 2 ounces (2 squares) semisweet chocolate, coarsely chopped
  - 1 tablespoon butter
  - ¼ cup heavy cream
  - 1 teaspoon light corn syrup
  - Confectioners' sugar
  - Fresh strawberries

1. Prepare filling according to package directions. Chill for 1 hour.

2. To prepare pastry, in a heavy saucepan, heat water, butter, and salt over medium-high heat until mixture boils and butter has completely melted. Reduce heat to low. Add flour all at once, stirring until mixture forms a ball and pulls away from sides of pan. Remove from heat. Cool for 10 minutes.

3. Add eggs, 1 at a time, beating well after each addition. Cool for 10 minutes. Gently stir in chocolate chips until just combined. (Do not overstir.)

4. Preheat oven to 400°F. Grease a large baking sheet. Drop dough into 10 mounds, 5 inches apart, on prepared baking sheet. Spread each mound into a 5 x 3¼-inch rectangle, piling dough on top and slightly rounding sides.

5. Bake eclairs until golden, 35 minutes. Transfer to a wire rack to cool. Make a 1-inch-long slit on side of each eclair.

6. To prepare frosting, in the top of a double boiler set over simmering (not boiling) water, melt chocolate and butter, stirring until smooth. Remove from heat.

7. In a small saucepan, bring cream and corn syrup to a boil over medium heat. Reduce heat to low; cook, stirring, 2 minutes.

8. Remove pan from heat; stir in chocolate mixture until well blended. Cool completely.

9. Slice eclairs in half lengthwise. Pull out any uncooked dough. Spoon ¼ cup filling into bottom half of each eclair. Replace tops. Spread with frosting. Dust tops with confectioners' sugar. Garnish with strawberries.

Miniature Chocolate Eclairs

No store-bought eclairs can compare to these bite-size pastries with their rich chocolate center.

25 minutes preparation, 45 minutes baking

Makes 12 eclairs

Filling:

- 1 package (about 3½ ounces) instant chocolate pudding and pie filling
- 2 cups milk

Pastry:

- 4 ounces (1 stick) butter
- 1 cup water
- ⅛ teaspoon salt
- 1 cup all-purpose flour
- 3 large eggs

Frosting:

- 2 tablespoons butter
- 2 ounces (2 squares) semisweet chocolate
- 1 cup confectioners' sugar
- 2 tablespoons milk
- 1 teaspoon vanilla extract

1. Prepare filling according to package directions. Chill for 1 hour.

2. To prepare pastry, in a heavy saucepan, heat butter, water, and salt over medium-high heat until mixture boils and butter has melted. Reduce heat to low. Add flour all at once, stirring until mixture forms a ball and pulls away from sides of pan. Remove from heat. Cool for 10 minutes.

3. Add eggs, 1 at a time, beating well after each addition. Cool for 10 minutes.

4. Preheat oven to 400°F. Grease a baking sheet. Drop dough into 12 mounds, about 5 inches apart, on prepared baking sheet.

5. Spread each mound into a 4 x ½-inch rectangle, piling dough on top and slightly rounding sides.

6. Bake eclairs until golden, 35 minutes. Remove from oven; make a 1-inch-long slit on side of each eclair. Reduce oven temperature to 375°F. Bake for 10 minutes. Transfer to a wire rack to cool.

7. To prepare frosting, heat butter and chocolate over low heat, stirring until melted. Remove from heat. Stir in sugar, milk, and vanilla until smooth.

8. Slice eclairs in half. Spoon about 1 tablespoon filling into bottom half of each eclair. Replace tops. Spread with frosting.

Cook's Tip

A wire rack lets air circulate below and around the food so it cools without becoming soggy.

White Chocolate Eclairs

These delectable pastries are sure to impress tea and dinner party guests.

45 minutes preparation plus cooling and standing, 25-30 minutes baking

Makes 10 eclairs

Ingredients:
- 2/3 cup milk
- 3 ounces (¾ stick) butter
- ¼ teaspoon salt
- 1 cup all-purpose flour
- 5 large eggs

Filling:
- 3 ounces white chocolate, finely chopped
- 1 cup heavy cream

Frosting and Garnish:
- 1 cup confectioners' sugar
- 2 tablespoons water
- Fresh raspberries, strawberries, or blackberries
- Sprigs of fresh mint

1. In a medium, heavy saucepan, heat milk, butter, and salt over medium-high heat until mixture boils and butter has melted.

2. Reduce heat to low. Add flour all at once, stirring until mixture forms a ball and pulls away from sides of pan. Remove from heat. Cool for 10 minutes.

3. Add eggs, 1 at a time, beating well after each addition. Cool for 10 minutes.

4. Preheat oven to 400°F. Grease a baking sheet.

5. Drop dough into 10 mounds on prepared baking sheet, 3 inches apart. Spread each mound into a 4½ x 1-inch rectangle, piling dough on top and slightly rounding sides.

6. Bake eclairs until golden, 25-30 minutes. Make a 1-inch-long slit on side of each eclair.

7. Turn off oven; leave oven door slightly open. Let eclairs cool for 1 hour.

8. To prepare filling, in the top of a double boiler set over simmering (not boiling) water, heat white chocolate and ¼ cup cream, stirring frequently, until melted and smooth. Remove from heat. Cool completely.

9. Beat remaining cream at medium speed until just thickened. Beat in white chocolate mixture until soft peaks form.

10. Cut eclairs in half lengthwise. Pull out any uncooked dough. Spoon filling into eclair bottoms. Replace tops.

11. To prepare frosting, mix together confectioners' sugar and water until smooth. Spread frosting on top of eclairs. Let stand until frosting has set. Garnish eclairs with fresh berries and sprigs of fresh mint.

Cook's Tip

White chocolate needs careful handling. Heating it with a little cream or milk prevents lumps forming as it melts.

Pies & Tarts

"Easy as pie" is not just a trite phrase. While it probably originated to mean something easy to eat, there is nothing simpler than making one from scratch, especially if you have a food processor for preparing the dough.

The trick to producing light, flaky pastry is to not overwork the dough, rolling it out evenly the first time and baking it at the proper temperature. Once you've seen how easy it is, you may never buy commercial piecrusts again.

Brownie Fudge Pie

This very rich pie contains some unexpected ingredients that provide a special, subtle flavor.

20 minutes preparation, 58-65 minutes baking

Makes 8 servings

Ingredients:

½ package (10-11 ounces) piecrust mix

Filling:

3 ounces (3 squares) unsweetened chocolate, coarsely chopped

2 ounces (½ stick) butter, softened

3 large eggs

1¼ cups granulated sugar

2 teaspoons instant coffee powder

3 tablespoons light corn syrup

3 tablespoons milk

2 tablespoons peanut butter

1 teaspoon vanilla extract

½ cup chopped walnuts (2 ounces)

1. Preheat oven to 425°F.

2. Prepare piecrust mix according to package directions.

3. On a floured surface, using a floured rolling pin, roll dough into an 11-inch circle. Fit into a 9-inch pie pan, pressing to fit the sides. Trim excess dough, leaving a ¾-inch overhang. Fold overhang under; flute edges.

4. Bake crust until just set, 8-10 minutes. Remove from oven. Reduce temperature to 350°F.

5. To prepare filling, in a double boiler set over simmering (not boiling) water, melt chocolate and butter, stirring until smooth. Remove from heat. Cool slightly.

6. Beat eggs at high speed until light and fluffy. At medium speed, beat in sugar, coffee powder, corn syrup, milk, peanut butter, and vanilla. Beat in chocolate mixture. Stir in nuts. Pour into crust.

7. Bake pie until top puffs up, 50-55 minutes. Transfer pan to a wire rack to cool. (Center of pie will sink slightly.)

Cook's Tip

Either creamy or chunky peanut butter can be used to make the brownie filling. For a special treat, serve this pie with a flavored whipped cream and fresh raspberries.

Chocolate-Almond Meringue Pie

This pie features a crisp meringue crust and a creamy chocolate and almond-flavored filling.

25 minutes preparation plus standing and cooling, 45-50 minutes baking   Makes 8 servings

Ingredients:

- 2 large egg whites
- ¼ teaspoon cream of tartar
- ⅛ teaspoon salt
- ½ cup granulated sugar
- 1 teaspoon vanilla extract
- ½ cup finely chopped almonds, toasted (about 2 ounces)

Filling:

- 4 ounces (4 squares) semisweet chocolate, coarsely chopped
- 2 tablespoons water
- 2 tablespoons almond-flavored liqueur or water
- 2 teaspoons vanilla extract
- ½ teaspoon almond extract
- 1 cup heavy cream
- 2 tablespoons granulated sugar

Garnish:

- ⅓ cup blanched, slivered almonds, toasted (about 1¼ ounces)
- 1½ cups whipped cream

1. Preheat oven to 300°F. Grease a 9-inch pie pan.

2. Beat egg whites at medium speed until foamy. Add cream of tartar and salt, beating until soft peaks form. Gradually add sugar and vanilla, beating until stiff, but not dry, peaks form. Fold in nuts.

3. Spoon meringue into prepared pan. Spread meringue evenly over bottom and sides of pan, creating a shallow crust. Bake until firm and dry, 45-50 minutes. Turn off oven; let meringue stand in oven with door closed to dry for 2 hours or overnight.

4. To prepare filling, in a double boiler set over simmering (not boiling) water, heat chocolate, water, liqueur, vanilla, and almond extract until melted and smooth. Remove pan from heat. Cool for 15 minutes.

5. Beat cream at medium speed until foamy. Gradually add sugar, beating until soft peaks form. Fold chocolate mixture into cream. Spoon filling into prepared crust.

6. To garnish, sprinkle nuts on top. Using a pastry bag fitted with a star tip, pipe cream in a decorative border.

Cook's Tip

Meringue will become soggy if chilled too long. For best results, serve this pie at room temperature shortly after assembling. For best results, use a wet knife to slice pie.

Chocolate Custard Pie

Serve everyone a big piece of this rich pie and watch them savor every delicious mouthful.

35 minutes preparation plus cooling and chilling, 20 minutes baking   Makes 6 servings

Ingredients:
    Package (10-11 ounces) piecrust
      mix

Filling:
    1 cup granulated sugar
    8 ounces (2 sticks) butter, softened
    3 ounces (3 squares) unsweetened
      chocolate, melted
    2 tablespoons almond-flavored
      liqueur or water
    ½ teaspoon vanilla extract
    ½ teaspoon ground cinnamon
    3 large eggs

Topping and Garnish:
    2 cups heavy cream
    ½ cup confectioners' sugar
    ½ teaspoon vanilla extract
    Chocolate curls

1. Preheat oven to 350°F. Prepare piecrust mix according to package directions.

2. On a floured surface, using a floured rolling pin, roll dough into an 11-inch circle. Fit dough into a 9-inch tart pan with a removable bottom. Trim dough even with pan edges. Prick dough several times with a fork. Line with aluminum foil; fill with pie weights or dried beans.

3. Bake crust for 10 minutes. Remove foil and weights. Bake until golden, 10 minutes more. Transfer pan to a wire rack to cool completely.

4. To prepare filling, beat together sugar and butter at medium speed until light and fluffy. Beat in melted chocolate, liqueur, vanilla, and cinnamon. Add eggs, 1 at a time, beating well after each addition. Spoon filling into prepared crust; smooth top. Chill for 3 hours or overnight.

5. To prepare topping, beat cream at medium speed until foamy. Add confectioners' sugar and vanilla, beating until soft peaks form.

6. Using a pastry bag fitted with a star tip, pipe topping over filling. Garnish with chocolate curls.

Cook's Tip
Refrigerate this pie until ready to serve.

Chocolate Mousse Cake

Impress dinner party guests by recreating this popular restaurant dessert in your own home.

30 minutes preparation plus cooling and chilling, 45 minutes baking

Makes 10 servings

Ingredients:

Crust:

1 cup chopped walnuts
(4 ounces)

1 cup chopped hazelnuts or
almonds (4 ounces)

2 ounces (½ stick) butter, softened

Filling:

1 pound semisweet chocolate,
coarsely chopped

1 cup heavy cream

6 large eggs

1 teaspoon vanilla extract

½ cup all-purpose flour

⅓ cup granulated sugar

Garnish:

1 cup whipped cream

1 cup fresh raspberries

1. Preheat oven to 325°F.

2. To prepare crust, mix together nuts and butter. Press evenly over bottom and up sides of a 9-inch springform pan.

3. To prepare filling, in a medium saucepan, heat chocolate and cream over low heat, stirring constantly, until chocolate is melted and smooth. Cool to room temperature, 10 minutes.

4. Beat together eggs and vanilla at low speed until foamy. At high speed, gradually beat in flour and sugar until thick, for 8-10 minutes.

5. Fold one-third of egg mixture into melted chocolate mixture. Fold chocolate mixture, one-quarter at a time, into remaining egg mixture. Spread batter in prepared pan; smooth top.

6. Bake cake until puffed around outer edges, 45 minutes. Transfer pan to a wire rack to cool for 30 minutes. Remove sides of pan.

7. Chill cake for 4 hours or overnight. Garnish with whipped cream and fresh raspberries before serving.

Chocolate Walnut Pie

Rich is the word for this amazing nut-filled dessert.

40 minutes' preparation plus cooling, 35 minutes baking

Ingredients:

    1 unbaked 9-inch piecrust

Filling:

    ½ cup granulated sugar

    1 cup heavy cream

    ½ cup light corn syrup

    1 teaspoon vanilla extract

    2 ounces (½ stick) butter, softened

    6 ounces (6 squares) semisweet
        chocolate, coarsely chopped

    2 cups coarsely chopped walnuts
        (8 ounces)

    2 large eggs, lightly beaten

Topping and Garnish:

    2 ounces (2 squares) semisweet
        chocolate, melted

    Whipped cream

    2 tablespoons chopped walnuts

    Sprigs of fresh mint

1. Preheat oven to 400°F. Place oven rack in lower third of oven.

2. To prepare filling, in a large skillet, heat sugar over medium-high heat until bubbles appear. Reduce heat to low; cook without stirring until mixture turns a deep golden color, 10 minutes. Remove from heat.

3. Stir in cream, corn syrup, and vanilla. Stir in butter, chocolate, and nuts. Pour a small amount of cream mixture into eggs.

4. Stir egg mixture into mixture in skillet until well blended. Pour filling into piecrust.

5. Bake pie for 15 minutes. Reduce temperature to 350°F.

6. Bake pie until set, 20 minutes more. Transfer pan to a wire rack to cool completely.

7. For topping, drizzle top of pie with melted chocolate. Using a pastry bag fitted with a star tip, pipe whipped cream around edges. Sprinkle nuts over cream. Garnish with mint sprigs.

Cook's Tip

When making your favorite piecrust recipe, add ½ teaspoon freshly ground nutmeg to enhance the flavor.
This pie is at its best when served chilled.

Chocolate Silk Pie

This silky-smooth pie is ideal for a special occasion dessert.

1 hour preparation plus chilling and cooling, 20-25 minutes baking

Ingredients:
- 1⅓ cups all-purpose flour
- ½ cup chopped almonds (2 ounces)
- ¼ cup firmly packed brown sugar
- ¼ teaspoon salt
- 4 ounces (1 stick) chilled butter, cut into small pieces
- 1 large egg yolk, lightly beaten
- 2 tablespoons ice water

Filling:
- 4 ounces (1 stick) butter, softened
- ⅓ cup firmly packed brown sugar
- ⅛ teaspoon salt
- 2 ounces (2 squares) unsweetened chocolate, melted and cooled
- 1 teaspoon vanilla extract
- 4 large egg yolks
- ⅓ cup granulated sugar
- 2 tablespoons rum extract
- ½ cup heavy cream

Garnish:
- Strawberry halves
- Sprigs of fresh mint

1. Mix together flour, nuts, brown sugar, and salt. Using a pastry blender, cut butter into flour mixture until coarse crumbs form.

2. Add egg yolk and water to flour mixture, 1 tablespoon at a time, tossing with a fork until a dough forms. Shape dough into a disk, wrap in plastic wrap, and chill for 15 minutes.

3. On a floured surface, using a floured rolling pin, roll dough into an 11-inch circle. Fit dough into a 9-inch pie pan, pressing to fit the sides. Trim excess dough, leaving a 1-inch overhang. Fold overhangs under; flute edges. Prick bottom and sides of dough with a fork. Chill for 30 minutes.

4. Preheat oven to 400°F.

5. Line dough with aluminum foil; fill with pie weights or dried beans. Bake crust for 10 minutes. Remove foil and weights. Reduce temperature to 350°F. Bake crust until golden, 10-15 minutes more. Transfer pan to a wire rack to cool.

6. To prepare filling, beat together butter, brown sugar, and salt at medium speed until light and fluffy. Beat in melted chocolate and vanilla.

7. In the top of a double boiler set over simmering (not boiling) water, beat together egg yolks, granulated sugar, and rum extract. Cook, stirring constantly, until smooth and thickened. Remove from heat.

8. Stir chocolate mixture into egg mixture. Beat until completely cooled, 5 minutes.

9. Beat cream at high speed until stiff peaks form. Stir one-quarter of whipped cream into chocolate mixture. Fold in remaining whipped cream.

10. Pour filling into prepared crust. Run a small spatula over top of filling to form a swirl pattern. Chill for 1 hour.

11. Arrange strawberry halves, cut-sides up, around edges of pie. Arrange remaining strawberry halves and sprigs of fresh mint in center of pie.

Fabulous Brownie Pie

Quick and easy, this chocoholic's dream dessert is great for almost any occasion.

15 minutes preparation plus cooling, 25 minutes baking　　　　　Makes 8 servings

Ingredients:

- 4 ounces (1 stick) butter, cut into small pieces
- 2 ounces (2 squares) unsweetened chocolate, coarsely chopped
- 1 cup granulated sugar
- ¾ cup all-purpose flour
- 2 large eggs
- 1 teaspoon vanilla extract
- ⅛ teaspoon salt
- ½ cup coarsely chopped walnuts (about 2 ounces)
- Whipped cream
- Finely chopped walnuts
- Chocolate curls

1. Preheat oven to 350°F. Grease a 9-inch pie pan.

2. In a saucepan, heat butter and chocolate over low heat until melted and smooth.

3. Beat together chocolate mixture, sugar, flour, eggs, vanilla, and salt at medium speed until blended. Stir in nuts. Pour batter into prepared pan.

4. Bake pie until set, 25 minutes. Transfer pan to a wire rack to cool completely.

5. To garnish, using a pastry bag fitted with a star tip, pipe whipped cream rosettes over top of pie. Sprinkle nuts over rosettes. Arrange chocolate curls on top.

Cook's Tip

Unused whipped cream can be stored in the freezer. Simply put the leftovers in small paper cups, cover, and place in transparent freezer bags. Thaw and use as needed.

Alternatively, drop dollops of whipped cream onto a sheet of aluminum foil, then freeze them, uncovered, until firm. Transfer the dollops to an airtight freezer container and freeze until needed. Use the dollops to top desserts—they will thaw quickly when placed on individual servings.

Crusty Brownie Cups

These individual brownie pies are great for an informal buffet, a picnic, or the kids' lunch.

40 minutes preparation plus cooling, 30 minutes baking — Makes 1 dozen cups

Ingredients:

> 1 package (15 ounces) ready-to-use
> refrigerated piecrust dough
> (2 sheets)

Filling:

> 4 ounces (1 stick) butter, cut into
> small pieces
> 3 ounces (3 squares) unsweetened
> chocolate, coarsely chopped
> ¾ cup sifted all-purpose flour
> ½ teaspoon salt
> 1 cup granulated sugar
> 3 large eggs
> 1½ teaspoons vanilla extract
> 1 cup coarsely chopped pecans,
> toasted (about 4 ounces)

Topping:

> ½ cup coarsely chopped pecans
> (about 2 ounces)

1. Preheat oven to 325°F. Grease 12 standard size muffin-pan cups.

2. On a floured surface, unfold dough sheets. Cut six 5-inch circles from each sheet. Fit circles into prepared cups. Flute edges.

3. To prepare filling, in a small saucepan, heat butter and chocolate over low heat, stirring constantly, until melted and smooth. Remove from heat. Cool completely.

4. Mix together flour and salt.

5. Beat together sugar and eggs at medium speed until light and fluffy. Beat in chocolate mixture and vanilla.

6. At low speed, beat flour mixture into chocolate mixture, ½ cup at a time, until blended and smooth. Stir in nuts.

7. Spoon batter into piecrusts, filling cups three-quarters full. Sprinkle nuts on top.

8. Bake cups until a toothpick inserted in the centers comes out almost clean, 30 minutes. Transfer pan to a wire rack to cool completely.

Cook's Tip

Look for no-roll, ready-to-use dough sheets in the refrigerated section of the supermarket.

Frozen Mocha Pie

Elegant, rich, and "make-ahead," this is the perfect party dessert.

1 hour preparation plus cooling, chilling, and freezing, 30 minutes baking   Makes 10 servings

Crust:

½ cup finely chopped pecans
(about 2 ounces)

½ cup granulated sugar

4 large egg whites

Mocha Cream:

4 large egg yolks

3 tablespoons granulated sugar

¼ cup strong black coffee

4 ounces (4 squares) semisweet
chocolate, coarsely chopped

1 teaspoon vanilla extract

1½ cups heavy cream

Topping and Garnish:

1 ounce (1 square) semisweet
chocolate, coarsely chopped

½ cup heavy cream

2 teaspoons granulated sugar

1. Preheat oven to 400°F. Grease an 8- or 9-inch springform pan.

2. To prepare crust, mix together nuts and sugar.

3. Beat egg whites at high speed until stiff, but not dry, peaks form. Fold in nut mixture. Spread mixture in prepared pan; smooth top.

4. Place pan in oven. Immediately reduce oven temperature to 350°F. Bake crust until golden brown, 30 minutes. Transfer pan to a wire rack to cool slightly.

5. Carefully loosen crust by running a metal spatula around sides of pan. Cool crust in pan completely.

6. To prepare mocha cream, in the top of a double boiler set over simmering (not boiling) water, beat together egg yolks, sugar, and coffee until thick and foamy, 10 minutes. Add chocolate; stir until melted and well blended. Stir in vanilla. Transfer to a clean bowl; chill for 15 minutes.

7. Beat cream at medium speed until soft peaks form; fold into chocolate mixture.

8. Spread mocha cream on top of crust in pan. Freeze for 4 hours or overnight.

9. To prepare topping, in the top of a double boiler set over simmering (not boiling) water, melt chocolate, stirring until smooth. Let cool until beginning to thicken, 10 minutes.

10. Using the tip of a teaspoon or a plastic-lined pastry bag fitted with a fine writing tip, make 10 loops of chocolate on waxed paper. Chill until firm, 10 minutes.

11. Remove sides of pan. Drizzle remaining chocolate over center of mocha cream.

12. In a small bowl, beat together cream and sugar at medium speed until soft peaks form. Using a pastry bag fitted with a large star tip, pipe a decorative border on top of pie.

13. Using the tip of a small knife, remove chocolate loops from waxed paper; place loops, standing, in whipped cream border. Serve pie at room temperature, or refreeze until ready to serve.

Lemon Black Bottom Pie

This delightful layered custard pie is the bottom-line in great desserts.

40 minutes preparation plus standing, cooling, and chilling   Makes 8 servings

Ingredients:

1 9-inch graham cracker crust

Filling:

1 envelope unflavored gelatin

¼ cup cold water

1½ cups milk

3 tablespoons cornstarch

4 large egg yolks

1 cup granulated sugar

⅛ teaspoon salt

¼ cup fresh lemon juice

2 tablespoons light rum or water

1 tablespoon grated lemon peel

3 ounces semisweet chocolate, coarsely chopped

1 teaspoon vanilla extract or lemon extract

1 cup heavy cream

Garnish:

Chocolate shavings

Lemon slice

1. To prepare filling, in a small bowl, sprinkle gelatin over cold water. Let stand until softened, 5-10 minutes.

2. Mix together ½ cup milk, cornstarch, and egg yolks.

3. In a small saucepan, bring remaining milk, ⅔ cup sugar, and salt to a simmer over medium heat. Stir egg yolk mixture into milk mixture.Cook, stirring constantly, until mixture thickens, 3 minutes. Transfer 1 cup custard to another small bowl. Set aside.

4. Add softened gelatin to remaining custard in saucepan; stir until gelatin is dissolved. Stir in lemon juice, rum, and lemon peel. Remove from heat.

5. In the top of a double boiler set over simmering (not boiling) water, melt chocolate, stirring until smooth.

6. Stir melted chocolate and vanilla into reserved custard in small bowl. Spoon chocolate custard evenly into crust. Chill until just set, 15 minutes.

7. Beat together cream and remaining sugar at high speed until soft peaks form. Fold two-thirds of whipped cream into lemon custard. Spoon lemon custard over chocolate custard layer in crust; smooth top. Chill until firm, 2 hours.

8. Using a pastry bag fitted with a star tip, pipe reserved whipped cream around border of crust. Arrange chocolate shavings inside whipped cream border. Garnish with a lemon slice and a dollop of whipped cream.

Cook's Tip

For a crunchy base, bake crust in a preheated 350°F oven until lightly colored and fragrant, 8 minutes. Transfer crust to a wire rack to cool completely.

Mississippi Mud Pie

This incredibly rich and gooey pie is guaranteed to satisfy anyone with a sweet tooth.

20 minutes preparation, 1 hour chilling, 35-45 minutes baking   Makes 10 servings

Crust:

1¼ cups all-purpose flour

1 tablespoon granulated sugar

½ teaspoon salt

½ teaspoon baking powder

3 ounces (¾ stick) chilled butter,
  cut into small pieces

1 large egg, lightly beaten

Filling:

⅔ cup dark corn syrup

⅔ cup granulated sugar

4 ounces (4 squares) semisweet
  chocolate, chopped

2 ounces (½ stick) butter

3 large eggs

Garnish:

Chocolate shavings (optional)

1. To prepare the crust, in a medium bowl, mix together flour, sugar, salt, and baking powder.

2. Using a pastry blender or 2 knives, cut the butter into the flour mixture until coarse crumbs form. Add the beaten egg, tossing with a fork until a slightly dry dough forms.

3. Turn dough out onto a lightly floured surface and knead quickly 3 or 4 times until smooth. Shape dough into a disk, wrap in plastic wrap, and chill in the refrigerator for at least 1 hour.

4. Preheat the oven to 350°F. On a lightly floured surface, using a lightly floured rolling pin, roll the dough into a 12-inch circle. Fit the dough into a 9-inch pie pan, pressing to fit the sides. Trim excess dough, leaving a 1-inch overhang. Fold overhang under; flute edges. Chill crust while preparing filling.

5. To prepare the filling, in a medium saucepan, stir together the corn syrup and sugar. Bring to a boil over medium heat. Remove the pan from the heat. Stir in the chocolate and butter. Let stand for 1 minute to melt. Beat until smooth.

6. In a large bowl, beat eggs. Gradually beat in the chocolate mixture until well blended. Pour the filling into the crust.

7. Bake the pie until the filling is set, 35-45 minutes. Transfer the pie to a wire rack to cool completely. Sprinkle with the chocolate shavings and chill until ready to serve.

Mocha Angel Pie

Absolutely heaven-sent, this fabulously rich dessert is for special occasions only.

45 minutes preparation plus standing, cooling, and chilling, 45-50 minutes baking   Makes 6 servings

Meringue:
  2 large egg whites
  ⅛ teaspoon cream of tartar
  ⅛ teaspoon salt
  ½ cup granulated sugar
  1 teaspoon vanilla extract
  ⅓ cup chopped pecans (1¼ ounces)
Filling:
  4 ounces semisweet chocolate,
    coarsely chopped
  2 tablespoons water
  2 teaspoons instant coffee powder
  1 cup heavy cream
  1 tablespoon confectioners' sugar
  ½ teaspoon vanilla extract
Garnish:
  Unsweetened cocoa powder
  Confectioners' sugar

1. Preheat oven to 200°F. Grease a 9-inch pie pan. Dust with flour; tap out excess.

2. To prepare meringue, beat together egg whites, cream of tartar, and salt at high speed until foamy. Gradually add sugar; continue beating until stiff, but not dry, peaks form. Stir in vanilla and nuts.

3. Spoon meringue into prepared pan. Spread meringue evenly over bottom and sides of pan, creating a shallow crust. Bake until firm and dry, 45-50 minutes. Turn off oven; let meringue stand in oven with door closed to dry for 2 hours.

4. Meanwhile, prepare filling. In a small saucepan, heat chocolate and water over low heat, stirring constantly, until melted. Stir in coffee powder. Cool until thickened, 30 minutes.

5. Beat together cream, confectioners' sugar, and vanilla at medium speed until soft peaks form. Fold in chocolate mixture.

6. Dust meringue with cocoa powder and confectioners' sugar. Using a pastry bag fitted with a star tip, pipe mounds of filling over top of meringue. Chill for 2 hours.

Cook's Tip
Serve pie the day it is made; if stored overnight, the meringue will lose its crispness.

Ultra-Rich Chocolate Pie

A chocolate lover's favorite, this dark and delicious pie is an easy sweet success.

30 minutes preparation plus chilling and cooling, 1 hour 5 minutes baking   Makes 10 servings

Ingredients:

- 1¼ cups all-purpose flour
- ½ teaspoon salt
- 4 ounces (1 stick) chilled butter, cut into small pieces
- 2-3 tablespoons ice water

Filling:

- 1½ cups granulated sugar
- 4 ounces (1 stick) butter
- 2 ounces (2 squares) semisweet chocolate, coarsely chopped
- 3 large eggs, lightly beaten
- 1 tablespoon white vinegar
- 1 teaspoon vanilla extract
- ⅛ teaspoon salt

Topping and Garnish:

- 1 cup whipped cream
- Fresh strawberries

1. In a large bowl, mix together flour and salt. Using a pastry blender or 2 knives, cut butter into flour mixture until coarse crumbs form.

2. Add water, 1 tablespoon at a time, tossing with a fork until a soft dough forms. Shape dough into a disk, wrap in plastic wrap, and chill for 1 hour.

3. On a floured surface, using a floured rolling pin, roll dough into an 11-inch circle. Fit dough into a 9-inch pie pan, pressing to fit the sides. Trim excess dough, leaving a 1-inch overhang. Fold overhang under; flute edges. Chill 30 minutes.

4. Preheat oven to 375°F. Prick dough with a fork. Line with aluminum foil; fill with pie weights or dried beans.

5. Bake crust for 15 minutes. Remove foil and weights. Bake until light golden, 10 minutes more. Transfer pan to a wire rack to cool slightly. Reduce oven temperature to 325°F.

6. To prepare filling, in a medium saucepan, heat sugar and butter over medium heat, stirring, until sugar has dissolved. Remove from heat. Add chocolate; stir until melted and smooth.

7. Stir eggs, vinegar, vanilla, and salt into chocolate mixture. Pour filling evenly into prepared crust.

8. Bake pie until crust is golden and filling is set, 40 minutes. Transfer pan to a wire rack to cool.

9. Using a pastry bag fitted with a star tip, pipe cream rosettes around edge of pie. Garnish with strawberries.

Cook's Tip

To make a strawberry fan, using a small, sharp knife, slice a strawberry several times at a slight angle, leaving the top intact. Gently fan the strawberry open.

Banana-Chocolate Tart

A rich chocolate cream covers a layer of sticky caramel bananas in this glorious tart.

30 minutes preparation, 20 minutes baking plus cooling Makes 6-8 servings

Ingredients:

1 cup all-purpose flour

Pinch of salt

1 ounce (¼ stick) butter, cut into
small pieces

2 tablespoons solid vegetable
shortening, cut into small pieces

Filling:

7 ounces (7 squares) semisweet
chocolate, broken into squares

⅔ cup double or whipping cream

1 tablespoon butter

2 tablespoons light corn syrup

2 large bananas, sliced

Confectioners' sugar, to sprinkle

1. Sift the flour and salt into a large bowl. Using a pastry blender or 2 knives, cut butter and shortening into flour mixture until coarse crumbs form. Add 1-2 tablespoons chilled water and mix to form a soft, but not sticky, dough. Knead for a few seconds until smooth, then wrap and chill for 10 minutes. On a floured surface, using a floured rolling pin, roll dough into an 11-inch circle. Fit dough into a 9-inch pie pan with a removable bottom, pressing to fit the sides. Trim excess dough, leaving 1 inch overhang. Fold overhang under; flute edges.

2. Preheat oven to 375°F. Prick dough with a fork. Line with aluminium foil; fill with pie weights or dried beans.

3. Bake crust for 15 minutes. Remove foil and weights. Bake until golden, 10 minutes more. Transfer pan to wire rack to cool.

4. To prepare filling, melt the chocolate in a small heatproof bowl set over a pan of gently simmering water, stirring occasionally. Let cool for 15 minutes, then, using a balloon whisk, gradually whisk in the cream.

5. Heat the butter and corn syrup in a skillet until bubbling. Add the sliced bananas, reserving a few slices for decoration. Cook in the syrup mixture for 1 minute.

6. Transfer the bananas to the crust and spread evenly over the base of the tart. Cool, then spread the chocolate mixture over the surface. Decorate with the banana slices and sprinkle with the confectioner's sugar.

Chocolate-Marzipan Tart

This delicious, stunning tart is easier to prepare than you might think.

1 hour preparation plus cooling and standing, 20-22 minutes baking   Makes 8 servings

Ingredients:

- 4 ounces (1 stick) butter, softened
- 8 ounces marzipan, grated
- 3 tablespoons cake flour
- 3 large eggs, separated

Glaze, Topping, and Frosting:

- 2 tablespoons light corn syrup
- 2 ounces (½ stick) butter, softened
- 1 tablespoon half-and-half
- 5 ounces (5 squares) semisweet chocolate, coarsely chopped
- 1 cup confectioners' sugar
- 2 ounces (2 squares) unsweetened chocolate, melted
- 2 teaspoons milk
- ½ teaspoon almond extract
- 8 chocolate candies
- 3 teaspoons water
- ½ teaspoon peppermint extract

1. Preheat oven to 375°F. Grease an 8-inch round cake pan.

2. Beat butter at medium speed until light and fluffy. Beat in marzipan until blended. Beat in flour. Add egg yolks, 1 at a time, beating well after each addition.

3. Using clean beaters, beat egg whites at medium speed until stiff, but not dry, peaks form. Fold one-third beaten egg whites into batter. Fold in remaining whites. Spoon batter into prepared pan; smooth top.

4. Bake tart until golden, 20-22 minutes. Transfer pan to a wire rack to cool slightly. Turn tart out onto rack to cool completely.

5. To prepare glaze, in a medium saucepan, heat corn syrup, 2 tablespoons butter, and half-and-half over medium heat until mixture boils. Remove from heat. Stir in chopped semisweet chocolate until melted and smooth. Cool slightly. Spread glaze evenly over tart. Let stand until set.

6. To prepare topping, beat together ½ cup confectioners' sugar, remaining butter, melted unsweetened chocolate, milk, and almond extract at medium speed until light and fluffy.

7. Using a pastry bag fitted with a star tip, pipe topping around edges of tart. Arrange chocolate candies on top.

8. To prepare frosting, mix together remaining confectioners' sugar, water, and peppermint extract until smooth.

9. Using a small pastry bag fitted with a fine writing tip, pipe icing in small dots around edges of tart and in centers of candies.

Chocolate-Buttercrunch Tart

This light meringue tart is full of crunch and a creamy chocolate flavor.

30 minutes preparation plus standing and chilling, 1 hour baking

Makes 12 servings

Ingredients:

3 large egg whites

⅛ teaspoon salt

1 cup granulated sugar

2 tablespoons unsweetened cocoa powder

Filling:

1 cup heavy cream

4 ounces (4 squares) semisweet chocolate, coarsely chopped

Topping and Garnish:

1½ cups heavy cream

2 tablespoons confectioners' sugar

4 ounces chocolate-covered buttercrunch candy, coarsely chopped

Unsweetened cocoa powder

1. Preheat oven to 250°F. Line a baking sheet with aluminum foil.

2. Beat egg whites and salt at medium speed until foamy. Gradually add sugar, beating until stiff, but not dry, peaks form. Fold in cocoa powder.

3. Spoon meringue onto prepared baking sheet. Using a spoon, shape meringue into an 8-inch circle, spreading meringue higher at outside edges, creating a shallow crust.

4. Bake meringue until firm and dry, 1 hour. Turn off oven; let meringue stand in oven with door closed to dry for 2 hours.

5. Meanwhile, prepare filling. In a saucepan, heat cream over medium heat until bubbles appear around edges of pan. Remove from heat. Stir in chocolate until melted and smooth. Chill for 2 hours, stirring occasionally.

6. Beat filling at medium speed until soft peaks form. Spoon filling into prepared shell.

7. To prepare topping, beat cream at medium speed until soft peaks form. Gradually add sugar, beating until stiff, but not dry, peaks form. Reserve half of whipped cream.

8. Fold buttercrunch candy into remaining whipped cream. Spread buttercrunch mixture over filling; smooth top. Spread reserved whipped cream on top and sides of tart. Dust with cocoa powder.

Cook's Tip

Substitute coarsely chopped almonds for the buttercrunch.

Chocolate-Meringue Tart

A crunchy meringue topping adds an appealing texture to this lighter-than-air dessert.

45 minutes preparation plus cooling, 30-33 minutes baking   Makes 12 servings

Ingredients:

1¼ cups all-purpose flour
1 teaspoon baking powder
¼ teaspoon salt
4 ounces (1 stick) butter, softened
1 cup granulated sugar
2 large egg yolks
1 teaspoon vanilla extract

Topping and Garnish:

2 large egg whites
1 cup granulated sugar
1 tablespoon unsweetened cocoa
   powder
4 ounces (4 squares) semisweet
   chocolate, melted
½ cup blanched, slivered almonds
   (about 2 ounces)

1. 1 Preheat oven to 350°F. Grease a 13 x 9-inch baking pan.

2. 2 Mix together flour, baking powder, and salt.

3. 3 Beat together butter and sugar at medium speed until light and fluffy. Beat in egg yolks and vanilla. At low speed, beat in flour mixture until combined. Spread batter evenly in prepared pan.

4. 4 Bake cake until golden, 15 minutes. Transfer pan to a wire rack to cool completely.

5. 5 To prepare topping, using clean beaters, beat egg whites at high speed until foamy. Gradually add sugar and cocoa powder, beating until stiff, but not dry, peaks form.

6. 6 Spread melted chocolate evenly over cake.

7. 7 Spread topping evenly over chocolate to sides of pan; smooth top.

8. 8 Bake tart until topping is lightly browned, 15-18 minutes. Transfer pan to a wire rack to cool slightly. Sprinkle nuts over warm tart; cool completely.

Cook's Tip

For a buffet party, slice this tart into small pieces and serve like a bar cookie. Serve this tart with sliced fresh fruit, such as strawberries or bananas.

Chocolate-Nut Caramel Tart

This dark and delectable dessert has a rich candy bar flavor.

1 hour preparation plus cooling and chilling, 10 minutes baking · · · · · · · · · · · · · · · · Makes 18 servings

Ingredients:
- 1 cup (4 ounces) chocolate wafer cookie crumbs
- 3 tablespoons butter, melted

Filling:
- ⅔ cup granulated sugar
- ½ cup milk
- ⅓ cup light corn syrup
- ¼ cup condensed milk
- 3 tablespoons butter
- ⅓ cup coarsely chopped pecans (about 1¼ ounces)
- ½ teaspoon vanilla extract
- ½ cup fresh or frozen, thawed blueberries, drained

Topping:
- 4 cups confectioners' sugar
- 8 ounces (8 squares) semisweet chocolate, melted and cooled
- 4 ounces (1 stick) butter, melted and cooled
- 2 large eggs
- 1 teaspoon vanilla extract

Garnish:
- 1½ cups heavy cream
- 3 tablespoons granulated sugar
- 2 tablespoons unsweetened cocoa powder
- Chocolate shavings

1. Preheat oven to 350°F. Grease a 9-inch spring form pan.

2. Mix together cookie crumbs and melted butter. Press crumb mixture evenly over bottom of prepared pan.

3. Bake crust for 10 minutes. Transfer pan to a wire rack to cool.

4. To prepare filling, in a heavy saucepan, mix together sugar, milk, corn syrup, condensed milk, and butter. Cook milk mixture over medium heat, stirring occasionally, until mixture reaches 240°F on a candy thermometer (soft ball stage), 10 minutes. Remove from heat. Stir in nuts and vanilla.

5. Pour filling over prepared crust. Cool completely. Sprinkle blueberries on top.

6. To prepare topping, beat together confectioners' sugar, melted chocolate, melted butter, eggs, and vanilla at medium speed until light and fluffy. Spread topping evenly over filling. Chill for 2 hours.

7. To prepare garnish, beat cream at medium speed until just thickened. Gradually beat in sugar and cocoa powder until soft peaks form. Place tart on a plate. Remove sides of pan.

8. Using a pastry bag fitted with a plain tip, pipe cream around edges of tart. Sprinkle chocolate shavings on top.

Cook's Tip

If you don't have a candy thermometer, you can use this test to see if the sugar mixture is ready in Step 4: Use a wet teaspoon to take a little of the mixture and drop it into a cup of cold water. It should form a soft paste that you can roll into a squashy ball between your thumb and forefinger.

Chocolate-Pear Tart

An unbaked filling makes this chocolate-custard pie decidedly easy to prepare.

20 minutes preparation, 25 minutes baking, plus cooling

Makes 4-6 servings

Ingredients:

½ package (10 ounces) piecrust
   mix

Filling and Topping:

2 ounces (½ stick) butter

1 tablespoon unsweetened cocoa
   powder

2 tablespoons cornstarch

1 can (5-ounce) evaporated milk

4 ounces (4 squares) semisweet
   chocolate, broken into squares

1 can (14-ounce) pear halves in
   natural juice

½ teaspoon ground cinnamon

Sprig of fresh mint, to garnish

1. Prepare piecrust mix according to package directions.

2. On a floured surface, using a floured rolling pin, roll dough into an 11-inch circle. Fit dough into a 9-inch pie pan with a removable bottom, pressing to fit the sides. Trim excess dough, leaving a 1-inch overhang. Fold overhang under; flute edges.

3. Preheat oven to 375°F. Prick dough with a fork. Line with aluminum foil; fill with pie weights or dried beans.

4. Bake crust for 15 minutes. Remove foil and weights. Bake until light golden, 10 minutes more. Transfer pan to a wire rack to cool completely.

5. For the filling, put the butter, cocoa, cornstarch, evaporated milk, and chocolate into a heavy-bottomed saucepan. Drain the pears and pour the juice into the saucepan.

6. Heat the chocolate mixture over low heat, stirring constantly with a small whisk or wooden spoon, until thick and smooth. Pour into the pastry case and let cool completely.

7. Slice the pear halves and arrange over the filling. Sprinkle the cinnamon on top of the pears and put the mint sprig in the middle. Chill until ready to serve.

Chocolate Linzer Tart

A rich chocolate crust gives this jelly-filled tart an extra dimension.

15 minutes preparation plus chilling, 25 minutes baking

Ingredients:

1⅓ cups all-purpose flour

⅓ cup unsweetened cocoa powder

⅓ cup firmly packed brown sugar

¼ teaspoon salt

4 ounces (1 stick) chilled butter, cut into small pieces

2 tablespoons chilled solid vegetable shortening, cut into small pieces

⅓ cup ice water

Filling:

3 cups (2 pounds) raspberry jelly

1. In a medium bowl, mix together flour, cocoa powder, brown sugar, and salt. Using a pastry blender or 2 knives, cut butter and shortening into flour mixture until coarse crumbs form.

2. Add water, 1 tablespoon at a time, tossing with a fork until a dough forms. Shape dough into a disk, wrap in plastic wrap, and chill for 1 hour.

3. Preheat oven to 375°F. On a floured surface, using a floured rolling pin, roll two-thirds of dough into an 11-inch round. Fit into a 9-inch springform pan. Spread raspberry jelly evenly over dough.

4. On a floured surface, using a floured rolling pin, roll remaining dough into a 10-inch square. Cut into 1-inch-wide strips. Arrange 8 strips in a lattice pattern over filling. Trim excess dough. Arrange 2 strips around edge of lattice.

5. Bake tart until crust is set and filling bubbles, 25 minutes. Transfer pan to a wire rack to cool slightly. Remove sides of pan; cool completely.

Cook's Tip

For variety, use strawberry-rhubarb or blackberry jelly instead of raspberry.

Chocolate-Walnut Tartlets

These elegant little nut tartlets are perfect for a bridal shower or garden tea party.

30 minutes preparation plus chilling, 20-25 minutes baking

Makes 18 tartlets

Ingredients:

- 1½ cups all-purpose flour
- 2 tablespoons firmly packed light brown sugar
- ¾ teaspoon salt
- 4 ounces (1 stick) chilled butter, cut into small pieces
- 3 tablespoons ice water
- ¾ cup semisweet chocolate chips

Filling:

- ¾ cup all-purpose flour
- ¾ cup finely ground walnuts (about 3 ounces)
- 3 ounces (¾ stick) butter, softened
- ½ cup granulated sugar
- 1 tablespoon fresh lemon juice
- 1 teaspoon vanilla extract
- 3 large eggs

1. In a medium bowl, mix together flour, brown sugar, and salt. Using a pastry blender or 2 knives, cut butter into flour mixture until coarse crumbs form.

2. Add water, 1 tablespoon at a time, tossing with a fork until a dough forms. Shape dough into a disk, wrap in plastic wrap, and chill for 2 hours.

3. Preheat oven to 375°F. Spray 18 standard size muffin-pan cups with vegetable cooking spray.

4. On a floured surface, using a floured rolling pin, roll dough to a 1/8-inch thickness. Using a 2½-inch floured round cookie cutter, cut dough into circles. Gather trimmings, roll to a 1/8-inch thickness and cut out more circles. Fit 1 circle into each prepared cup. Sprinkle 2 teaspoonfuls of chocolate chips in each pastry shell.

5. To prepare filling, beat together flour, ground nuts, butter, sugar, lemon juice, and vanilla at medium speed until well blended. Add eggs, 1 at a time, beating well after each addition.

6. Spoon filling evenly into each pastry shell. Spread to edges.

7. Bake tartlets until golden, 20-25 minutes. Transfer pan to a wire rack to cool for 10 minutes. Transfer tartlets to rack to cool completely.

Cook's Tip

For variety, fill the bottom of each tartlet with 1 teaspoon of apple butter or jelly.

Fudgy Chocolate-Hazelnut Tart

Ground hazelnuts give this tart's gooey filling an added dimension.

30 minutes preparation, 35-40 minutes baking plus cooling

Ingredients:

11 graham crackers

2 ounces (½ stick) butter, melted

Filling:

4 ounces (1 stick) butter, softened

½ cup firmly packed brown sugar

½ teaspoon vanilla extract

½ cup ground hazelnuts (2 ounces)

1½ teaspoons baking powder

½ teaspoon salt

1 cup all-purpose flour

9 ounces cocoa powder, unsweetened

½ cup milk

Topping and Garnish:

2 ounces (½ stick) butter, softened

Confectioners' sugar

1 teaspoon unsweetened cocoa powder

1 tablespoon milk

18 whole hazelnuts

1 ounce semisweet chocolate, melted

1. Crush the crackers and mix with the melted butter. Press over the base and side of an 8-inch springform pan. Chill until required.

2. Preheat oven to 350°F. In a mixing bowl, beat together the softened butter and brown sugar with an electric beater or a wooden spoon, until pale and fluffy.

3. Stir the vanilla extract and ground hazelnuts into the creamed mixture. Sift in the flour, baking powder, salt, and cocoa powder and mix well. Stir in the milk until smooth.

4. Spoon the filling into the pan and level the surface. Bake for 35-40 minutes, or until firm. Put the dish on a wire rack and cool completely.

5. For the topping, put the butter and confectioners' sugar into a bowl and beat until pale and fluffy. Mix together the cocoa powder and milk and beat into the creamed mixture.

6. Spoon the topping into a pastry bag fitted with a star-shaped tip. Pipe swirls around the edge of the tart and in the center. Put whole hazelnuts around the edge.

7. Spoon the melted chocolate into a clean pastry bag fitted with a small plain tip and pipe over the hazelnuts.

Mandarin-Chocolate Tartlets

Chocolate pastry shells filled with smooth custard make a quick and easy dessert.

35 minutes preparation, 25-30 minutes baking plus chilling

Makes 6 tarts

Ingredients:

2 cups plain flour

3 tablespoons unsweetened cocoa powder

Pinch of salt

3 ounces (¾ stick) butter, diced

2 tablespoons superfine sugar

5 tablespoons ice water

2 ounces (2 squares) semisweet chocolate, melted

Filling:

2 cups heavy cream

3 large eggs

6 tablespoons superfine sugar

2 tablespoons cornstarch

2 tablespoons all-purpose flour

1 teaspoon vanilla extract

Finely grated peel of 1 orange

Topping and Garnish:

2 cans (10½-ounce) mandarin orange segments in fruit juice, drained

2 tablespoons superfine sugar

Sprigs of fresh mint

1. In a medium bowl, mix together the flour, cocoa powder, and salt. Using a pastry blender or 2 knives, cut butter into flour mixture until coarse crumbs form. Mix in the sugar. Add water, 1 tablespoon at a time, tossing with a fork until a dough forms. Shape dough into a disk, wrap in plastic wrap, and chill for 1 hour.

2. Divide the dough into 6 equal pieces. On a floured surface, using a floured rolling pin, roll out each piece to line a 4½-inch tartlet pan with a removable bottom. Preheat oven to 375°F. Prick dough with a fork. Line with aluminum foil; fill with dried beans. Bake tartlets for 15 minutes. Remove foil and beans. Bake until light golden, 10 minutes more. Transfer pans to a wire rack to cool completely.

3. To prepare filling, warm the cream in a pan over low heat until almost boiling. Meanwhile, beat the eggs and sugar in a large bowl until pale and thick. Sift in the cornstarch and flour and mix well. Stir in the hot cream.

4. Put the mixture back in the pan and return to the heat. Slowly bring the custard to a boil, stirring constantly, until thickened. Remove from the heat and stir in the vanilla extract and orange peel. Transfer the custard to a bowl and cover the surface with plastic wrap. Let cool.

5. Brush the melted chocolate over the inside of each cooled tartlet shell. Let set.

6. Divide the custard between the tartlet cases. Arrange the orange sections on top and sprinkle with the sugar. Put the tartlets under a hot broiler for 5-6 minutes, or until the sugar bubbles. Cool, then garnish with mint sprigs.

Chocolate-Peppermint Tart

Refreshing peppermint is the surprise flavor in this mousse-filled tart.

20 minutes preparation, 20-25 minutes baking plus cooling

Serves 6-8

Ingredients:

¾ package (15 ounces)
   refrigerated piecrust dough

Filling and Garnish:

4 ounces (4 squares) semisweet
   chocolate, coarsely chopped

2 large eggs, separated

¾ cup heavy cream

¾ teaspoon peppermint extract

 sprigs of fresh mint

1. On a floured surface, using a floured rolling pin, roll dough into a 10-inch circle. Fit dough into an 8-inch pie pan, pressing to fit sides. Trim excess dough.

2. Preheat oven to 375°F. Prick dough with a fork. Line with aluminum foil; fill with pie weights or dried beans. Bake crust for 15 minutes. Remove foil and weights. Bake until light golden, 10 minutes or more. Transfer pan to a wire rack to cool completely.

3. To prepare filling, melt the chocolate in a heatproof bowl set over a pan of simmering water. Do not let the water boil or touch the bowl. Remove from the heat and let cool slightly.

4. Beat the egg yolks into the chocolate. Set aside to cool.

5. In a bowl, whip the cream until soft peaks form. Reserve 2 tablespoons for garnish. Fold the remaining cream and peppermint extract into the chocolate mixture.

6. In a clean, dry bowl, beat the egg whites until stiff peaks form. Gently fold into the chocolate mixture. Spoon into the crust and level the surface. Chill for 2 hours, or until the filling is set.

7. To serve the tart, add fresh mint sprigs for decoration and dust with confectioners sugar.

Quick Breads, Muffins & Coffee Cakes

When you're looking for a sweeter start to the day than your normal breakfast toast, something to serve when it is your turn for a coffee morning, or a nutritious lunchbox treat for the kids, these recipes will all fit the bill.

But be warned—not only will you be able to put them together and bake them quickly, these tasty breads also have a habit of disappearing in a hurry!

Chocolate-Cherry Bread

This great quick bread is perfect for breakfast, or as a picnic companion for dessert.

15 minutes preparation, 50 minutes baking   Makes 1 loaf

Ingredients:

3 cups plus 1 tablespoon
 all-purpose flour

1 teaspoon baking powder

½ teaspoon salt

½ teaspoon ground cinnamon

2 ounces (½ stick) butter, softened

½ cup granulated sugar

½ cup firmly packed brown sugar

1 large egg

1 cup milk

1 cup coarsely chopped dried
 cherries (6 ounces)

2 ounces (2 squares) semisweet
 chocolate, coarsely chopped

1. Preheat oven to 375°F. Grease a 9 x 5-inch loaf
   pan.

2. Mix together 3 cups flour, baking powder, salt, and
   cinnamon.

3. Beat together butter, granulated sugar, and brown
   sugar at medium speed until light and fluffy.
   Beat in egg and milk. At low speed, beat in flour
   mixture, ½ cup at a time, until combined.

4. Toss cherries with remaining flour. Fold cherries
   and chocolate into batter. Spread batter in prepared
   pan; smooth top.

5. Bake loaf until golden and a toothpick inserted in
   the center comes out clean, 50 minutes. Transfer
   pan to a wire rack to cool slightly. Loosen loaf by
   running a metal spatula around sides of pan. Turn
   out onto rack to cool completely.

Chocolate Chip-Banana Bread

This sweet quick bread is wonderful with tea and fits the bill for an easy dessert as well.

20 minutes preparation, 70-75 minutes baking

Makes 1 loaf

Ingredients:

2 cups all-purpose flour

1 cup semisweet chocolate chips

¾ cup granulated sugar

2 teaspoons baking powder

½ teaspoon salt

2 large, ripe bananas, mashed

⅓ cup vegetable oil

2 large eggs

2 teaspoons vanilla extract

1. Preheat oven to 350°F. Grease an 8½ x 4½-inch loaf pan. Dust with flour; tap out excess.

2. Mix together flour, chocolate chips, sugar, baking powder, and salt.

3. Stir together mashed bananas, oil, eggs, and vanilla.

4. Make a well in the center of flour mixture. Add banana mixture all at once to well, tossing with a fork until dry ingredients are just moistened. (Do not overmix.) Spoon batter into prepared pan; smooth top.

5. Bake loaf until a toothpick inserted in the center comes out clean, 70-75 minutes. Transfer pan to a wire rack to cool slightly.

6. Loosen loaf by running a metal spatula around sides of pan. Turn loaf out onto rack to cool completely.

Cook's Tip

If you're using a 9 x 5-inch loaf pan instead of an 8½ x 4½-inch pan, reduce the baking time to 60 minutes.

Chocolate-Raisin Muffins

No frosting is necessary on these wonderfully sweet and rich treats.

35 minutes preparation, 30 minutes baking

Makes 1 dozen muffins

Ingredients:

- 4 ounces (1 stick) butter
- 3 ounces (3 squares) unsweetened chocolate, coarsely chopped
- ⅔ cup all-purpose flour
- ¼ teaspoon baking powder
- ⅛ teaspoon salt
- 1 cup plus 2 tablespoons granulated sugar
- 2 large eggs
- 1½ teaspoons vanilla extract
- ¼ cup milk
- ¼ cup chocolate-covered raisins

Topping:

- ½ cup chocolate-covered raisins

1. Preheat oven to 325°F. Grease 12 standard size muffin-pan cups or line with paper liners.

2. In a small saucepan, cook butter and chocolate over low heat, stirring frequently, until melted and smooth.

3. Mix together flour, baking powder, and salt.

4. Beat together sugar and eggs at high speed until light and fluffy. At low speed, beat in chocolate mixture and vanilla until blended.

5. Alternately beat in flour mixture and milk until combined. Stir in chocolate-covered raisins.

6. Spoon batter into prepared pan, filling each cup two-thirds full.

7. For topping, sprinkle remaining chocolate-covered raisins on top.

8. Bake muffins until a toothpick inserted in the centers comes out clean, 30 minutes.

9. Transfer pan to a wire rack to cool slightly. Turn muffins out onto rack to cool completely.

Lemon-Chocolate Marble Muffins

These moist, chocolate-rich muffins make great picnic fare.

30 minutes preparation, 20 minutes baking

Makes 1 dozen muffins

Ingredients:

- 1 cup all-purpose flour
- ¾ teaspoon baking powder
- ⅛ teaspoon salt
- 4 ounces (1 stick) butter, softened
- ½ cup granulated sugar
- 2 large eggs
- 1 large egg yolk
- 2 teaspoons vanilla extract or almond extract
- 1 tablespoon fresh lemon juice
- 1 teaspoon grated lemon peel
- 1 tablespoon milk
- ¼ teaspoon baking soda
- 2 ounces (2 squares) semisweet chocolate, melted

1. Preheat oven to 350°F. Grease 12 standard size muffin-pan cups or line with paper liners.

2. Mix together flour, baking powder, and salt.

3. Beat together butter and sugar at medium speed until light and fluffy. Add eggs and egg yolk, 1 at a time, beating well after each addition.

4. At low speed, beat in flour mixture, ½ cup at a time, until blended. Beat in 1 teaspoon vanilla, lemon juice, and lemon peel. Divide batter in half.

5. Mix together milk, remaining vanilla, and baking soda.

6. Stir melted chocolate into milk mixture. Stir chocolate mixture into half of batter. Spoon chocolate batter evenly into prepared pan. Spoon lemon batter evenly over chocolate batter.

7. Using a knife, swirl through batter to create a marble pattern.

8. Bake muffins until tops are firm and a toothpick inserted in the centers comes out clean, 20 minutes.

9. Transfer pan to a wire rack to cool slightly. Turn muffins out onto rack to cool completely.

Chocolate Chunk Muffins

The tantalizing aroma of these muffins will be a wake-up call to chocolate-loving sleepyheads.

15 minutes preparation, 18-20 minutes baking   Makes 1 dozen muffins

Ingredients:

- 2 cups all-purpose flour
- ½ cup granulated sugar
- 1 tablespoon baking powder
- ½ teaspoon salt
- 1 cup milk
- ⅓ cup vegetable oil
- 1 large egg
- 1 teaspoon vanilla extract
- 4 ounces (4 squares) semisweet chocolate, coarsely chopped

1. Preheat oven to 400°F. Grease 12 standard size muffin-pan cups or line with paper liners.

2. Mix together flour, sugar, baking powder, and salt.

3. Mix together milk, oil, egg, and vanilla.

4. Make a well in the center of flour mixture. Add milk mixture all at once to well, tossing with a fork until dry ingredients are just moistened. Stir in chocolate. (Do not overmix.) Spoon batter into prepared pan, filling cups three-quarters full.

5. Bake muffins until tops are firm and golden, 18-20 minutes. Transfer pan to a wire rack to cool slightly. Turn muffins out onto rack to cool completely.

Cook's Tip

Don't panic if the muffin batter is a little lumpy. The batter consistency adds to the muffins' light texture.

Chocolate-Orange Muffins

For an ideal combination of flavors, whip up a batch of these wonderful muffins.

20 minutes preparation, 18-20 minutes baking

Makes 1 dozen muffins

Ingredients:

2 cups all-purpose flour
1 cup chocolate chips (6 ounces)
¼ cup granulated sugar
1 tablespoon baking powder
½ teaspoon salt
½ cup orange juice
½ cup milk
⅓ cup vegetable oil
1 large egg
1 teaspoon grated orange peel

1. Preheat oven to 400°F. Grease 12 standard size muffin-pan cups or line with paper liners.

2. Mix together flour, chocolate chips, sugar, baking powder, and salt.

3. Mix together orange juice, milk, oil, egg, and orange peel.

4. Make a well in the center of flour mixture. Add milk mixture all at once to well, tossing with a fork until dry ingredients are just moistened. (Do not overmix.)

5. Spoon batter into prepared pan, filling cups three-quarters full.

6. Bake muffins until tops are firm and golden, 18-20 minutes. Transfer pan to a wire rack to cool slightly. Turn muffins out onto rack to cool completely.

Cook's Tip

For a nutty flavor, add ¼ cup coarsely chopped pecans to the batter.

Marzipan-Chocolate Muffins

If you're a marzipan lover, these sweet and unusual muffins are perfect for you.

15 minutes preparation plus cooling, 18-20 minutes baking   Makes 1 dozen muffins

Ingredients:

1¾ cups all-purpose flour

3 tablespoons unsweetened cocoa powder

3 tablespoons firmly packed light brown sugar

3 tablespoons granulated sugar

2½ teaspoons baking powder

½ teaspoon baking soda

½ teaspoon salt

1 cup buttermilk

2 large eggs

Topping and Garnish:

1 tablespoon unsweetened cocoa powder

18 ounces marzipan

1. Preheat oven to 375°F. Grease 12 standard size muffin-pan cups or line with paper liners.

2. Mix together flour, cocoa powder, brown sugar, granulated sugar, baking powder, baking soda, and salt.

3. Mix together buttermilk and eggs.

4. Make a well in the center of flour mixture. Add buttermilk mixture all at once to well, tossing with a fork until dry ingredients are just moistened. (Do not overmix.)

5. Spoon batter into prepared pan, filling cups three-quarters full.

6. Bake muffins until tops are firm and golden, 18-20 minutes. Transfer pan to a wire rack to cool slightly. Turn muffins out onto rack to cool completely.

7. To prepare topping, sprinkle a floured surface with cocoa powder. Divide marzipan into 12 equal pieces. Using a floured rolling pin, roll each piece into a 6-inch circle.

8. Place a muffin in the center of each circle. Fold marzipan over muffins; press seams to seal. Using a small knife, pierce muffins several times.

Cook's Tip

For added sweetness, sprinkle tops with granulated sugar.

Chocolate-Walnut Bread

Chock-full of chocolate and walnuts, this buttery spiral will brighten up a weekend brunch.

45 minutes preparation plus resting and rising, 30-40 minutes baking   Makes 1 loaf

Ingresients:

1 package active dry yeast

1 tablespoon plus 1 teaspoon granulated sugar

1 teaspoon salt

¼ cup warm water (105°-115°F)

1 cup warm milk (105°-115° F)

3 tablespoons butter, melted and cooled

4 cups all-purpose flour

Filling:

¾ cup coarsely chopped walnuts (about 3 ounces)

½ cup granulated sugar

⅓ cup unsweetened cocoa powder

1½ ounces (1½ squares) semisweet chocolate, finely chopped

2 ounces (½ stick) butter, softened

Topping:

⅓ cup confectioners' sugar

¼ cup all-purpose flour

1 teaspoon ground cinnamon

¼ teaspoon ground nutmeg

2 tablespoons chilled butter, cut into small pieces

¼ cup coarsely chopped walnuts (about 1 ounce)

1 tablespoon butter, melted

1. In a large bowl, dissolve yeast, sugar, and salt in warm water and warm milk. Let stand until foamy, 5-10 minutes.

2. Stir melted butter into yeast mixture. Using a heavy-duty electric mixer fitted with a paddle attachment and set on low speed, beat in flour, ½ cup at a time, until a soft dough forms.

3. On a floured surface, knead dough until smooth and elastic, 5-10 minutes, adding more flour to prevent sticking. Place dough in a large greased bowl, turning to coat. Cover loosely with a damp cloth; let rest for 30 minutes.

4. To prepare filling, mix together nuts, sugar, cocoa powder, and chocolate.

5. Grease a baking sheet. On a floured surface, using a floured rolling pin, roll dough into a 20 x 10-inch rectangle. Spread butter over dough to within 1 inch of edges. Sprinkle filling over butter; press in slightly.

6. Brush 1 long side of dough with water. Starting with a long side, roll up dough, jelly-roll style. Pinch seam to seal. Coil loaf into a spiral; fold ends under. Place loaf, seam-side down, on prepared baking sheet.

7. Cover loosely with a damp cloth; let rise in a warm place until doubled, 1 hour.

8. To prepare topping, in a medium bowl, mix together confectioners' sugar, flour, cinnamon, and nutmeg. Using a pastry blender or 2 knives, cut chilled butter into flour mixture until coarse crumbs form. Stir in nuts.

9. Preheat oven to 375°F. Brush loaf top with melted butter. Sprinkle with topping. Bake loaf until golden and bottom sounds hollow when tapped, 30-40 minutes. Transfer loaf to a wire rack to cool completely.

Soufflés, Custards & Fruit Crisps

These sublime desserts cross the range from creamy to crunchy, from favorite childhood puddings to elegant extravaganzas, from those served piping hot from the oven to icy frozen delights, and from those that require little preparation at all to more complex presentations.

The one common factor (aside from chocolate) is that all of these recipes make perfect sweet endings to a meal, from a casual family lunch to the most formal dinner party.

Pear-Chocolate Soufflés

Light-as-air chocolate soufflés studded with chunks of sweet pear.

35 minutes preparation, 25 minutes baking

Makes 6 soufflés

Ingredients:

2 ounces (½ stick) butter

1 large pear, pared, cored, and chopped

¼ cup superfine sugar

½ cup all-purpose flour

1¼ cups milk

4 ounces (4 squares) semisweet chocolate, coarsely chopped

4 large eggs, separated

1. Preheat oven to 350°F. Grease six 6-ounce custard cups.

2. Melt the butter in a heavy-based saucepan. Add the chopped pears and cook for 1 minute. Add the sugar and cook for another minute, or until the sugar dissolves.

3. Remove the pan from the heat and stir in the flour. Stir in the milk, a little at a time. Return to the heat and cook, stirring constantly with a wooden spoon, until thickened. Remove from the heat and stir in the chocolate. Let cool for 10 minutes.

4. In a large, clean bowl, beat the egg whites with an electric beater until stiff peaks form.

5. Stir the egg yolks into the chocolate and pear mixture, then fold in the egg whites. Divide the mixture evenly between the custard cups. Transfer the dishes to a large baking sheet.

6. Bake for 25 minutes, or until the soufflés are well risen and set in the center. Serve immediately.

Cook's Tip

For one large dessert, bake in a 5–cup, straight-sided soufflé dish for 40 minutes. If you are entertaining, you can prepare the soufflé mixture in advance. The mixture will sit happily in the custard cups before being baked.

Hot Chocolate Soufflé

Here's an easy soufflé classic to add to your dessert repertoire.

30 minutes preparation plus cooling, 45 minutes baking

Makes 6 servings

Ingredients:

½ cup plus 1 tablespoon granulated sugar

1 cup milk

3 tablespoons all-purpose flour

⅛ teaspoon salt

3 ounces (3 squares) unsweetened chocolate, coarsely chopped

2 tablespoons butter

2 teaspoons vanilla extract

6 large eggs, separated

¼ teaspoon cream of tartar

Topping:

Confectioners' sugar

1. Grease a 6-cup straight-sided soufflé dish. Sprinkle dish evenly with 1 tablespoon sugar.

2. In a saucepan, mix together milk, remaining sugar, flour, and salt. Add chocolate. Cook over medium heat, stirring constantly, until chocolate is melted and mixture thickens, 2 minutes. Remove from heat. Stir in butter and vanilla. Cool completely.

3. Preheat oven to 350°F. Place in lower third of oven rack. Remove other racks.

4. Stir egg yolks into chocolate mixture.

5. Beat together egg whites and cream of tartar at high speed until stiff, but not dry, peaks form. Fold one-quarter of beaten egg whites into chocolate mixture. Fold in remaining whites.

6. Pour chocolate mixture into prepared soufflé dish. Place dish in a shallow roasting pan. Pour enough boiling water into roasting pan to come halfway up sides of dish.

7. Bake soufflé until light and puffy, 45 minutes. (Center will be soft and somewhat runny. For a firmer soufflé, bake 5 minutes more.) Remove dish from roasting pan. Dust top with confectioners' sugar.

Cook's Tip

Placing the rack in the lower third of the oven can help the soufflé rise more effectively. The dish will get a concentrated blast of heat that will give the soufflé the upward push it will need to rise nicely.

White Chocolate Soufflé

This elegant dessert is very easy to prepare and stunning to behold.

30 minutes preparation, 40 minutes baking

Makes 6 servings

Ingredients:

¼ cup plus 1 tablespoon granulated sugar

3 tablespoons butter

3 tablespoons all-purpose flour

1¼ cups milk

8 ounces (8 squares) white chocolate, coarsely chopped

2 teaspoons vanilla extract

6 large eggs, separated

⅛ teaspoon cream of tartar

Garnish:

Confectioners' sugar

Wrap strip around dish so collar stands about 3 inches above rim.

1. Preheat oven to 375°F. Place rack in lower third of oven. Remove other racks. Grease a 2½-quart soufflé dish. Sprinkle bottom and sides with 1 tablespoon sugar.

2. Tear off a 24-inch strip of waxed paper. Fold paper lengthwise into a 24 x 6-inch strip. Wrap strip around outside of dish so collar stands about 3 inches above rim. Secure collar with tape.

3. In a medium saucepan, melt butter over medium heat. Stir in flour. Cook, stirring constantly, for 1 minute. Gradually stir in milk. Cook milk mixture over low heat, stirring constantly, until thickened and smooth, 2-3 minutes. Remove from heat.

4. Stir in white chocolate until melted and smooth. Stir in vanilla.

5. Beat egg yolks at medium speed until thickened. Gradually beat in white chocolate mixture.

6. Using clean beaters, beat egg whites at high speed until foamy. Gradually beat in remaining sugar and cream of tartar until stiff, but not dry, peaks form.

7. Fold one-quarter beaten egg whites into white chocolate mixture. Fold in remaining whites. Spoon white chocolate mixture into prepared dish; smooth top.

8. Bake soufflé until top is puffed and golden, 40 minutes.

9. Remove collar. Dust with confectioners' sugar. Serve immediately.

Cook's Tip

Serve the soufflé with a quick raspberry sauce: In a blender or food processor fitted with the metal blade, process 2 cups fresh or frozen, thawed raspberries until smooth.

Chocolate Popovers with Custard

Serve these tender, cakelike popovers with custard for a delightfully unusual dessert.

30 minutes preparation plus cooling, 40 minutes baking

Makes 6 servings

Ingredients:
1½ cups sifted all-purpose flour
3 tablespoons unsweetened cocoa powder
3 tablespoons granulated sugar
1½ cups milk
3 large eggs
1½ tablespoons vegetable oil

Custard:
½ cup granulated sugar
2 tablespoons cornstarch
2 cups milk
2 large egg yolks, lightly beaten
2 tablespoons butter, cut into small pieces
1 teaspoon almond extract
1 teaspoon vanilla extract

Garnish:
Confectioners' sugar
Fresh raspberries

1. Preheat oven to 425°F. Grease a 6-cup popover pan or 6 standard size muffin-pan cups.

2. Mix together flour, cocoa powder, and sugar. Stir in milk, eggs, and oil until blended. Pour batter into prepared pan, filling cups two-thirds full.

3. Bake popovers for 20 minutes. Reduce oven temperature to 350°F.

4. Bake popovers until puffed, 20 minutes more. Using a thin knife, loosen edges of popovers. Transfer pan to a wire rack to cool slightly. Turn popovers out onto rack to cool completely.

5. To prepare custard, in a small saucepan, mix together sugar and cornstarch. Stir in milk. Cook over medium heat, stirring constantly, until sugar dissolves and sauce thickens, 4-5 minutes. Remove from heat.

6. Stir a small amount of hot custard into egg yolks. Stir egg yolk mixture back into saucepan. Cook, stirring constantly, until thickened, 2 minutes. Remove from heat. Stir in butter, almond extract, and vanilla.

7. Spoon warm custard evenly onto dessert plates. Place a popover in the center of each plate. Dust popovers with confectioners' sugar. Garnish with raspberries.

Cook's Tip

These popovers and the custard may be served warm or chilled. They are especially nice because they will hold their shape and not deflate.

Chocolate Bread Pudding

This easy-to-prepare pudding is sure to satisfy even the most discerning chocoholic.

20 minutes preparation plus chilling, 45-55 minutes baking   Makes 6 servings

Ingredients:

    16 slices day-old egg bread, crusts
       removed, cut into 1-inch cubes

Custard:

    5 ounces (5 squares) semisweet
       chocolate, coarsely chopped

    1 cup milk

    1 cup half-and-half

    2 large eggs

    1 large egg yolk

    ¼ cup granulated sugar

    1 teaspoon coffee extract

    2 teaspoons vanilla extract

Garnish:

    Confectioners' sugar

1. Grease an 8-inch square baking dish.

2. Spread bread cubes in bottom of prepared baking dish.

3. To prepare custard, in the top of a double boiler set over simmering (not boiling) water, heat chocolate, stirring constantly, until melted and smooth. Remove from heat. Stir in milk and half-and-half.

4. Mix together eggs, egg yolk, sugar, coffee extract, and vanilla. Stir in chocolate mixture. Pour custard over bread cubes. Chill for 1 hour.

5. Preheat oven to 350°F. Bake pudding until set, 45-55 minutes. Transfer baking dish to a wire rack to cool slightly. Dust with confectioners' sugar.

Cook's Tip

For a hot fudge sauce, mix together 6 ounces melted semisweet chocolate, 2 ounces (½ stick) melted butter, and ½ teaspoon coffee extract.

Chocolate Charlotte

A chocolate mousse is surrounded by a wall of ladyfingers in this dramatic dessert.

50 minutes preparation plus cooling and chilling   Makes 6-8 servings

Ingredients:

    15 ladyfingers

Filling:

    4 ounces semisweet chocolate, coarsely chopped

    1¼ cups milk

    3 large egg yolks

    1 teaspoon vanilla extract

    1 package unflavored gelatin

    1¼ cups heavy cream

    6 tablespoons confectioners' sugar

    2 large egg whites

Garnish:

    2 ounces (2 squares) semisweet chocolate, made into curls (see page 185)

1. Grease a 5-cup charlotte mold or 8-inch springform pan. Line the sides of the pan with ladyfingers, flat side in.

2. To prepare the filling, in the top of a double boiler set over simmering (not boiling) water, melt the chocolate. Remove from the heat and let cool.

3. In a saucepan, heat chocolate, milk, and egg yolks over low heat, stirring constantly until smooth. Remove from heat and add vanilla.

4. Sprinkle gelatin over chocolate mixture. Let stand until softened, 5-10 minutes.

5. In a bowl, beat the cream with the confectioners' sugar until it forms soft peaks. In a clean bowl, beat the egg whites at high speed until stiff, but not dry, peaks form. Stir a little of the cream and egg whites into the chocolate mixture, then gently fold in the remaining cream and egg whites. Smooth the top and garnish with the chocolate curls.

6. Turn the chocolate mixture into the prepared mold and chill for at least 4 hours or overnight, until completely set.

7. To serve, remove the mold and tie a ribbon around the charlotte if desired.

Chocolate-Orange Creme Brulée

These creamy custards are flavored with orange and topped with a caramelized sugar crust.

20 minutes preparation plus chilling and cooling, 30-45 minutes baking   Makes 5 servings

Ingredients:

- 6 ounces (6 squares) semisweet chocolate, coarsely chopped
- 2 cups heavy cream
- 4 large egg yolks, lightly beaten
- 2 tablespoons orange juice
- 2 teaspoons grated orange peel

Topping:

- ⅓ cup granulated sugar

Garnish:

- Whipped cream
- Chocolate shavings
- Strips of orange peel

1. Preheat oven to 325°F.

2. In a saucepan, heat together chocolate and cream, stirring frequently, until melted and smooth. Bring to a boil. Remove from heat.

3. Gradually add chocolate mixture to egg yolks, stirring constantly. Stir in orange juice and orange peel.

4. Strain custard through a fine strainer. Pour evenly into five 8-ounce custard cups. Place custard cups in a shallow roasting pan. Pour enough boiling water into roasting pan to come halfway up sides of cups.

5. Bake custards until just set, 30-45 minutes. Remove from pan. Chill for at least 1 hour or overnight.

6. Preheat broiler. Place broiler rack 4 inches from heat.

7. Place custard cups back into a shallow baking pan. Sprinkle a thin layer of sugar over each custard. Place pan under broiler. Broil custards until sugar bubbles and turns golden in color, 2-3 minutes.

8. Transfer cups to a wire rack to cool. Garnish with whipped cream, chocolate shavings, and strips of orange peel.

Mochaccino Custard Pots

Like all custard desserts, these luscious little pots of cream can be made ahead for a party.

30 minutes preparation, 25-30 minutes baking   Makes 6 custards

Ingredients:

 1 cup heavy cream
 1 cup milk
 1 vanilla bean, split lengthwise,
    or 1½ teaspoons vanilla extract
 2 teaspoons instant coffee
    powder, preferably espresso
 2½ ounces (2½ squares)
    semisweet chocolate, coarsely
    chopped
 2 large eggs
 2 large egg yolks
 ⅓ cup granulated sugar

Garnish:

 Whipped cream
 Chocolate-covered coffee beans

1. In a heavy saucepan, mix together cream, milk, and vanilla bean, if using. Bring to a boil.

2. Pour ½ cup of hot cream mixture into a small glass measuring cup. Add instant coffee; stir until dissolved. Add coffee mixture and chocolate to remaining hot cream mixture; stir until chocolate has melted and mixture is smooth.

3. Preheat oven to 300°F.

4. Beat together eggs, egg yolks, and sugar. Gradually pour hot cream mixture into egg mixture, beating constantly. Stir in vanilla extract, if using. Strain mixture into a large glass measuring cup.

5. Place six 4-ounce custard cups in a shallow baking pan. Fill cups with custard mixture. Place pan on rack in middle of oven; pour enough hot water into pan to come halfway up sides of cups.

6. Bake custards until set but still slightly wobbly in center, 25-30 minutes. Transfer cups to a wire rack to cool. Garnish each with whipped cream and coffee beans. Chill until ready to serve.

Cook's Tip

For more flavorful custard, remove cream mixture from heat, cover, and let vanilla bean steep for 30 minutes.

Soufflés, Custards & Fruit Crisps   177

Black & White Chocolate Parfaits

Layers of white and semisweet chocolate mousse are stylishly presented in parfait glasses.

20 minutes preparation plus chilling

Makes 4 parfaits

Ingredients:

- 4 ounces (4 squares) semisweet chocolate, coarsely chopped
- 4 ounces (4 squares) white chocolate, coarsely chopped
- 4 large eggs, separated
- 2 tablespoons brandy or rum
- 1¼ cups whipping cream

Garnish:

Chocolate curls
(see page 185)

1. In the top of a double boiler set over simmering (not boiling) water, melt the semisweet chocolate. Remove from the heat and let cool. In a separate pan, melt the white chocolate in the same way.

2. Put 2 egg yolks and 1 tablespoon brandy or rum into each bowl of chocolate. Beat with a wooden spoon until smooth. Let cool slightly.

3. In a clean bowl, whip half the cream until stiff peaks form. Divide between the chocolate mixtures and fold in.

4. In another clean bowl, beat the egg whites with an electric whisk until stiff peaks form. Divide evenly between the chocolate mixtures and fold in.

5. Fill four 6-ounce parfait glasses with alternate layers of plain and white chocolate mousse. Chill for at least 2 hours, or until set.

6. Whip the remaining cream until stiff peaks form. Spoon into a pastry bag fitted with a large star-shaped tip. Pipe a large swirl on the top of each mousse. Decorate with the chocolate curls.

Double Chocolate Pudding Cups

Make this all-American favorite for a special family gathering or a formal dinner party.

40 minutes preparation plus chilling   Makes 4 servings

Pudding:
- ½ cup granulated sugar
- ⅓ cup unsweetened cocoa powder
- 2 tablespoons cornstarch
- 2 cups heavy cream
- 2 large egg yolks
- 2 tablespoons butter, melted
- 2 tablespoons chocolate cream liqueur or 1 teaspoon chocolate extract
- 4 (1.4 ounce) chocolate-covered toffee bars, chopped (1 cup)
- ⅓ cup coarsely chopped pecans, toasted (about 1¼ ounces)

Chocolate Cups:
- 16 ounces white chocolate, coarsely chopped

Garnish:
- 1 cup whipped cream

Using the back of a spoon, spread melted chocolate up sides of foil.

1. To prepare pudding, in a medium, heavy saucepan, mix together sugar, cocoa powder, and cornstarch. Stir in cream and egg yolks. Bring to a boil over medium heat, stirring constantly, until thickened, 1 minute.

2. Remove from heat. Add butter and liqueur, stirring until melted and smooth. Cover the surface with plastic wrap. Chill for 30 minutes.

3. To prepare chocolate cups, cut out four 9-inch aluminum foil squares. Fit each square into an 8-ounce custard cup; flute sides of foil. Spray foil with vegetable cooking spray.

4. In the top of a double boiler set over simmering (not boiling) water, heat chocolate, stirring, until melted and smooth.

5. Pour ¼ cup melted chocolate into each custard cup. Using the back of a spoon or a pastry brush, spread chocolate evenly up sides of foil. Chill until set, 3-4 hours.

6. Carefully remove foil from custard cups.

7. Stir toffee bars and nuts into pudding. Spoon pudding into cups, dividing evenly.

8. Using a pastry bag fitted with a star tip, pipe a whipped cream rosette in the center of each pudding.

Rocky Road Pudding

Flavored with coffee liqueur, this pudding is reminiscent of the popular rocky road ice cream.

Ingredients:

- 1 cup milk
- 1 cup half-and-half
- ½ cup granulated sugar
- ⅓ cup unsweetened cocoa powder
- 2 tablespoons cornstarch
- ⅛ teaspoon salt
- 2 large egg yolks
- 3 tablespoons butter
- 2 tablespoons coffee-flavored liqueur

Filling and Topping:

- 1 cup miniature marshmallows
- ½ cup coarsely chopped almonds (about 2 ounces)

1. In a medium saucepan, mix together milk, half-and-half, sugar, cocoa powder, cornstarch, and salt. Stir in egg yolks, 1 at a time, beating well after each addition.

2. Bring cocoa mixture to a boil over medium heat, stirring constantly. Boil for 1 minute. Remove from heat. Stir in butter and liqueur. Strain custard through a fine strainer into a bowl.

3. Spoon half of the pudding evenly into 4 dishes. Sprinkle half the marshmallows and half the nuts over pudding. Spoon remaining pudding into dishes. Top with remaining marshmallows and nuts. Chill for 3-4 hours.

Cook's Tip

If desired, substitute warm black coffee for the liqueur.

Cherry-Chocolate Crisp

Inspired by chocolate-covered cherries, this luscious dessert is absolutely mouth-watering.

20 minutes preparation, 45 minutes baking   Makes 6 servings

Ingredients:

4 cans (17 ounces each) pitted,
  tart cherries, drained
½ cup granulated sugar
1½ tablespoons all-purpose flour
6 ounces (6 squares) semisweet
  chocolate, coarsely chopped

Topping:

½ cup all-purpose flour
¼ cup granulated sugar
¼ cup firmly packed light brown
  sugar
Pinch of salt
2 ounces (½ stick) chilled butter,
  cut into small pieces

1. Preheat oven to 375°F.

2. Mix together cherries, sugar, and flour. Spread evenly in an ungreased 10-inch baking dish. Sprinkle chocolate over top.

3. To prepare topping, in a medium bowl, mix together flour, granulated sugar, brown sugar, and salt. Using a pastry blender or 2 knives, cut butter into flour mixture until coarse crumbs form.

4. Sprinkle topping evenly over cherry filling.

5. Bake crisp until filling bubbles and topping is browned, 45 minutes. Transfer baking dish to a wire rack to cool slightly.

Cook's Tip

If you're fond of crust, double the topping ingredients.

Serve this crisp warm from the oven with a generous scoop of chocolate or cherry ice cream.

Holiday & Celebration Desserts

Here you will find new and exciting ideas for every situation: a special valentine treat for your sweetheart, a pie for your favorite leprechauns, a cake for the Easter bunny, Mother's and Father's Day delights, and wholesome treats for the neighborhood trick-or-treaters. Or perhaps you'd like a happy ending for family Thanksgivings or special Christmas celebrations? Plus ideas abound for children's birthday parties, weddings, and anniversaries, and all those really special occasions that demand a luxurious dessert to show how much you care.

Decorating with Chocolate

Chocolate is not only a treat to eat, it also makes wonderful garnishes.

The rich, smooth taste of chocolate is loved by almost everyone. But chocolate is more than just a flavoring for brownies, cakes, ice creams, and mousses, it's also terrific for making garnishes and dramatic cake decorations.

Composition of Chocolate

Chocolate is made from cocoa beans that are dried, roasted, and ground to a paste called chocolate liquor. The type and blend of beans, specific methods of roasting and refining, the ratio of cocoa butter and cocoa solids, and the amount of added sugar all contribute to the flavor of a particular chocolate. The taste of chocolates, even those in the same category, vary greatly from brand to brand. Taste several to find one you like best. The finest quality chocolates always have a high percentage of cocoa butter.

Types of Chocolate

Unsweetened chocolate, or plain chocolate, contains a minimum of 50 percent and a maximum of 58 percent cocoa butter. It is primarily used for baking.

Both bittersweet and semisweet chocolate are made from plain chocolate with some sugar added. European brands of bittersweet chocolate tend to be richer-tasting and less sweet than most American brands of semisweet chocolate.

Sweet chocolate has a higher percentage of sugar than bittersweet or semisweet and is used mostly by the candy industry.

Milk chocolate is made from lightly roasted beans and includes powdered milk. It is rarely used for baking. White chocolate contains cocoa butter but no cocoa solids and technically is not really chocolate at all. Look for it under the name "white coating," and always read the label to see that it is made from cocoa butter and not vegetable fat.

Cocoa powder is what remains when all the cocoa butter is extracted from the chocolate liquor. Dutch-processed cocoa has alkali added to produce a milder tasting, darker cocoa. Non-alkalized brands are lighter in color, but they have a stronger chocolate flavor.

Storing Chocolate

Store chocolate in a dry place with good air circulation and an ideal temperature of about 65°F. Wrap chocolate in foil or plastic wrap and store away from anything with a strong odor. Dark chocolate and cocoa stay fresh for many years. Milk chocolate and white chocolate have high amounts of fat and can turn rancid in as little as six months.

Chocolate that has not been properly stored may develop a whitish film called "bloom." This happens when the cocoa butter rises to the surface, or when water condenses on the surface of the chocolate and dissolves some of the sugar. Bloomed chocolate can be used for baking and melting, but it should not be used to make decorations.

Melting Chocolate

Chocolate scorches easily and must be melted very slowly. Milk chocolate and white chocolate can develop lumps if they are overheated. Be sure the container the chocolate is melted in is completely dry, unless the recipe specifies that a liquid should be added. If chocolate comes in contact with water or steam while it is melting, it will tighten and refuse to melt. If this happens, stir shortening or vegetable oil into the chocolate, 1 teaspoon at a time, until it becomes smooth. Note that this can affect the texture of the final recipe.

Microwave ovens do a great job of melting chocolate, or you can use a conventional oven heated to 250°F. Chop the chocolate, put it in a heatproof bowl, and melt in the warm oven, stirring occasionally until smooth. If chocolate is to be combined with melted butter or another liquid, you can eliminate the risk of scorching by melting chocolate in a food processor. First, chop the chocolate using the metal blade of the food processor.

Pour the butter or other liquid through the feed tube while the machine is running and process until smooth, 20-30 seconds.

To stencil, mask top of cake with a dusting of cocoa powder. Lay stencil gently on top of cake. Dust over it with powdered sugar. Very carefully lift the stencil from the top of the cake. Do not let the sugar spill onto the design, as it will be very difficult to fix.

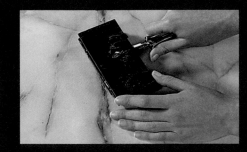

To make curls, using a vegetable peeler, shave sides of a piece of chocolate. Store in refrigerator if you're not going to use immediately.

To make leaves, wash and dry leaves. Using a pastry brush, spread cooled melted chocolate evenly on the top side of each leaf.

Wipe the edge and bottom of the leaf clean of any excess chocolate. Place the leaves on a tray and refrigerate until completely set.

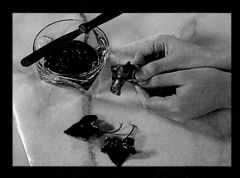

Carefully peel away leaf. Store leaves between waxed paper layers in an airtight container in refrigerator.

Halloween Brownie Cake

Let little trick-or-treaters help decorate this Halloween favorite.

40 minutes preparation plus cooling, 55-60 minutes baking

Makes 12 servings

Ingredients:

1 cup all-purpose flour

1 teaspoon baking powder

⅛ teaspoon salt

1 cup granulated sugar

2 tablespoons firmly packed light brown sugar

1 teaspoon vanilla extract

5 large eggs

7 ounces (7 squares) semisweet chocolate, melted

4 ounces (1 stick) butter, melted

3 tablespoons heavy cream

Frosting and Filling:

1 package (16 ounces) confectioners' sugar, sifted

1 package (8 ounces) cream cheese

4 ounces (1 stick) butter, softened

5 tablespoons unsweetened cocoa powder

2 teaspoons vanilla extract

Garnish:

32 pieces candy corn

1. Preheat oven to 325°F. Grease an 8-inch square cake pan. Dust with flour; tap out excess.

2. Mix together flour, baking powder, and salt.

3. Beat together granulated sugar, brown sugar, and vanilla at medium speed until light and fluffy.

4. Beat in eggs, 1 at a time, beating well after each addition. Beat in melted chocolate, melted butter, and cream.

5. At low speed, beat in flour mixture, ½ cup at a time, until blended and smooth. Pour batter into prepared pan; smooth top.

6. Bake cake until a toothpick inserted in the center comes out clean, 55-60 minutes.

7. Transfer pan to a wire rack to cool for 15 minutes. Loosen cake by running a metal spatula around sides of pan. Turn cake out onto rack to cool completely.

8. To prepare frosting, beat together confectioners' sugar, cream cheese, butter, cocoa powder, and vanilla at low speed until blended and smooth.

9. Slice cake in half horizontally. Spread bottom layer with some frosting. Top with remaining layer. Spread remaining frosting over top and sides. Garnish with candy corn.

Chocolate-Dipped Easter Egg Cookies

Kids will enjoy helping to make these adorable treats for the Easter basket.

40 minutes preparation, 1 hour chilling, 10-12 minutes baking   Makes 2 dozen cookies

Ingredients:

3 cups all-purpose flour

½ teaspoon salt

8 ounces (2 sticks) butter, softened

1 cup smooth or chunky peanut butter

½ cup firmly packed dark brown sugar

½ cup granulated sugar

2 large eggs

2 teaspoons vanilla or almond extract

Decoration:

1 pound (16 squares) semisweet chocolate, coarsely chopped

Assorted candy décors

1. Preheat oven to 325°F. Line a baking sheet with aluminum foil.

2. Mix together flour and salt.

3. Beat together butter, peanut butter, brown sugar, and granulated sugar at medium speed until light and fluffy.

4. Add eggs, 1 at a time, beating well after each addition. Beat in vanilla. At low speed, beat in flour mixture, 1 cup at a time, beating well after each addition, until a dough forms. Shape dough into a disk, wrap in plastic wrap, and chill for 1 hour.

5. Roll dough into 1½-inch balls. On a flat surface, shape each ball into an egg shape, with bottom side flat. Place cookies, 2 inches apart, on prepared baking sheet.

6. Bake cookies until just set, 10-12 minutes. Transfer cookies to a wire rack to cool.

7. In a saucepan, melt chocolate over low heat, stirring constantly. Dip bottom half of each cookie into chocolate, letting excess drip back into pan.

8. Immediately press candies into chocolate-covered portion to decorate as desired. Place on waxed paper. Chill until set.

Cook's Tip

For white Easter egg cookies, use white melting drops, available from specialty baking shops. Do not use regular white chocolate as it will not melt properly.

Store Easter egg cookies in a single layer in an airtight container in the refrigerator.

Chocolate-Orange Easter Cake

This showstopping chocolate-orange cake will add a heavenly note to the Easter festivities.

1 hour preparation, 20-25 minutes baking

Makes 10 servings

Ingredients:

1 cup all-purpose
flour

½ cup unsweetened
cocoa powder

1¼ teaspoons baking
powder

¾ teaspoon baking
soda

8 large eggs,
separated

1⅓ cups
confectioners' sugar

Filling:

1 package unflavored
gelatin

1 large egg

⅓ cup granulated
sugar

2 cups orange juice

1 tablespoon grated
orange peel

1 cup chilled heavy
cream

Frosting and Garnish:

2 ounces (½ stick)
butter, softened

¼ cup light or dark
corn syrup

¼ teaspoon vanilla
extract

⅛ teaspoon salt

½ cup unsweetened
cocoa powder

3 tablespoons milk

2 cups confectioners'
sugar

Marzipan decorations
(optional)

1. Preheat oven to 350°F. Grease bottom and sides of a 9-inch springform pan. Dust with flour; tap out excess.

2. Mix together flour, cocoa powder, baking powder, and baking soda.

3. Beat egg yolks at medium speed until thick. Add confectioners' sugar; beat well. Fold in flour mixture.

4. Beat egg whites until stiff, but not dry, peaks form. Fold into egg yolk mixture. Pour batter into prepared pan.

5. Bake cake until a toothpick inserted in the center comes out clean, 20-25 minutes. Transfer pan to a wire rack to cool. Remove sides of pan.

6. To prepare filling, in a medium saucepan, mix together gelatin, egg, sugar, orange juice, and orange zest. Cook over medium heat, stirring, until slightly thickened, 2 minutes. Remove pan from heat; place in a bowl filled with ice water. Stir mixture until thick and cool, 5 minutes.

7. Beat cream at medium speed until soft peaks form. Fold into orange juice mixture.

8. To prepare frosting, beat butter at medium speed until creamy. Beat in corn syrup, vanilla, and salt. Stir in cocoa powder. Alternately beat in milk and confectioners' sugar until smooth and creamy.

9. Using a serrated knife, slice cake horizontally into 3 layers. Place 1 layer on a serving plate. Spread with half of filling. Repeat with second layer and filling. Top with third layer. Spread with frosting. Decorate with marzipan.

Chocolate Pecan Pie

Let this rich classic take center stage on your Thanksgiving dessert buffet table.

25 minutes preparation plus chilling and cooling, 45 minutes baking

Makes 8 servings

Ingredients:
1½ cups all-purpose flour
2 teaspoons granulated sugar
¼ teaspoon salt
2 ounces (½ stick) chilled butter,
    cut into small pieces
3 tablespoons chilled solid vegetable
    shortening, cut into small pieces
¼ cup ice water

Filling:
3 ounces (3 squares) semisweet
    chocolate, coarsely chopped
2 tablespoons butter
½ cup granulated sugar
1¼ cups light corn syrup
¼ cup bourbon (optional)
4 large eggs
1½ cups pecan halves (6 ounces)

Glaze and Garnish:
1 egg, lightly beaten
Whipped cream
Coarsely chopped pecans

1. In a large bowl, mix together flour, sugar, and salt.

2. Using a pastry blender or 2 knives, cut butter and shortening into flour mixture until coarse crumbs form. Add water, 1 tablespoon at a time, tossing with a fork until a soft dough forms. Shape dough into a disk, wrap in plastic wrap, and chill for 30 minutes.

3. On a floured surface, using a floured rolling pin, roll dough into a 12-inch circle. Fit dough into a 10-inch pie plate. Trim overhang. Fold edges under.

4. Gather trimmings; roll to a ⅛-inch thickness. Cut out enough small pastry leaves to cover edges of pie.

5. To prepare filling, in the top of a double boiler set over simmering (not boiling) water, heat chocolate and butter, stirring constantly, until melted and smooth. Cool slightly.

6. Beat together sugar, corn syrup, and bourbon at medium speed until blended. Beat in eggs, 1 at a time, beating well after each addition. Stir in melted chocolate mixture and nuts.

7. Pour filling into crust. Brush edges with water; arrange pastry leaves around edges. Brush edges and leaves with beaten egg.

8. Preheat oven to 375°F. Bake pie until filling is set, 45 minutes. Transfer pie to a wire rack to cool completely. Garnish with whipped cream and sprinkle with nuts.

Cook's Tip
For a nuttier flavor, toast the nuts. In a small skillet, cook nuts over medium heat, stirring occasionally, for 5 minutes. Do not add oil to the skillet.

Classic Yule Log

The presentation of this traditional French treat can sometimes upstage old St. Nick himself.

1 hour preparation plus cooling, chilling, and standing, 15 minutes baking · Makes 10 servings

Ingredients:
½ cup sifted cake flour
¼ cup unsweetened
    cocoa powder
1 teaspoon baking
    powder
¼ teaspoon salt
½ cup granulated sugar
3 large eggs, separated
¼ cup milk
Confectioners' sugar

Filling:
1½ cups whipped cream

Frosting:
2 cups heavy cream
8 ounces (8 squares)
    semisweet chocolate,
    melted
2 ounces (½ stick)
    butter, softened

Garnish:
Confectioners' sugar
½ teaspoon green food
    coloring
1 package (8 ounces)
    marzipan
Cinnamon red-hot
    candies
Candy snowmen

1. Preheat oven to 350°F. Grease a 15 x 10-inch jelly roll pan. Line with waxed paper. Grease paper.

2. Sift together flour, cocoa powder, baking powder, and salt.

3. Beat together granulated sugar and egg yolks at high speed until light and fluffy. At low speed, alternately beat milk and flour mixture into egg mixture.

4. Using clean beaters, beat egg whites at high speed until stiff, but not dry, peaks form. Fold one-third of beaten whites into batter. Fold in remaining whites. Spread batter in prepared pan; smooth top.

5. Bake cake until set, 15 minutes. Dust a clean cloth with confectioners' sugar. Turn cake out onto prepared cloth. Remove waxed paper. Trim cake edges.

6. Starting with a long side, roll up cake, jelly-roll style. Transfer, seam-side down, to a wire rack to cool for 30 minutes.

7. Unroll cake; remove cloth. Spread cream over cake to within 1 inch of edges. Re-roll cake. Place, seam-side down, on serving plate.

8. To prepare frosting, in a small saucepan, bring cream, melted chocolate, and butter to a boil over medium heat, stirring vigorously until blended. Remove from heat. Let stand until set.

9. Spread frosting over top and sides of cake.

10. To prepare garnish, dust work surface with confectioners' sugar. Knead food coloring into marzipan until blended. Using a rolling pin dusted with confectioners' sugar, roll marzipan to a 1/8-inch thickness. Using a small knife, cut out leaves.

11. Arrange leaves, cinnamon candies, and snowmen on top of cake and around plate. Dust with confectioners' sugar.

Easter Bunny Meringue Tart

The sweet little March hare on this luscious, custard-filled dessert is good enough to eat.

50 minutes preparation plus chilling and standing, 45 minutes baking   Makes 8 servings

Ingredients:
½ cup granulated sugar
1 tablespoon cornstarch
1 cup half-and-half
2 large egg yolks, lightly beaten
2 tablespoons grated orange peel
¼ teaspoon almond extract

Meringue:
4 large egg whites
¾ cup granulated sugar
¼ cup finely ground almonds
   (about 1 ounce)
1 tablespoon unsweetened cocoa powder
1 teaspoon vanilla extract

Topping and Garnish:
1 tablespoon unsweetened cocoa powder
6 ounces marzipan
1 ounce milk chocolate, melted

1. Mix together sugar and cornstarch.

2. In the top of a double boiler set over simmering (not boiling) water, heat half-and-half until bubbles appear around edges. Stir in sugar mixture and egg yolks. Cook, stirring constantly, until custard thickens, 5 minutes. Stir in orange peel and almond extract. Remove from heat. Chill custard, stirring occasionally, until thickened, 2 hours.

3. Preheat oven to 225°F.

4. To prepare meringue, beat egg whites at high speed until foamy. Gradually add sugar, beating until stiff, but not dry, peaks form. Fold in nuts, cocoa powder, and vanilla.

5. Line 2 baking sheets with waxed paper. Spread meringue into two 9-inch rounds on prepared baking sheets.

6. Bake meringues until firm and dry, 45 minutes. Turn off oven. Let meringues stand in oven until dry and crisp, 1 hour.

7. Place 1 meringue circle on a serving plate. Spoon custard over top. Place remaining meringue circle on top.

8. To prepare topping, dust tart with cocoa powder. Trace an 8-inch bunny rabbit onto a sheet of waxed paper. Using scissors, cut out tracing. Place marzipan between 2 pieces of plastic wrap. Roll into an 8-inch round. Remove top plastic wrap.

9. Place tracing over marzipan. Using a sharp knife, cut out rabbit. Using a flat metal spatula, place rabbit on top of tart.

10. Using a pastry brush dipped in melted chocolate, paint tips of ears, an eye, nose, paws, and tail onto rabbit.

Grasshopper Pie

Reward grown-up leprechauns on St. Patrick's Day with this richly spirited dessert.

30 minutes preparation, 4½ hours chilling

Makes 8 servings

Ingredients:

1 9-inch baked chocolate-cookie
   crumb crust

1 package unflavored gelatin

½ cup cold water

⅓ cup plus 3 tablespoons
   granulated sugar

3 large eggs, separated

⅓ cup green crème de menthe

2 tablespoons crème de cacao

½ cup chilled heavy cream

2 drops green food coloring

Chocolate Shamrocks and Garnish:

2 ounces semisweet chocolate,
   coarsely chopped

Whipped cream

1. In a saucepan, sprinkle gelatin over water; let stand for 3 minutes. Stir in 1/3 cup of sugar and egg yolks. Cook over low heat, stirring constantly, just until thickened. Do not boil. Stir in crème de menthe and crème de cacao until blended. Chill until mixture is very thick but not set, 30 minutes.

2. Beat egg whites at high speed until foamy. Gradually beat in remaining sugar until stiff, but not dry, peaks form.

3. Beat cream at medium speed until soft peaks form.

4. Fold beaten egg whites and whipped cream into gelatin mixture. Fold in food coloring. Pour mixture into crust. Chill until set, at least 3 hours.

5. To prepare chocolate shamrocks, draw 3 shamrock patterns on a piece of white paper. Place on a baking sheet; cover with waxed paper.

6. In a small saucepan, melt chocolate over very low heat, stirring constantly. Remove from heat. Stir occasionally until cool to touch. Using a pastry brush, thickly spread chocolate over patterns. Chill until set, 1 hour. Peel waxed paper from shamrocks.

7. Garnish pie with whipped cream. Top with chocolate shamrocks.

Halloween Sugar Cookies

Let the kids help with cutting out and decorating these terrifying cookies.

45 minutes preparation plus chilling, cooling, and standing, 12 minutes baking per batch   Makes 4 dozen cookies

Ingredients:

 3 cups all-purpose flour
 1 teaspoon pumpkin pie spice
 ½ teaspoon salt
 6 ounces (1½ sticks) butter,
  softened
 ⅔ cup granulated sugar
 2 tablespoons maple syrup
 1 teaspoon vanilla extract
 2 large eggs

Topping:

 2 ounces (2 squares) semisweet
  chocolate, melted

1. Mix together flour, pumpkin pie spice, and salt.

2. Beat together butter, sugar, maple syrup, vanilla, and eggs at medium speed until light and fluffy.

3. At low speed, beat flour mixture into butter mixture, ½ cup at a time, until a dough forms. Shape dough into a disk and wrap in plastic wrap, and chill for 2½ hours.

4. Preheat oven to 350°F. Grease 2 baking sheets.

5. On a floured surface, using a floured rolling pin, roll dough to a ¼-inch thickness.

6. Using floured 3½-inch Halloween cookie cutters, cut out cookies.

7. Gather trimmings, roll to a ¼-inch thickness, and cut out more cookies.

8. Place cookies, 1 inch apart, on prepared baking sheets.

9. Bake cookies until golden, 12 minutes. Transfer baking sheets to wire racks to cool slightly. Transfer cookies to racks to cool completely.

10. Using a pastry bag fitted with a plain writing tip, pipe chocolate decorations on top of cookies. Let stand until set.

Anniversary Cake

Celebrate your special day with family, friends, and this exquisite cake.

4 hours preparation plus cooling, 30-40 minutes baking   Makes 25-30 servings

Chocolate Filling:
- 1½ cups heavy cream
- 6 ounces (6 squares) semisweet chocolate

Cake:
- Two separate batches of batter
- For each batch of batter:
- 2½ cups cake flour
- 2½ teaspoons baking powder
- 1¼ teaspoons salt
- 5 ounces (1¼ sticks) butter, softened
- 1¼ cups granulated sugar
- 3 large eggs
- 1½ teaspoons vanilla extract
- 1 cup milk

Orange Filling:
- 2 cups confectioners' sugar, sifted
- 8 ounces (2 sticks) butter, softened
- 2½ tablespoons heavy cream
- 1 tablespoon grated orange peel

Frosting:
- 1 large egg white
- 1¼ cups confectioners' sugar

Topping and Decorations:
- 4 pounds marzipan
- 2 drops red food coloring
- 2 drops green food coloring
- Silver dragées; chocolate leaves

1. To prepare chocolate filling, in a small saucepan, heat cream until bubbles appear around edges of pan. Remove from heat. Stir in chocolate until smooth. Chill for 2 hours, stirring occasionally.

2. To prepare first batch of batter, preheat oven to 350°F. Grease a 10-inch round cake pan (at least 2 inches deep) with a circle of waxed paper. Butter paper and dust pan with flour; tap out excess.

3. In a bowl, sift together flour, baking powder, and salt.

4. Using a heavy-duty electric mixer fitted with the paddle attachment and set on medium speed, beat together butter and sugar until light and fluffy. Add eggs to butter mixture, 1 at a time, beating well after each addition. Add vanilla.

5. At low speed, alternately beat in flour mixture and milk until blended.

6. Pour batter into prepared pan and smooth top. Bake cake in middle of oven until toothpick inserted in the center comes out clean, 35-40 minutes.

7. Transfer pan to a wire rack to cool slightly, 5-10 minutes.

8. Loosen cake by running a metal spatula around sides of pan. Turn cake out onto rack to cool completely. Peel off waxed paper.

9. Prepare second batch of batter. Grease a 6-inch round cake pan and an 8-inch round cake pan (both at least 2 inches deep) with circles of waxed paper. Butter paper and dust pans with flour; tap out excess. Repeat Steps 3 to 5.

10. Pour 1¾ cups batter into prepared 6-inch pan and smooth top. Pour remaining batter into prepared 8-inch pan. Bake both 6- and 8-inch cakes in middle of oven until a toothpick inserted in the centers comes out clean, 30–35 minutes for the smaller cake; 35-40 minutes for the larger cake.

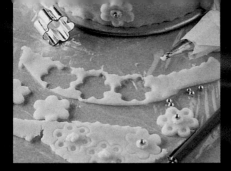

Spread the orange and chocolate fillings evenly between the layers of each cake.

Use a pastry wheel to cut out marzipan strips. Place marzipan rounds on top of cakes and strips around sides.

Using a 1-inch flower-shaped cookie cutter, cut out flowers. Using icing as "glue," attach flowers and decorations to cake.

11. Transfer pans to a wire rack to cool slightly, 5-10 minutes.

12. Loosen cakes by running a metal spatula around sides of pan. Turn cake out onto rack to cool completely. Peel off waxed paper.

13. To prepare orange filling, beat together confectioners' sugar and butter at medium speed until light and fluffy. Beat in cream and orange peel.

14. Beat chocolate filling at medium speed until soft peaks form.

15. To prepare icing, using clean beaters, beat egg white at medium speed until foamy. Beat in confectioners' sugar until stiff, but not dry, peaks form.

16. Cut each cake horizontally into 3 layers. Place 1 large layer on waxed paper. Spread some orange filling over top. Top with another large layer; spread with some chocolate filling. Top with remaining large layer. Repeat layering with remaining cakes, orange filling, and chocolate filling. Keep the 3 cakes separate.

17. Cut out 3 circles of cardboard to fit beneath each cake. Place cakes on top of circles.

18. To prepare topping, knead red food coloring into ⅔ cup marzipan until color is even. Knead green food coloring into one 3-ounce piece of marzipan until color is even. Wrap each piece in plastic wrap.

19. Divide remaining marzipan in half. Wrap 1 half in plastic wrap. Roll remaining half between 2 sheets of plastic wrap to a ⅛-inch thickness. Using a decorative pastry wheel, cut out three 2¼-inch-wide strips of marzipan. Arrange strips around sides of each cake. Trim excess; wrap trimmings in plastic wrap.

20. Unwrap remaining marzipan and divide it into one 11-ounce piece, one 9-ounce piece, and one 7-ounce piece. Place each piece between 2 sheets of plastic wrap; roll each piece into a circle 1½-inches larger than each cake. Remove top sheets of plastic; trim edges with a pastry wheel.

21. Place marzipan circles on top of cakes. Stack cakes, with cardboard rounds, on top of each other. Cover whole cake with plastic wrap.

22. To prepare decorations, using a small knife, cut colored marzipan into flowers and leaves. Roll colored trimmings into long thin ropes; twist together. Roll out reserved uncolored marzipan trimmings between 2 sheets of plastic wrap to a ⅛-inch thickness. Using a 1-inch flower-shaped cookie cutter, cut out flowers.

23. Using a pastry bag fitted with a writing tip, pipe icing into center of each flower. Top with a dragée. Using the back of a ballpoint pen, press a pattern in flower petals.

24. 24 Unwrap cake. Arrange marzipan decorations and chocolate leaves on top and sides of cake, as pictured, using icing as "glue." Press some dragées onto sides of cake. Cover cake until ready to serve.

Black Forest Cake

This classic cake is sure to be a success for any occasion.

45 minutes preparation, 20-25 minutes baking plus cooling

Makes 6-8 servings

Ingredients:

- 4 ounces (1 stick) butter
- ½ cup superfine sugar
- 4 large eggs
- ¾ cup ground almonds (3 ounces)
- 4 ounces (4 squares) semisweet chocolate, melted
- ½ cup all-purpose flour
- 6 tablespoons cornstarch
- 2 teaspoons baking powder

Filling and Topping:

- 6 tablespoons kirsch or rum
- 3 tablespoons black cherry jelly
- 1 can (16-ounce) cherries, drained
- 2 cups heavy cream, whipped
- 4 ounces chocolate curls, to decorate

1. Grease three 8-inch round cake pans. Line with waxed paper. Preheat oven to 350°F.

2. In a bowl, beat together the butter and sugar until pale and fluffy. Beat in the eggs, almonds, and melted chocolate.

3. Sift the flour, cornstarch, and baking powder over the mixture and fold in with a large spoon.

4. Divide the mixture between the pans and bake until a toothpick inserted into the centers comes out clean, 20-25 minutes. Turn out onto a wire rack to cool completely. Remove the waxed paper.

5. Sprinkle each cake with 2 tablespoons kirsch or rum. Spread a layer of jelly, cherries, and half of the whipped cream over 2 of the cakes. Put one on top of the other and top with the remaining cake.

6. Spread the remaining cream over the cake. Press on the chocolate curls and serve.

Cook's Tip

The quickest way to make the chocolate curls is to use a swivel-bladed vegetable peeler —simply make shavings from the side of a well-chilled chocolate bar. Store this cake in an airtight container in the refrigerator and eat within 36 hours.

Celebration Chocolate Cake

This gorgeous chocolate cake is the perfect finale for an elegant New Year's party.

1 hour preparation plus cooling, 30 minutes baking

Makes 12 servings

Ingredients:

½ cup unsweetened cocoa powder
½ teaspoon instant coffee powder
½ cup boiling water
1 cup sour cream
2¼ cups all-purpose flour
1½ teaspoons baking soda
½ teaspoon salt
1⅔ cups granulated sugar
4 ounces (1 stick) butter, softened
2 large eggs
1 tablespoon vanilla extract
1 tablespoon raspberry-flavored liqueur (optional)

Filling and Frosting:

½ cup raspberry jelly
1½ cups confectioners' sugar
½ cup milk
4 ounces (4 squares) semisweet chocolate, melted

Topping and Garnish:

½ cup chocolate sprinkles
1 cup prepared chocolate frosting

1. Preheat oven to 350°F. Line two 9-inch round cake pans with waxed paper.

2. Dissolve cocoa powder and coffee powder in boiling water. Cool to room temperature. Stir in sour cream.

3. Mix together flour, baking soda, and salt.

4. Beat sugar and butter at medium speed until smooth. Beat in eggs, vanilla, and liqueur. At low speed, alternately beat sour cream mixture and flour mixture into butter mixture until blended. Pour batter evenly into prepared pans; smooth tops.

5. Bake cakes until a toothpick inserted in the centers comes out clean, 30 minutes. Transfer pans to wire racks to cool slightly. Loosen cakes by running a metal spatula around edges of pans. Turn cakes out onto racks to cool completely.

6. Place 1 cake layer on a serving plate. Spread jelly on top. Place remaining cake layer on top.

7. To prepare frosting, mix together confectioners' sugar, milk, and melted chocolate. Spread frosting over top of cake.

8. Pat chocolate sprinkles around top edges of cake. Using a pastry bag fitted with a star tip, pipe chocolate frosting inside border.

Holiday & Celebration Desserts   197

Chocolate Box-Berry Cake

Strips of glossy chocolate surround a moist chocolate cake topped with fresh berries.

45 minutes preparation, 35-40 minutes baking plus cooling

Makes 8-10 servings

Ingredients:

- 4 ounces (1 stick) butter, softened
- ½ cup superfine sugar
- 1 cup all-purpose flour, sifted
- 2 teaspoons baking powder, sifted
- ½ teaspoon salt
- 1 tablespoon unsweetened cocoa powder, sifted
- 2 large eggs

Frosting and Decoration:

- 1 tablespoon unsweetened cocoa powder
- 3 ounces (¾ stick) butter, softened
- 1½ cups confectioners' sugar, sifted
- 5 ounces (5 squares) semisweet chocolate
- ½ pint fresh strawberries
- ½ pint fresh blueberries

1. Preheat oven to 325°F. Lightly grease a 7-inch square cake pan and line with waxed paper.

2. In a large mixing bowl, mix together the butter, superfine sugar, flour, baking powder, salt, cocoa, and eggs until well blended. Beat for 2-3 minutes, or until smooth and glossy.

3. Spoon the mixture into the prepared pan. Bake until a toothpick inserted in the center comes out clean, 35-40 minutes.

4. Cool in the pan for about 10 minutes, then turn out onto a wire rack. Remove the waxed paper and let cool completely.

5. For the frosting, mix together the cocoa powder and 1 tablespoon boiling water. Let cool. Add the butter and confectioners' sugar and beat until smooth.

6. Spread out the melted chocolate on a piece of waxed paper. Leave until just set. Cut the chocolate into 4 strips to fit the sides of the cake.

7. Put the cake on a serving plate. Spread the top and sides of the cake with two-thirds of the frosting. Press the strips of chocolate onto the sides.

8. Put the remaining frosting in a pastry bag fitted with a star tip. Pipe swirls of frosting around the top of the cake. Fill the center with the strawberries/blueberries.

Chocolate-Chestnut Cakes

These rich, moist cakes are great for a Christmas buffet.

25 minutes preparation plus cooling, 15-20 minutes baking

Makes 30 cupcakes

Ingredients:

- 8 ounces (8 squares) semisweet chocolate, coarsely chopped
- 8 ounces (2 sticks) butter, softened
- 5 large eggs, separated
- 1 cup granulated sugar
- 1 teaspoon vanilla extract
- 1 teaspoon almond extract
- ½ cup all-purpose flour
- 1 can (15½-ounce) chestnut purée

Topping:

- ¼ cup confectioners' sugar

1. Preheat oven to 350°F.

2. Grease 30 standard size muffin-pan cups or line with paper liners. In a medium saucepan, heat chocolate and butter over low heat, stirring constantly, until melted and smooth. Remove from heat.

3. Beat together egg yolks and ½ cup sugar at medium speed until light and fluffy. Beat in melted chocolate mixture, vanilla, and almond extract. At low speed, beat in flour and chestnut purée until combined.

4. Using clean beaters, beat egg whites at high speed until foamy. Gradually add remaining sugar, beating until stiff, but not dry, peaks form. Fold one-quarter of beaten egg whites into chocolate mixture. Fold in remaining whites. Spoon batter into prepared pans, filling cups two-thirds full.

5. Bake cupcakes until set, 15-20 minutes. Transfer pans to wire racks to cool slightly. Turn cupcakes out onto racks to cool completely.

6. Dust with confectioners' sugar.

Cook's Tip

Chestnut purée can be found in specialty food stores.

Chocolate-Hazelnut Shortbread Hearts

Show the sweetness of your love by giving your Valentine these scrumptious hazelnut cookies.

15 minutes preparation, 30 minutes chilling, 8-10 minutes baking per batch   Makes 2 dozen cookies

Ingredients:

> 12 ounces (3 sticks) butter,
> softened
> 1¼ cups confectioners' sugar
> 3 tablespoons hazelnut liqueur or
> 1 teaspoon almond extract
> 1 teaspoon vanilla extract
> 3 cups all-purpose flour

Garnish:

> 1½ cups hazelnuts, toasted, skins
> removed, and chopped
> (6 ounces)

Frosting:

> 6 ounces (6 squares) semisweet
> chocolate, coarsely chopped
> 1 tablespoon hazelnut liqueur or
> 1 teaspoon almond extract
> 1 teaspoon milk

1. Preheat oven to 350°F. Beat together butter and confectioners' sugar at medium speed until light and fluffy. Beat in liqueur and vanilla.

2. Gradually beat flour into butter mixture until a smooth, very soft dough forms. Shape dough into a ball, wrap in plastic wrap, and chill until firm, 30 minutes.

3. On a floured surface, using a floured rolling pin, roll dough to a ½-inch thickness. Using a 2-inch heart-shaped cookie cutter, cut dough into hearts; reserve trimmings. Place cookies, 1 inch apart, on a nonstick baking sheet. Repeat as directed with trimmings.

4. Bake cookies until just golden, 8-10 minutes. Transfer cookies to a wire rack to cool.

5. Meanwhile, prepare frosting. In top of a double boiler set over simmering (not boiling) water, melt chocolate. Remove from heat. Stir in liqueur and milk until smooth.

6. Dip each cookie halfway into frosting. Sprinkle each cookie with about ½ tablespoon of chopped nuts. Transfer cookies to a sheet of waxed paper to cool completely.

Cook's Tip

To toast and skin hazelnuts, spread nuts in a baking pan. Bake in a 350°F oven, stirring occasionally, until toasted, 10-15 minutes. Turn nuts out onto a cloth towel. Rub off and discard papery skins.

Chocolate-Nut Soufflé Torte

Celebrate a special New Year's Eve with this rich soufflélike dessert.

25 minutes preparation plus cooling, 35 minutes baking   Makes 12 servings

Ingredients:

7½ ounces (7½ squares) semisweet chocolate, coarsely chopped

8 ounces (2 sticks) butter, cut into small pieces

1 teaspoon vanilla extract

1 teaspoon almond extract

5 large eggs, separated

1 cup granulated sugar

⅔ cup ground hazelnuts or walnuts (about 2½ ounces)

⅓ cup all-purpose flour

⅛ teaspoon cream of tartar

Topping:

2 tablespoons confectioners' sugar

1. Preheat oven to 375°F. Grease a 9-inch springform pan. Dust with flour; tap out excess.

2. In a medium saucepan over low heat, melt together chocolate and butter. Cool slightly. Stir in vanilla and almond extract.

3. Beat together egg yolks and ¾ cup sugar at medium speed until light and fluffy. Beat in chocolate mixture, nuts, and flour.

4. Using clean beaters, beat together egg whites and cream of tartar at medium speed until foamy. Gradually beat in remaining sugar until stiff, but not dry, peaks form.

5. Fold one-quarter beaten egg whites into batter. Fold in remaining whites. Spoon batter into prepared pan; smooth top.

6. Bake cake until a toothpick inserted in the center comes out almost clean, 35 minutes.

7. Transfer pan to a wire rack to cool slightly. Loosen cake by running a metal spatula around sides of pan. Remove sides of pan. Transfer cake to wire rack to cool completely.

8. Place cake on a serving plate. Dust with confectioners' sugar.

Cook's Tip

The center of this cake will fall slightly as it begins to cool.

Chocolate-Ice Cream Cake

This chocolate cake filled with kiwi fruit ice cream makes a memorable dessert.

45 minutes preparation, 30 minutes baking plus freezing   Makes 8-10 servings

Ingredients:

  5 ounces (5 squares) semisweet
     chocolate
  2 ounces (½ stick) butter, melted
  3 large eggs, separated
  ⅓ cup firmly packed brown sugar
  ½ cup all-purpose flour
  ½ cup ground hazelnuts (2 ounces)

Ice Cream:

  3 large egg yolks
  1 cup confectioners' sugar
  1½ cups heavy cream
  4 tablespoons kirsch
  3 kiwi fruits, peeled and mashed

Garnish:

  1 cup heavy cream
  2 tablespoons superfine sugar
  ½ teaspoon vanilla extract
  4 ounces (4 squares) semisweet
     chocolate, grated
  2 kiwi fruits, sliced

1. Preheat oven to 350°F. Grease a 8½-inch springform cake pan and line the base with waxed paper. Put the melted chocolate and butter into a small bowl and mix together. Set aside.

2. In a bowl, beat together the egg yolks and sugar until thick and fluffy. Beat in the chocolate mixture. Fold in the flour and nuts.

3. Beat the egg whites until stiff peaks form. Fold into the cake mixture. Spoon the mixture into the pan and bake until a toothpick inserted in the center comes out clean, 30 minutes. Turn out onto a wire rack to cool. Chill the cooled cake.

4. To prepare the ice cream, beat together the egg yolks and confectioners' sugar until thick and fluffy.

5. In another bowl, beat together the cream and

kirsch until soft peaks form. Fold into the egg yolk mixture. Fold in the mashed kiwi fruit.

6. Cut the chilled cake horizontally in half. Put a half in the base of the springform pan. Pour the ice cream mixture on top and smooth the top. Cover with the remaining cake and freeze for 4-5 hours, or until frozen.

7. To garnish, turn the cake out onto a serving plate. Whip together the cream, sugar, and vanilla until soft peaks form. Put a quarter of the mixture into a pastry bag fitted with a star tip. Spread the remaining cream over the top and sides of the cake. Press the grated chocolate around the side.

8. Pipe swirls of cream around the top of the cake and decorate with kiwi slices.

Chocolate-Mint Sweetheart Pie

Perfect for a "Sweet 16" party, this rich and pretty pie is oh-so-easy to love...and make.

30 minutes preparation plus chilling
Makes 8 servings

Ingredients:

1 9-inch prepared piecrust, baked
and cooled

Filling:

¾ cup granulated sugar

4 ounces (1 stick) butter, softened

3 ounces (3 squares) unsweetened
chocolate, melted and cooled

1 teaspoon vanilla extract

½ teaspoon peppermint extract

3 large eggs

½ cup heavy cream

1 tablespoon granulated sugar

Garnish:

¼ cup heavy cream

Fresh strawberries

1. To prepare filling, beat together sugar and butter at medium speed until light and fluffy. Stir in melted chocolate, vanilla, and peppermint extract. Add eggs, 1 at a time, beating well after each addition.

2. Beat together cream and sugar at medium speed until soft peaks form. Fold cream into chocolate mixture. Spoon filling evenly into prepared piecrust. Chill for 4 hours.

3. For the garnish, beat cream at medium speed until soft peaks form. Using a pastry bag fitted with a star tip, pipe a rosette in the center of the pie. Arrange strawberries on top.

Cook's Tip

To glaze strawberries, heat ¼ cup strawberry or red currant jelly over low heat until dissolved. Arrange berries on top of pie. Brush with glaze.

Chocolate-Orange Cupcakes

Perfect for a birthday celebration, these dark chocolate cupcakes have a kiss of citrus flavor.

20 minutes preparation plus cooling and standing, 15-20 minutes baking   Makes 1 dozen cupcakes

Ingredients:

- 1¼ cups all-purpose flour
- ½ teaspoon baking powder
- ½ teaspoon baking soda
- ¼ teaspoon salt
- ¾ cup granulated sugar
- 3 ounces (¾ stick) butter, softened
- 2 large eggs
- 2 ounces (2 squares) unsweetened chocolate, melted and cooled
- 2 teaspoons grated orange peel
- 1 teaspoon vanilla extract
- ½ cup milk

Frosting:

- 2 cups confectioners' sugar
- ⅔ cup unsweetened cocoa powder
- 2 ounces (½ stick) butter, softened
- 3 tablespoons orange juice
- 1 tablespoon orange-flavored liqueur (optional)
- 1 teaspoon grated orange peel
- ½ teaspoon vanilla extract
- ⅛ teaspoon salt

1. Preheat oven to 350°F. Line 12 standard size muffin-pan cups with paper liners.

2. Mix together flour, baking powder, baking soda, and salt.

3. Beat together sugar and butter at medium speed until light and fluffy.

4. Add eggs, 1 at a time, beating well after each addition. Beat in melted chocolate, orange peel, and vanilla. At low speed, alternately beat in flour mixture and milk until blended.

5. Spoon batter into prepared pan, filling cups three-quarters full.

6. Bake cupcakes until tops spring back when lightly pressed, 15-20 minutes. Transfer pan to a wire rack to cool slightly. Turn cupcakes out onto a wire rack to cool completely.

7. To prepare frosting, mix together confectioners' sugar, cocoa powder, butter, orange juice, liqueur, orange peel, vanilla, and salt until light and fluffy.

8. Spread frosting evenly on top of cupcakes. Let stand until set.

Cook's Tip

Spread a thin layer of orange marmalade or apricot preserves over the cupcakes before frosting, if desired.

Chocolate Pavlova

A chocolate variation of an old classic, decorated with fruit and chocolate curls.

40 minutes preparation, 55 minutes baking plus standing

Ingredients:

- 3 large egg whites
- ¾ cup superfine sugar
- 1 teaspoon white wine vinegar
- 1 teaspoon cornstarch

Filling:

- 1 pound (16 squares) semisweet chocolate
- 1¼ cups heavy cream

Garnish:

- 4 ounces (4 squares) semisweet chocolate
- 1 pint fresh strawberries
- 2 ounces (2 squares) white chocolate
- 1 cup fresh raspberries

1. Preheat oven to 350°F. Draw a 9-inch circle on a piece of waxed paper and put upside-down on a baking sheet.

2. Beat the egg whites until very stiff. Gradually beat in the sugar. Fold in the vinegar and cornstarch.

3. Spread the meringue over the circle on the baking paper. Make a large hollow in the center of the meringue.

4. Bake for 5 minutes, then reduce oven temperature to 250°F and bake for 50 minutes more. Set aside to cool slightly. Carefully peel away the waxed paper and let meringue cool completely.

5. Meanwhile, make the filling. In the top of a double boiler set over simmering (not boiling) water, melt the chocolate. Heat the cream in a pan until almost boiling. Gradually whisk the cream into the melted chocolate until smooth. Set aside for 2-3 hours to thicken but not to set completely. Stir occasionally.

6. To prepare the garnish, melt the semisweet chocolate in a bowl set over a pan of simmering water. Using a vegetable peeler, scrape across the chocolate to form chocolate curls (see page 185).

7. Melt the remaining chocolate. Dip the strawberries into the melted chocolate and put on waxed paper to set completely. Make more chocolate curls with the white chocolate.

8. Put the meringue on a large serving plate and carefully spoon the filling into the hollow. Halve the strawberries and arrange on top of the filling with the raspberries and chocolate curls.

Chocolate Pudding Cake

This luscious dessert is the perfect treat for a Father's Day celebration.

30 minutes preparation plus cooling, 30-40 minutes baking

Makes 12 servings

Ingredients:

1 cup all-purpose flour
⅔ cup granulated sugar
¼ cup unsweetened
 cocoa powder
1 teaspoon baking soda
1 teaspoon baking
 powder
1/8 teaspoon salt
1 teaspoon instant
 coffee powder
1 tablespoon boiling
 water
½ cup milk
¼ cup vegetable oil
1 teaspoon vanilla
 extract

Topping:

⅔ cup granulated sugar
2 tablespoons
 unsweetened cocoa
 powder
1 cup boiling water

Sauce:

6 ounces (6 squares)
 semisweet chocolate,
 coarsely chopped
4 ounces (1 stick) butter,
 cut into small pieces
1 tablespoon light corn
 syrup

1. Preheat oven to 350°F. Grease an 8-inch square baking pan.

2. Mix together flour, sugar, cocoa powder, baking soda, baking powder, and salt.

3. Dissolve coffee powder in boiling water. Stir in milk, oil, and vanilla.

4. At low speed, beat flour mixture into milk mixture, ½ cup at a time, until blended and smooth. Spoon batter into prepared pan.

5. To prepare topping, mix together sugar and cocoa powder. Sprinkle sugar mixture evenly over batter.

6. Pour boiling water evenly over topping. (Do not mix.)

7. Bake cake until a toothpick inserted in the center comes out clean, 30-40 minutes. Transfer pan to a wire rack to cool slightly.

8. To prepare sauce, in the top of a double boiler set over simmering (not boiling) water, heat together chocolate, butter, and corn syrup until melted and smooth. Spoon sauce over cake.

Cook's Tip

This dessert is best served warm with a lightly sweetened whipped cream topping and fresh strawberry slices.

Chocolate Truffle Praline Cake

An indulgent gateau made with chocolate, cream, and crushed almond praline.

1 hour preparation, 20 minutes baking plus cooling and chilling　　　　　Makes 10-12 servings

Ingredients:

　2 large eggs
　6 tablespoons vanilla sugar
　½ cup all-purpose flour

Filling:

　5 tablespoons granulated sugar
　½ cup blanched almonds, toasted
　6 tablespoons orange-flavored
　　liqueur
　18 ounces (18 squares) semisweet
　　chocolate, coarsely chopped
　2½ cups heavy cream
　3 large egg yolks
　¼ cup superfine sugar
　Chocolate curls, to garnish
　(see page 185)

1. Preheat oven to 375°F. Grease a 9-inch springform cake pan. Dust the inside with flour and sugar.

2. Put the eggs and vanilla sugar into a bowl set over a pan of hot water. Beat for 10 minutes, or until thick ribbons form when the beaters are lifted.

3. Fold in the flour. Pour the mixture into the pan. Bake for 20 minutes, or until firm. Turn out onto a wire rack to cool. Clean the pan. Grease and line the base and side with waxed paper.

4. To prepare the filling, oil a baking sheet. Put the granulated sugar into a heavy saucepan. Heat gently, without stirring, until dissolved. Add the almonds and cook until golden. Spread onto the baking sheet to cool.

5. Break the nut mixture into small pieces. Put into a food processor and whizz for a few seconds to form a praline powder.

6. Put the cake back in the springform pan and sprinkle with 1 tablespoon liqueur. Put the chocolate and ⅔ cup cream into a double boiler, set over simmering (not boiling) water. Let the chocolate melt, stirring occasionally. Set aside.

7. Put the egg yolks and superfine sugar into a bowl set over a pan of hot water. Beat with an electric beater for 10 minutes, or until the beaters leave a trail on the surface when lifted.

8. Fold the chocolate mixture into the egg mixture. Fold in the crushed praline mixture. Whip the remaining cream until soft peaks form and fold in with the remaining liqueur.

9. Pour the mixture into the pan over the cake. Chill for 12 hours, or until set. Turn onto a serving plate, remove the waxed paper, and sprinkle with chocolate curls.

Chocolate Walnut Valentine Cake

Say "Be My Valentine" with this moist, heart-shaped dessert.

30 minutes preparation, 30 minutes baking   Makes 10 servings

Ingredients:

  1½ cups all-purpose flour
  1¼ teaspoons baking powder
  ¼ teaspoon salt
  ¾ cup granulated sugar
  4 ounces (1 stick) butter, softened
  2 large eggs
  ½ teaspoon maple extract
  ¼ cup milk
  ¼ cup mini semisweet chocolate
    chips
  ¼ cup coarsely chopped walnuts
    (about 1 ounce)

1. Preheat oven to 350°F. Line a 1-quart heart-shaped pan or an 8-inch round cake pan with waxed paper. Spray waxed paper with vegetable cooking spray.

2. Mix together flour, baking powder, and salt.

3. Beat together sugar and butter at medium speed until light and fluffy. Add eggs, 1 at a time, beating well after each addition. Beat in maple extract.

4. At low speed, alternately beat flour mixture and milk into butter mixture until blended. Stir in chocolate chips and nuts. Spoon batter into prepared pan; smooth top.

5. Bake cake until a toothpick inserted in the center comes out clean, 30 minutes. Transfer pan to a wire rack to cool slightly.

6. Loosen cake by running a metal spatula around sides of pan. Turn cake out onto rack. Remove paper. Cool completely.

Cook's Tip

To make a maple glaze, combine ¾ cup confectioners' sugar and ¼ cup maple syrup.

Death by Chocolate Cake

A chocoholic's dream, this delectable cake has a white and dark chocolate filling.

40 minutes preparation, 30 minutes baking plus cooling

Makes 10-12 servings

Ingredients:

8 ounces (8 squares) semisweet chocolate, coarsely chopped

6 ounces (1½ sticks) butter

4 large eggs

1 cup superfine sugar

1 cup all-purpose flour

1½ teaspoons baking powder

½ teaspoon salt

Filling:

6 ounces (6 squares) white chocolate, coarsely chopped

8 ounces (8 squares) semisweet chocolate, coarsely chopped

4 ounces (1 stick) butter

Glaze:

5 ounces (5 squares) semisweet chocolate, coarsely chopped

⅔ cup heavy cream

Chocolate curls, to decorate

1. Preheat oven to 350°F. Grease two 8-inch round cake pans. Line the bases with waxed paper.

2. To prepare the cake, put the semisweet chocolate and butter into a bowl. Set over a pan of hot water and let melt. Do not let the bottom of the bowl touch the water. Remove from the heat and set aside.

3. Beat together the eggs and sugar in a bowl set over a pan of simmering water for about 7 minutes, or until thick ribbons form when the beaters are lifted. Sift in the flour and fold in. Fold in the melted chocolate.

4. Divide the mixture evenly between the pans. Bake for 30 minutes, or until the cakes have risen and have a light crust. Cool in the pans for 10 minutes, then turn out onto a wire rack to cool.

5. To prepare the filling, melt the white chocolate in the top of a double boiler set over simmering water. Cut each cake horizontally in half. Spread the melted white chocolate over 2 of the layers. Reassemble the cakes.

6. Melt the semisweet chocolate in the top of a double boiler. Remove from the heat and set aside until the mixture is thick enough to spread. Use to sandwich the 2 cakes together.

7. To prepare the glaze, melt the semisweet chocolate. Put the cream into a small pan and bring to a boil. Remove from the heat and pour over the melted chocolate. Set aside for 10 minutes. Beat the mixture until thickened and smooth.

8. Spread the glaze over the cake. Let set. Add chocolate curls.

Fudge Valentine Heart

Show how much you care with this spectacular chocolate cake that's straight from the heart.

1 hour preparation plus cooling, 40 minutes baking   Makes 16 servings

Ingredients:

2¾ cups sifted all-purpose flour

2 tablespoons unsweetened cocoa powder

1 tablespoon baking powder

1 teaspoon baking soda

1 teaspoon salt

8 ounces (2 sticks) butter, softened

1¼ cups granulated sugar

1 cup firmly packed brown sugar

5 large eggs, separated

1½ cups milk

6 ounces (6 squares) unsweetened chocolate, melted and cooled

1 teaspoon vanilla extract

1 cup sour cream

Frosting and Garnish:

18 ounces (18 squares) semisweet chocolate, coarsely chopped

12 ounces (3 sticks) butter, softened

6 large eggs

2 teaspoons vanilla extract

1 cup whipped cream

Fresh raspberries

1. Preheat oven to 350°F. Grease a heart-shaped baking pan. Dust with flour; tap out excess.

2. Mix together flour, cocoa powder, baking powder, baking soda, and salt.

3. Beat together butter, granulated sugar, and brown sugar at medium speed until light and fluffy. Add egg yolks, 1 at a time, beating well after each addition. Beat in milk, chocolate, and vanilla. Alternately beat flour mixture and sour cream into chocolate mixture.

4. Using clean beaters, beat egg whites at high speed until stiff, but not dry, peaks form. Fold egg whites into batter. Spoon batter into prepared pan; smooth top.

5. Bake cake until a toothpick inserted in the center comes out clean, 40 minutes. Transfer pan to a wire rack to cool for 5 minutes. Turn cake out onto rack to cool completely.

6. To prepare frosting, in the top of a double boiler set over simmering (not boiling) water, melt chocolate, stirring until smooth. Cool for 10 minutes.

7. Beat butter at medium speed until smooth. Beat in eggs, 1 at a time, beating well after each addition. Beat in chocolate and vanilla until thick and fluffy.

8. Spread frosting on top and sides of cake. Using a fork, make a swirled pattern on top. Using a pastry bag fitted with a 1-inch star tip, pipe a chocolate rosette border around top of cake.

9. To prepare garnish, using a pastry bag fitted with a 1-inch star tip, pipe whipped cream rosettes inside chocolate rosette border.

10. Pipe a decorative edge around bottom of cake. Place raspberries on top of whipped cream rosettes.

Easy Chocolate Birthday Cake

All kids love chocolate—this party cake is a surefire success.

20 minutes preparation, 30-35 minutes baking plus cooling

Makes 10-12 servings

Ingredients:

8 ounces (2 sticks) butter

1 cup superfine sugar

2 cups all-purpose flour, sifted

3 tablespoons unsweetened cocoa
powder, sifted

4 teaspoons baking powder

½ teaspoon salt

4 large eggs

Filling and Frosting:

3 tablespoons apricot jelly, boiled
and strained

1 container (16-ounce) prepared
chocolate frosting

Garnish:

Chocolate buttons or other
chocolate decorations

Birthday candles

1. Preheat oven to 325°F. Line the base of two 8-inch square cake pans with waxed paper.

2. Put the butter, sugar, flour, baking powder, salt, cocoa, and eggs in a bowl. Mix together with a wooden spoon and beat for 1-2 minutes, or until smooth and glossy.

3. Spoon the mixture evenly into the prepared pans. Level the surface with the back of a spoon. Bake until a toothpick inserted in the center comes out clean, 30-35 minutes. Cool completely in the pans.

4. Turn out the cakes and remove the waxed paper. Put 1 cake on a serving plate. Brush evenly with the apricot jelly. Sandwich the cakes together.

5. Spread the frosting over the top and down the sides of the cake.

6. Arrange the chocolate buttons on top of the cake. Insert the birthday candles.

Fabulous Chocolate Ring

A spectacular chocolate ring cake, filled and frosted with buttercream.

40 minutes preparation, 1 hour baking plus cooling

Makes 8-10 servings

Ingredients:

- 8 ounces (2 sticks) butter, softened
- 1 cup superfine sugar
- 4 large eggs, beaten
- 2 cups all-purpose flour
- 1 tablespoon baking powder
- 1 teaspoon salt
- 3 ounces (3 squares) semisweet chocolate, melted
- 1 tablespoon unsweetened cocoa powder

Filling and Frosting:

- 3 ounces (¾ stick) butter, softened
- 1¾ cups confectioners' sugar
- 2 tablespoons orange-flavored liqueur or orange juice
- 1¼ cups heavy cream
- 1 tablespoon unsweetened cocoa powder, to dust
- Chocolate leaves, to garnish

1. Preheat oven to 350°F. Grease a 9-cup fluted ring pan or Kugelhopf mold. Dust the pan with flour and tap out excess.

2. Beat together the butter and superfine sugar until pale and fluffy. Gradually beat in the eggs, then fold in the flour, baking powder, and salt.

3. Put half the mixture into a bowl and stir in the melted chocolate and cocoa powder. Put alternate layers of the plain and chocolate mixtures in the pan. Drag a skewer through to create a marbled effect.

4. Bake until a toothpick inserted near the center comes out clean, 1 hour. Cool in the pan for 10 minutes. Turn out onto a wire rack to cool completely.

5. For the filling, beat together the butter and 1½ cups confectioners' sugar. Beat in the liqueur.

6. Slice the cake into 3 layers. Spread the filling over the bottom 2 layers. Reassemble the cake. Whip the cream with the remaining confectioners' sugar until soft peaks form. Spread three-quarters over the cake. Put the remainder into a pastry bag and pipe over the cake. Dust with the cocoa powder and garnish with the chocolate leaves.

Cook's Tip

To make the chocolate leaves, rinse 15 small rose leaves and dry thoroughly. Melt 1 ounce (1 square) semisweet chocolate. With a clean, dry paintbrush, coat the underside of each leaf with melted chocolate. Let set on waxed paper. When set, peel away the rose leaves.

Porcupine Cake

No one can resist this cute party cake.

40 minutes preparation, 1 hour baking plus cooling

Makes 12-14 servings

Ingredients:

8 ounces (8 squares) semisweet
 chocolate, coarsely chopped
1 cup all-purpose flour
2½ teaspoons baking powder
Pinch of salt
¼ tablespoon unsweetened cocoa
 powder
8 ounces (2 sticks) butter, softened
1 cup firmly packed light brown
 sugar
4 large eggs, beaten
¾ cup ground almonds (3 ounces)

Frosting and Garnish:

1¼ cups heavy cream
⅔ cup chocolate and hazelnut
 spread
Chocolate curls
Candy-coated chocolate, malted
 milk balls, or jelly beans

1. Preheat oven to 325°F. Grease a 10-inch (2½-quart) baking dish. Put the chocolate into a heatproof bowl, set over a pan of barely simmering water, and let melt.

2. Sift the flour, baking powder, salt, and cocoa powder into a mixing bowl. Beat in the butter, sugar, eggs, almonds, and melted chocolate until smooth. Spoon the mixture into the baking dish.

3. Bake for 1 hour, or until a toothpick inserted in the center comes out clean. Cool in the dish for 10 minutes, then turn out onto a wire rack to cool completely.

4. Cut one end of the cake into a point shape to form the porcupine's nose. Slice the cutouts in half to create the feet. Put the cake onto a serving plate and put the feet in place.

5. For the frosting, put the cream and chocolate spread into a bowl and whip until soft peaks form. Put three-quarters of the mixture into a pastry bag fitted with a small star tip. Pipe rosettes over the body. Spread the remaining icing over the feet and over the pointed end to form the head.

6. Stick the chocolate curls all over the porcupine's body. Use the candy decorations to make the nose and eyes. Chill until ready to serve.

Cook's Tip

Don't overbeat the cream and chocolate spread, or the mixture will separate.

Party Chocolate Cupcakes

Junior chefs can make their own personalized treats with these yummy chocolate cupcakes.

25 minutes preparation plus cooling, 15-20 minutes baking   Makes 2 dozen cupcakes

Ingredients:

8 ounces (2 sticks) butter, cut into small pieces
½ cup water
4 tablespoons unsweetened cocoa powder
2 cups all-purpose flour
2 cups granulated sugar
1 teaspoon baking soda
⅛ teaspoon salt
1 cup milk
1 tablespoon fresh lemon juice
2 large eggs
1 teaspoon vanilla extract

Frosting:

3 cups confectioners' sugar
2½ ounces (⅝ stick) butter, softened
¼ cup milk
1 teaspoon vanilla extract
2 tablespoons unsweetened cocoa powder

Decorations:

Shredded unsweetened coconut
Assorted candy-coated pieces
Candy sprinkles
Colored icing for piping

1. Preheat oven to 375°F. Line 24 standard size muffin-pan cups with paper liners.

2. In a saucepan, heat butter, water, and cocoa powder over medium heat, stirring constantly, until melted and smooth.

3. Mix together flour, sugar, baking soda, and salt. Mix together milk and lemon juice.

4. Alternately beat cocoa mixture and milk mixture into flour mixture at low speed until blended. Add eggs, 1 at a time, beating well after each addition. Beat in vanilla. Spoon batter into prepared pans, filling cups two-thirds full.

5. Bake cupcakes until set, 15-20 minutes. Transfer to wire racks to cool completely.

6. To prepare frosting, beat together confectioners' sugar, butter, and milk at medium speed until light and fluffy. Divide frosting in half. Stir vanilla into one half. Stir cocoa powder into remaining half.

7. Spread tops of cupcakes with frostings. Decorate as desired.

Valentine Chocolate Cake

Easy yet sophisticated, this cake is lovely served with fresh berries.

15 minutes preparation plus cooling, 30 minutes baking   Makes 10 servings

Ingredients:

- ½ cup sour cream
- 2 large eggs
- 1 teaspoon vanilla extract
- 1 cup all-purpose flour
- 6 tablespoons unsweetened cocoa powder
- 1 teaspoon baking powder
- 1/8 teaspoon salt
- ¾ cup (1½ sticks) butter, softened
- ¾ cup granulated sugar

Topping:

- ¼ cup confectioners' sugar

1. Preheat oven to 375°F. Grease an 8-inch round cake pan or springform pan. Dust with flour; tap out excess.

2. Mix together sour cream, eggs, and vanilla.

3. Mix together flour, cocoa powder, baking powder, and salt.

4. At low speed, beat together butter and sugar until light and fluffy. Alternately beat in sour cream mixture and flour mixture until blended and smooth. Pour batter into prepared pan; smooth top.

5. Bake cake until a toothpick inserted in the center comes out clean, 30 minutes. Transfer pan to a wire rack to cool for 10 minutes.

6. Turn cake out onto rack to cool completely.

7. For topping, place a heart-shaped doily over the cake. Dust with confectioners' sugar. Remove doily.

Rich White Chocolate Cake

Perfect for any celebration, this party cake is wickedly rich.

1 hour preparation, 50 minutes baking plus cooling

Makes 8-10 servings

Ingredients:

- 2 ounces (2 squares) white chocolate, chopped
- 3 large eggs, separated
- 4 ounces (1 stick) butter, softened
- ½ cup superfine sugar
- 1 cup all-purpose flour
- 2 teaspoons baking powder
- ½ teaspoon salt
- ¼ cup ground almonds (1 ounce)
- 1½ teaspoons milk

Filling, Topping, and Garnish:

- 1¼ cups heavy cream
- 4 tablespoons raspberry jelly
- 8 ounces (8 squares) white chocolate

1. Preheat oven to 350°F. Grease an 8-inch springform cake pan. Line the pan with waxed paper. Grease the paper.

2. Put the chocolate pieces into a heatproof bowl with 4 tablespoons boiling water. Melt over a pan of simmering water. Remove from the heat and beat in the egg yolks.

3. Beat the egg whites until soft peaks form. In a separate bowl, beat the butter and sugar until pale and fluffy. Mix in the chocolate mixture. Sift in the flour baking powder, salt, and almonds. Stir in the milk. Carefully fold in the egg whites.

4. Spoon into the pan and bake for 50 minutes, or until a toothpick inserted into the center comes out clean. Cool in the pan for 5 minutes, then turn out onto a wire rack to cool completely.

5. Slice the cake in half horizontally. Spread with jelly and sandwich together. To garnish, whip the cream until soft peaks form. Using a metal spatula, spread the cream over the cake in swirls.

6. For the chocolate curls, break the chocolate into a bowl set over a pan of water. Heat gently to melt, but be careful not to overheat. Pour the melted chocolate onto a marble slab or clean plastic board. Smooth level and let stand until firm and set.

7. For the curls, hold the tip of a sharp knife between the thumb and forefinger of one hand. Hold the handle with the other hand and carefully pull the knife horizontally through the set chocolate. Decorate the top and side of the cake with the curls. Chill until needed.

Wicked Witch Cupcakes

Trick-or-treaters will be bewitched by these lots-of-fun little cakes.

40 minutes preparation plus cooling and standing, 20 minutes baking

Makes 1 dozen cupcakes

Ingredients:

1½ cups all-purpose flour

½ cup unsweetened cocoa powder

1 teaspoon baking soda

½ teaspoon baking powder

½ teaspoon salt

1 cup granulated sugar

4 ounces (1 stick) butter, softened

2 large eggs

1¼ cups milk

Topping and Garnish:

1½ cups prepared vanilla frosting

12 ice cream cones

8 ounces (8 squares) semisweet chocolate, melted

2 teaspoons vegetable oil

12 chocolate wafer cookies

Licorice strings, jelly beans, and candy corn

1. Preheat oven to 350°F. Grease 12 standard size muffin-pan cups or line with paper liners.

2. Mix together flour, cocoa powder, baking soda, baking powder, and salt.

3. Beat together sugar and butter at medium speed until light and fluffy. Add eggs, 1 at a time, beating well after each addition.

4. At low speed, alternately beat in flour mixture and milk until blended. Spoon batter evenly into prepared pan, filling cups two-thirds full.

5. Bake cupcakes until a toothpick inserted in the centers comes out clean, 20 minutes. Transfer pan to a wire rack to cool slightly. Turn cupcakes out onto rack to cool completely.

6. For topping, spread frosting over tops of cupcakes.

7. To prepare garnish, using a serrated knife, cut off 3-inch tips from ice cream cones.

8. Mix together melted chocolate and oil. Place cookies on waxed paper. Spread some chocolate mixture over cookies. Spoon remaining chocolate over cones, covering completely. Place 1 cone on top of each cookie. Let stand until set.

9. Place hats on cupcakes. Cut licorice into assorted lengths. Decorate faces with licorice, jelly beans, and candy corn.

Index

Metric Equivalents

VOLUME

US or Imperial	Metric
⅛ teaspoon	0.5 milliliter
¼ teaspoon	1 milliliter
½ teaspoon	2 milliliters
1 teaspoon	5 milliliters
1 tablespoon (½ fluid ounce)	1 tablespoon (15 milliliters)
¼ cup (2 fluid ounces)	2 tablespoons (50milliliters)
⅓ cup (2 fluid ounces)	¼ cup (75 milliliters)
½ cup (2 fluid ounces)	⅓ cup (125 milliliters)
¾ cup (2 fluid ounces)	¾ cup (200 milliliters)
1 cup (2 fluid ounces)	1cup (250 milliliters)
1 pint (16 fluid ounces)	500 milliliters
1 quart (32 fluid ounces)	1 liter minus 3 tablespoons

WEIGHT

US or Imperial	Metric
¼ ounce	7 grams
½ ounce	15 grams
¾ ounce	20 grams
1 ounce	30 grams
6 ounces	170 grams
8 ounces (½ pound)	225 grams
12 ounces (¾ pound)	340 grams
16 ounces (1 pound)	450 grams
35 ounces (2¼ pounds)	1 kilogram

LENGTH

US or Imperial	Metric
½ inch	12 millimeters
1 inch	2.5 centimeters
6 inchs	15 centimeters
12 inchs (1 foot)	30 centimeters

TEMPERATURE

US or Imperial	Metric
0 °F (freezer temperature)	minus 18°C
32°F (temperature water freezes)	0°C
180°F (temperature water simmers)	82°C
212°F (temperature water boils)	100°C
250°F (low oven temperature)	120°C
350°F (moderate oven temperature)	180°C
425°F (hot oven temperature)	220°C
500°F (very hot oven temperature)	260°C

BAKING PAN SIZES

US or Imperial	Metric
8 x 1½-inch round cake pan	20 x 5-centimeter cake tin
9 x 1½-inch round cake pan	23 x 5-centimeter cake tin
11 x 7 x 1½-inch baking pan	28 x 18 x 4-centimeter baking tin
13 x 9 x 2-inch baking pan	30 x 20 x 3-centimeter baking tin
15 x 10 x 1-inch baking pan (jelly roll pan)	38 x25 x 2.5-centimeter baking tin (Swiss-roll tin)
9 x 5 x 3-inch loaf pan	25 x 7.5-centimeter loaf tin (Canada)
	19 x 12 x 9-centimeter loaf tin (Australia)
9-inch pie plate	23 x 3-centimeter pie plate
7- or 8-inch springform pan or loose bottom tin	20-centimeter springform tin
10-inch tube or Bundt pan	26-centimeter (15-cup capacity) ring tin

SUBSTITUTIONS

Amaretti	Almomd Flavored Macaroons
Apple Butter	Apple puree
Baking soda	Bicarbonate of soda
Buttercrunch candy	Honeycomb
Cake Flour	Sifted white flour
Chocolate, semi-sweet, bittersweet	Dark, semi-sweet and bittersweet chocolate are interchangeable in recipies; use any good quality cooking chocolate
Chocolate-mint candy	After-dinner mints
Cocoa powder, unsweetened	Pure cocoa powder
Coconut flakes	Shredded coconut
Cornstarch	Cornflour
Cranberries, dried, sweetened	Use dried unsweetened cranberries
Dragee	Sugared almond
Egg bread	Brioche
Flour, all-purpose	Plain household flour or white flour
Graham crackers	Substitute digestive biscuts
Granola	Muesli
Half and half	Equal parts cream and milk
Heavy cream	Pure Cream
Jelly	Jam
Maple extract	Maple syrup
Marshmallow extract	Spreadable marshmallow
Mint extract	Peppermint essence
Piecrust mix	Ready prepared or frozen pastry
Rasins, chocolate covered	plain rasins
Rasins, golden	Sultanas
Ratafia biscuits	Almond-flavored macaroons
Sugar, confectioners'	Icing sugar
Sugar, granulated	Ordinary white sugar
Sugar, superfine	Caster sugar
Vanilla extract	Vanilla essence